Items should be returned on or before the last date
shown below. Items not already requested by other
borrowers may be renewed in person, in writing or by
telephone. To renew, please quote the number on the
barcode label. To renew online a PIN is required.
This can be requested at your local library.
Renew online @ **www.dublincitypubliclibraries.ie**
Fines charged for overdue items will include postage
incurred in recovery. Damage to or loss of items will
be charged to the borrower.

niner.
Inde-
dent,
also
es.
2006
ed by
(BA
A in
ision
Dub-

ews-
le. A
Bel-
tory)

dent
and
blin

HELL AT THE

GATES

THE INSIDE STORY OF IRELAND'S FINANCIAL DOWNFALL

JOHN LEE &
DANIEL McCONNELL

MERCIER PRESS
IRISH PUBLISHER – IRISH STORY

MERCIER PRESS
Cork
www.mercierpress.ie

© John Lee & Daniel McConnell, 2016

ISBN: 978 1 78117 394 7

10 9 8 7 6 5 4 3 2 1

A CIP record for this title is available from the British Library

Printed and bound in the EU.

For Eliza and Kitty

Contents

ACKNOWLEDGEMENTS 9

PROLOGUE 11

1 'MY WAY' 15

2 NEW BOSS 43

3 FLYING AHEAD OF THE SUN 65

4 WILL YOU STILL NEED ME ... WHEN I'M SEVENTY? 93

5 CHAOS AND DISORDER 113

6 THE STATE OF THE NATION 143

7 EL CID 167

8 2010 – A FALSE DAWN 191

9 THE TWEET IS MIGHTIER THAN THE SWORD 215

10 BAILOUT 245

11 END GAME 271

EPILOGUE 303

INDEX 311

Acknowledgements

We would like to sincerely thank Joe Neville, our chief researcher, whose efforts were invaluable in the making of this book. We thank our editor, Maggie Armstrong, and Mary Feehan, Wendy Logue and all at Mercier Press for giving us the opportunity to write a book we have wanted to write for some time. In this vein, we also thank Dominic Perrem, who played a huge part in this book seeing the light of day.

We would like to express our deep gratitude to Independent News & Media (INM) and DMG Media Ireland for their permission to use photographs in the book, which add greatly to the finished product. In particular, we thank Ed McCann and David Conachy in INM, and Conor O'Donnell and James Meehan in the *Irish Mail on Sunday*.

To all who gave generously of their time, either for interviews or for fact checking, we are deeply grateful, as your contributions are the making of the book.

Daniel would like to thank his wife, Cathy, and daughter, Eliza, for their unending support and love; his siblings for their tolerance of him over many years; and his late parents, John and Ann.

John would like thank his wife, Lorraine, daughter, Kitty, and parents, Éamonn and Imelda, for all their love and support.

Both authors acknowledge the support of their colleagues in the Leinster House Press Gallery and, in particular, a former press colleague, John Drennan, for his enthusiasm in discussing everything except politics.

PROLOGUE

The title of this book is taken from a BBC radio interview that the late finance minister Brian Lenihan gave two months before his death at age fifty-two from cancer. Reflecting on his tumultuous time as minister for finance, Lenihan said: 'I believed I had fought the good fight and taken every measure possible to delay such an eventuality, and now hell was at the gates … I had had such a fierce struggle in the previous two-and-a-half years to bring my colleagues and the country with me on what had been a very difficult economic programme.' Even as he faced his mortality, Lenihan described with eloquence and flair the torrid period he and his party, and the country, had gone through.

Here, for the first time, Lenihan's colleagues – Brian Cowen, Eamon Ryan, Micheál Martin, Mary Harney and many others – tell the inside story of that doomed government in their own words. They provide a deeply honest, deeply personal, revelation-strewn account of their experiences in the white heat of an economic meltdown. This is not a financial and economic history, as that aspect is still playing itself out; it is unapologetically a political story. It is unlikely that any period of office in Irish history will be reflected upon by future historians and students of politics as intensely as that of the Cowen government. Here we record its voices.

The financial-turned-economic crisis, which had huge and long-lasting social implications for Ireland and her people, also changed the Irish political landscape for several generations. The implications for the Fianna Fáil party were immense. The Green Party's Dáil presence was wiped out. This book is an attempt to uncover and explain not only why major decisions were taken but also the motivations behind those decisions.

When former taoiseach Brian Cowen agreed to give an interview, we suspected that he was just doing us a courtesy and would go through the motions. Instead, in a hotel in Tullamore, he gave us an account of his years in office. Quiet and reflective, funny and emotional, he was devastating in his assessments of those times – and of himself. Cowen explained his thinking on matters from the 2008 bank guarantee to his public image and his refusal to address the nation, to not sacking Brian Lenihan when many of his own supporters urged him to over Lenihan's perceived disloyalty, to ultimately requesting a Troika bailout in 2010. He revealed the impact of the crisis on his family and described how they coped with the pressure. He opened up for the first time on dealing with Lenihan's cancer diagnosis and their complex relationship. Cowen also broke his silence on that infamous night at the Fianna Fáil think-in in Galway in 2010, and the botched Cabinet reshuffle of January 2011 which led to his downfall. His honesty and candour reveal a new side to the pilloried politician and provide an insight into his thinking throughout his turbulent reign as leader.

This book also tells of the extent to which the relationship between Cowen and Lenihan became strained and ultimately ended in mistrust and separation. It records how the men met to resolve their differences in a farewell meeting before Lenihan passed away.

Brian Lenihan's family told us of their knowledge of his ambitions and his struggles, and revealed how serious his leadership ambitions were, even when he knew he did not have long to live. From his political allies, we heard that he saw himself as a credible interim taoiseach in 2010, who could better lead Fianna

Fáil through a general election. Most of the quotes we include from Lenihan himself come from interviews and discussions with Danny McConnell before his death.

Micheál Martin, Fianna Fáil's leader, for the first time gave the definitive account of his decision in early 2011 to move against his embattled leader. Former Cabinet minister Willie O'Dea told us how the Green Party insisted on his resignation, for which O'Dea has not yet forgiven them: 'It was an absolutely nightmarish time for me, my very worst time in politics. I'm sorry I had to live through it. My overriding memory was it was the worst time in my life both in politics and out of politics. The lessons to be learned I suppose go back to the situation that preceded those three years. You have to maintain a strong economy and you can't be using the people's money to buy their votes. After every party there's a hangover!'

Former ministers spoke about how they were physically as-saulted by traumatised members of the public at the height of the crisis and how they cowered in their homes and hotels, far from the madding crowd. Civil servants and other sources close to the Cabinet, who wished to keep their anonymity, provided their sometimes withering reflections. The book also contains the visceral criticisms of several ministers about the treatment of Ireland at the hands of Jean-Claude Trichet of the European Central Bank and Dominic Strauss-Kahn of the International Monetary Fund.

At its core, we wanted this book to re-assess the decisions behind the actions of the most hated government in living memory, which was dumped out by the Irish people in 2011. We also wanted, given a slight remove in time, to assess the actions and decisions of Brian Cowen and Brian Lenihan, the two key figures of the period. In her interview, former government minister and

Lenihan's aunt Mary O'Rourke gave a fitting summation of those years: 'There was drama, tragedy, pathos, comedy, farce, love and death. It was like a Shakespearean drama.'

This book, we hope, is a credible account of what happened between the acts, behind the scenes.

John Lee and Daniel McConnell
September 2016

1

'MY WAY'

It was early 2008 and Bertie Ahern had dominated the Irish political landscape for over a decade. A political phenomenon, Ahern had beaten the odds to be elected taoiseach for a third time in May 2007, only the second Fianna Fáil leader to win three back-to-back general elections. But victory had been achieved under a cloud – the Tribunal of Inquiry into Certain Planning Matters and Payments, commonly known as the Mahon Tribunal. Ahern had, for more than a year, been dogged by damaging press leaks of his private evidence to the tribunal, which continued during the election campaign.

There was deep disquiet in the Fianna Fáil-led government over the impact Ahern's tribunal wrangling was having. The public was stunned at the leader's claim he had no bank accounts while finance minister, at the loaning of Fianna Fáil monies to his partner, Celia Larkin, for the purchase of a house, and at his explanation that one large unexplained sum of cash was won backing horses. But ultimately he survived the repeated disclosures of his Byzantine personal finances to achieve that election victory.

Back in office, Ahern remained under tribunal scrutiny and, in September 2007, the taoiseach himself took the stand at the tribunal. For months his leadership was mired in bizarre explanations of his personal financial situation following the separation from his wife, Miriam Ahern. However, it was the appearance at the tribunal of Ahern's former secretary, Grainne Carruth, in the spring of 2008 that ultimately triggered his downfall. Under questioning in the witness box, Carruth broke down and repeatedly said, 'I just want to go home.' It was immediately clear that Carruth had no knowledge that could help the tribunal, but the spectacle of a young, innocent mother being humiliated was a low for the tribunal and a fatal moment for Ahern. The leader's travails at the tribunal were taking their toll on Fianna Fáil's morale.

Since the start of 2008, finance minister and tánaiste Brian Cowen had become increasingly uneasy about the leader's position but nevertheless remained a loyal supporter. After Carruth's appearance at the tribunal, he returned from an official ministerial visit to the Far East and immediately called Ahern at his Dublin Central constituency headquarters, a former doctor's surgery in Drumcondra known as St Luke's.

'I was away around the St Patrick's Day time and when I came back the secretary had been in the tribunal and there was all that controversy,' says Cowen in an interview for this book. 'We met up; I had to talk to him about the Anglo stuff [anyway],' he continues, referring to the so-called 'Paddy's Day Massacre', when Irish bank shares suffered horrendous losses on the stock market.

The unceasing controversy over the Mahon Tribunal was making Ahern's position untenable. Cowen was seen by the Fianna Fáil parliamentary party as the natural successor to him. It has been speculated that Cowen pushed Ahern out at the St Luke's meeting, but he insists there was no overt attempt to oust his leader. However, the two old friends, without articulating it, had come to the same conclusion about Ahern's position. 'I was the tánaiste, so my view was he has to come to his own decisions on those sorts of matters,' says Cowen. 'I think there had been a motion in the Dáil before we left for that trip and I finished up the debate so I was very much in his corner.'

Cowen continued to defend his boss in the Dáil even though

the resistance was becoming futile. 'But at the end of the day he was a politician who read the situation himself, and he decided that he wanted to step down,' explains Cowen. 'So he told me privately, in a telephone conversation on the Sunday [before his resignation]. I said I'd go with whatever he felt himself but that it was a matter for himself at the end of the day. I suppose his political assessment was whether he wanted to continue; I'm sure he could have continued if he wanted to. I think he came to that conclusion … that he should probably go at that stage.'

Then Minister for Health Mary Harney, who had once been Ahern's tánaiste, says he rang her in advance to tell her of his intention to stand down. 'In the run in to his standing down there was enormous controversy … He phoned me the night before he resigned to tell me he was standing down the next morning. And in the morning when he told the government, it was very emotional,' she said when interviewed by the authors.

'I think the general feeling was he was doing the right thing for himself and the right thing for the government, that everybody was well aware of the huge contribution that he had made. And it wasn't the timing of his choice, as he has since acknowledged.'

On the morning of Wednesday 2 April 2008, Ahern, flanked by Cowen and other ministers, formally announced his intention to resign on the steps of Government Buildings. Despite the tears in public, many in government were quietly pleased the Ahern era was over.

Micheál Martin, who less than three years later would become Fianna Fáil's leader, backed Ahern's decision. 'I think at the time the Mahon Tribunal was winding towards its end and we had the various incidents towards the end, with Bertie's testimony … particularly with Grainne Carruth, her testimony; you had a huge impact. I think Bertie Ahern took the right decision to resign.'

The Mahon Tribunal caused the two men to fall out in the coming years, with Martin publicly criticising his former leader.

Ahern had agreed a programme for a rainbow coalition government with the Green Party, the Progressive Democrats and Independents Jackie Healy-Rae, Beverley Flynn, Michael Lowry and Finian McGrath. Yet less than a year into the government, Fianna Fáil's main coalition partners, the Green Party, too, had grown tired of Ahern's troubles and were glad to see him go.

Eamon Ryan, then the Green Party minister for communications, energy and natural resources, says Ahern's tribunal fiasco was damaging to the government. 'I was glad when he stepped down, I thought it was right, in my mind it was just making it [his position] untenable, so my kind of sense when I heard the news was well, that's inevitable, and it's probably right.'

Secure in the knowledge that he would be the next taoiseach, Brian Cowen was prepared to allow Ahern an extended lap of honour as he exited. Ahern was scheduled to address the United States Congress on 30 April and Cowen felt that was 'a high point for him'.

On 6 May 2008 Ahern formally resigned. Brian Lenihan and Mary Coughlan nominated Cowen to be the next leader of Fianna Fáil and he was elected unopposed as its seventh leader and president. The following day, 7 May, Cowen was elected by Dáil Éireann as the new taoiseach by eighty-eight votes to seventy-six. He told the Dáil he was 'deeply honoured' and would take up the role with 'a genuine sense of humility'.

Cowen, a former solicitor, had a soaring intelligence and command of detail, and was an everyman who appeared to like a pint and a song. He was the darling of the backbenchers, who saw him as a combative and fierce defender of the party. He also represented a break from the past.

Cowen, not an emotionally demonstrative man, seemed relaxed on becoming the country's twelfth taoiseach. 'I knew it was a very big job and it was one that the party wanted me to do,' he said, 'but it's a big change going from a number two position to a number one position. It's a big difference. It's interesting, the minute you become taoiseach everyone starts calling you Taoiseach. There's a sense of respect obviously but there is also a sense of distance; you're expected to rise above the fray, and it's a new sense of authority that you don't realise until you're there.' Cowen's inability to separate himself from his close friends in the parliamentary party would cause him difficulties in the future.

Micheál Martin, an ambitious politician in his own right, seemed content to allow Cowen to go forward without a contest. 'I was happy for Brian Cowen to become taoiseach … and I supported him at the time. I had dealt with him as enterprise minister. I found him very matter of fact to deal with.

'If you had your homework done, if you had your material, if you were trying to get support for various initiatives [he'd help],' Martin claims.

Willie O'Dea, then defence minister, was another admirer of the Offaly TD. 'There was no question of anybody else being seriously considered, to the best of my recollection. It was a very smooth transition. There was a sense of relief; this man was a very competent guy, you know, he had proven himself. He had widespread support among the grass roots of the party and he was the right man to take the helm at a difficult time,' O'Dea remembers.

Others privately, however, were not as enamoured with Cowen's uncontested elevation. Former education minister Mary O'Rourke was uncomfortable that Cowen was appointed without a contest. 'It was all so smooth. Bertie anointed him, we all anointed him,' she recalls with the colourful turn of phrase that makes her such a compelling conversationalist.

'I know at the time Dermot Ahern was annoyed, he was miffed ... He felt there should have been some sort of a contest,' she adds. Critics in Fianna Fáil say that, in hindsight, the lack of a contest removed the chance to closely scrutinise Cowen and his leadership qualities.

Some ministers weren't even consulted, says Éamon Ó Cuiv, former minister for community, rural and Gaeltacht affairs and a grandson of party founder Éamon de Valera. 'As it happened, when Bertie Ahern announced that he was retiring I was in the air somewhere between Australia and America. By the time I got to New York that day, effectively Brian Cowen was the uncrowned king. I would not have been particularly close to Brian Cowen. I would not necessarily have chosen Brian Cowen.' Ó Cuiv echoes the opinion that Dermot Ahern had also wanted a contest: 'By that afternoon the job was done without a challenge. The only one I heard of [who was upset] was Dermot.'

Ó Cuiv also felt there were problems with Cowen's style of leadership. 'I would have seen him as very orthodox, as in maybe he would have taken the official line quite a bit. So, my reservations would be more of him being too swayed by officials.'

Bertie Ahern was a charismatic leader but he also used considerable charm when easing through difficult political measures. Cowen was a blunt man and Ó Cuiv foresaw problems there, too. He was following a leader who had been 'purely political' and had avoided confrontation. 'I also was not convinced that he had great people-handling skills. As in skills you would need around handling people politically, because he did not have the personal skills that Bertie Ahern would have.'

John McGuinness, the outspoken Kilkenny junior minister

for trade, became Cowen's most vocal critic but, while he didn't like the manner of his appointment, he admired Cowen. At first. 'I think that it was wrong the way it happened, that he was singled out and that there was no contest. But having said that, he had proved himself in the past in the Dáil in terms of debates. No one questioned his ability or his intelligence, or his understanding of government and policy.'

Cowen was a rural taoiseach from the old Albert Reynolds 'Country and Western' wing of Fianna Fáil. On entering the Dáil in 1984, when he was elected to his recently deceased father Ber Cowen's Laois–Offaly seat, Brian Cowen had firmly aligned himself with Reynolds' supporters. They were ingeniously christened by Charlie Haughey as the 'Country and Western' wing because of their preponderance in rural and western constituencies, and also thanks to Reynolds' honky-tonk TV appearance in the 1980s, dressed in cowboy gear, singing a Jim Reeves ballad which went 'put your sweet lips a little closer to the phone …'.

Having been elected taoiseach, Cowen's first job was to pick his Cabinet. His approach to his Cabinet formation marked out the differences in this new era. For one thing, there were no leaks – no colleagues or journalists had prior knowledge of the Cabinet.

There were gasps when Cowen's team walked into the Dáil Chamber behind him on Wednesday 7 May. Cowen fondly recalls the surprise as he led his Cabinet to their seats: 'I like the idea of a bit of suspense, that there is a sense of expectation … I didn't tell any of my colleagues what positions they were getting until the day I was appointed, with one exception. I told Brian Lenihan beforehand that he was being appointed to Finance … I told him a bit sooner, I knew he'd have to get into the zone for that but he was the one exception.' To the new leader, the appointment of a sophisticated TD from a Dublin constituency as minister for finance made solid sense.

Lenihan's appointment was a surprise for some. The Dublin West TD's family had hoped that he would be kept at the Department of Justice where he had, belatedly in the eyes of many, been promoted by Ahern in the summer of 2007. His brother, Conor Lenihan, says there was surprise in the family at the appointment, as barrister Brian had been less than a year in his dream job in Justice. 'He was extremely happy in the Department of Justice, he got on very well with the officials there,' he recalls. 'I think he did regret leaving Justice, he was very happy there, it was the kind of ministry which he would obviously enjoy given his legal background. I think he was surprised when Cowen asked him to be minister for finance.'

Éamon Ó Cuiv was also caught on the hop by Lenihan's promotion. 'Yeah, that surprised me because of his background, which was the law.' Ó Cuiv feels that the strong dynasty influences in traditional Irish politics, and electoral concerns wherein locality can trump ability, resulted in the wrong men in the wrong jobs. He believes that the taoiseach–minister for finance axis should be a good cop, bad cop one and Cowen had prospered as the bad cop in the past.

'Normally the minister for finance, you see it with [Michael] Noonan and so on, are people like [Ray] MacSharry, [Seán] McEntee in the old days … The minister for finance would be an enforcer,' says Ó Cuiv. 'I suppose the normal thing would be that the taoiseach would be a crowd-pleaser. Personality wise, I think Cowen had it the other way round.' Ó Cuiv thinks Lenihan was too nice, too conciliatory.

Revealing the somewhat chaotic nature of appointing ministers, Cowen recalls the frantic pace of phone calls to ministers that day. 'I had to hurriedly get people into the Sycamore Room [in Government Buildings]. They knew they were going to be in the Cabinet but then they didn't know what positions they were getting and there was sort of a little bit of expectation. So that's it, it was a bit different.'

Cowen had toyed with the idea of making Lenihan tánaiste in a bid to shore up support for Fianna Fáil in Dublin, but he struggled with who he would put into Finance. Among those he considered for the post were Micheál Martin, Dermot Ahern and Noel Dempsey, but all were deemed unsuitable.

Micheál Martin says he didn't canvass Cowen for promotion to Finance. 'I didn't lobby for anything or ask for anything.' He was as surprised as Lenihan when Cowen announced his Cabinet line-up. 'I had a very good relationship with Brian [Lenihan], and Brian came to me at the time and says, "Jeez, I thought you'd be the minister for finance", but we kind of had chats about it. I thought that Brian Cowen had to do what he had to do to bring in freshness and new faces and create his own stamp on the Cabinet.

'Obviously Finance is the most important portfolio in Cabinet, has a constitutional underpinning of its role no other Cabinet ministry has. That said, I understood the need that Brian [Cowen] had to create a freshness to the new Cabinet ... So I had no great issues when Brian Lenihan became minister for finance and Mary Coughlan was brought in as tánaiste.'

If there was surprise at Lenihan's elevation to Finance, Cowen's choice of tánaiste initially perplexed many. However, the appointment was welcomed as a real sign of progression in Irish politics. Not only was she a woman, she was a young, family woman whose easy, personable style made her popular among the parliamentary party. With a relatively low profile, Coughlan was another dynasty politician. Like Cowen in Laois–Offaly and Lenihan in Dublin West, Coughlan was elected to fill the constituency seat vacated by the premature death of her father (Donegal South-West), and Coughlan and Cowen shared a kinship. Their families were political families. As minister for agriculture, fisheries and food she had performed well. She had an informal manner dealing with the large farming lobby groups, and she held her own in a very male-dominated arena. Coughlan's promotion to tánaiste was seen as a major boost to the agenda of rural Ireland. Moreover, Cowen could trust her and she was ready to be loyal to him. As well as making Coughlan tánaiste, he moved her to the economically sensitive Department of Enterprise, Trade and Employment.

Gender was an increasingly important consideration when composing a Cabinet, and, at first, many welcomed the rare appointment of a woman to a senior Cabinet role. Of the 166 TDs, just twenty-two were women, which, at 13%, compared very badly internationally. Politics, like many of the professions in Ireland, for a long time had a greater proportion of men than women. Yet in politics, unlike many other professions, the gender balance was getting worse. Later, a 'gender quota', requiring that 30% of party candidates are female, was introduced to address the imbalance. This was necessary because there is a lot of aggression and political infighting in local political organisations and, often, professional women are reluctant to get involved. Moreover, the selection process is largely dominated by men, who put forward those who have done them favours in the past – other men. Any institution dominated by a particular group will naturally discriminate in favour of others in that group and outgoing TDs often play a role in selecting their successor – in many cases that means a man choosing a man. And even if women can ignore viciousness at a local level, national politics in Ireland is not family friendly. The Dáil sits late every Wednesday, and during political crises it can sit late every night. For many rural TDs this means staying in a Dublin hotel, away from your family.

Mary Hanafin and Mary Coughlan prospered in Fianna Fáil, that most male dominated of parties, but they were exceptions. Part of Coughlan's success was that she was able to curse and tell bawdy jokes with the men. But this didn't stop them turning on her when times got tough. She did not perform very well as tánaiste, and much of the reason for this was because she was a relatively inexperienced minister. While she had performed well in Agriculture, the demands on her in the new job were on another level, which even some of her supporters, like Dara Calleary, felt got on top of her. 'I think, unfortunately, Mary got stuck in to various battles. She did the Trade Missions, IDA etc. I often felt that she took on too much.' She was also thrown into the role at a time when a seasoned, conciliatory figure was needed. Yet many journalists who covered the period also witnessed a large degree of jealousy from male politicians in their attitude to Coughlan – many resented a woman for being promoted ahead of them. In this account others speak for her, as Coughlan was one of the very few Cabinet ministers who declined to give an interview for the book.

Initially, some praised Cowen for his inspired choices in completing the Fianna Fáil 'triumvirate' as he, Lenihan and Coughlan became known in the party. However, Willie O'Dea, who was seen as a close ally of Cowen and was tipped for higher office, stayed at Defence and was slightly disappointed. But, as he tells us, 'beggars can't be choosers'. The high-profile Limerick TD, who was the country's best vote-getter in 2007, was bemused at Cowen's selection of Lenihan and Coughlan. 'I remember being surprised,' he reveals. 'I mean, Lenihan proposed him as taoiseach and Mary Coughlan seconded. Because I knew Brian [Cowen] had been very close to Mary Coughlan I didn't realise he was in any way close to Lenihan at the time.'

Dermot Ahern became minister for justice, his fourth senior Cabinet position. Martin Cullen moved to Arts, Sport and Tourism, Micheál Martin went to Foreign Affairs and Noel Dempsey continued as minister for transport. Éamon Ó Cuiv remained minister for community, rural and Gaeltacht affairs, and Mary Harney stayed at the Department of Health. Pat Carey, a Dublin TD originally from Kerry, was appointed government chief whip, and Brendan Smith became minister for agriculture and food.

The two Green Party Cabinet ministers retained their portfolios. John Gormley stayed as minister for the environment, heritage and local government, and Eamon Ryan as minister for communications, energy and natural resources.

The only member of Cowen's closest group of Fianna Fáil parliamentary party friends promoted to Cabinet was Cork's Batt O'Keeffe. He became minister for education and science.

Mary Hanafin, a former schoolteacher, and a deputy who appeared to be in an almost perpetual state of disapproval at the shortcomings of others, frowned at Cowen's reputation as one of the lads. He frowned at her performance in Education and she was given Social and Family Affairs. 'I think she saw it as a demotion, it was generally seen as a demotion …' says O'Dea. 'A lot of our backbenchers had been complaining about Mary, they regarded her attitude as somewhat high-handed. I must say I didn't find that myself personally, but there were a lot of complaints.

'At Education you're always bringing people in about schools, and everybody wants a new extension, a new school and this and that. The backbenchers told me they found her very dismissive and they found the experience of bringing up a group of people from their constituency to meet the minister wasn't getting the votes for them, probably the opposite!'

Many thought Cowen should have ignored the mutterings from the backbenchers and appointed Hanafin, who represented Dún Laoghaire, as tánaiste instead of Coughlan. 'I do think it was a slight mistake. I'm not saying that Mary Coughlan was a mistake or a problem, although she did get into difficulties when in the job,' says Conor Lenihan. 'I think he might have been better off selecting Mary Hanafin, as a Dublin-based deputy, to be his tánaiste. And I think that would have been my thinking prior to when he selected his Cabinet. He needed a much stronger anchor in Dublin because Bertie Ahern had been so dominant in the Dublin electoral area.'

Brian Lenihan, because of his lack of financial expertise in the midst of a crisis, and Mary Coughlan, because of her lack of economic prowess in that same crisis, were subsequently criticised as appointments. Coughlan, indeed, was targeted viciously by the opposition and the media. However, Cowen, who was to admit to many mistakes in his interviews for this book, does not recant on his Cabinet selection. 'I stand over the decisions I made. Mary [Coughlan] was a very good colleague, we had this sort of situation in the past where having a woman in a prominent position is good, it reflects the modern country we live in I suppose, so I'd no problem with those appointments at all … I was happy with them.'

With his new Cabinet in place, Cowen headed home to Offaly to celebrate his becoming taoiseach. It was 10 May 2008 and he'd been taoiseach for three days. The triumphant Cowen homecoming meandered through Edenderry, Tullamore and his hometown, Clara, at the easy pace of the Brosna River. Cowen belted out songs in the towns of the county. There was a celebratory mood that day, a mix of relief, hope and expectation.

'The record shows, I took the blows, and did it my way ...' he sang from the back of a lorry in Tullamore.

Many of his parliamentary party colleagues and a large group of journalists joined him in Offaly that day and enjoyed the sun, beer and songs. And the party continued long into the night.

'Every taoiseach has had a homecoming of sorts, so I think they were doing what was traditional,' says Micheál Martin. 'Let's face it, when somebody becomes a taoiseach there is enormous pride. Ireland does local pride – the hometown, the village, the parish.

'I can understand it, right. But the storm clouds were gathering and in hindsight, looking back, I can see where people are [critical]. But I didn't take much notice of it at the time at all.'

While the scenes from the streets of Tullamore were lapped up by the rural TDs, many of the party's urban TDs winced at what they were seeing. As the images of Cowen's celebrations were beamed over the airwaves, some watched uneasily as their new figurehead blithely ignored the cameras to drink a few pints of Guinness and play to the crowd during his homecoming.

Mary Hanafin was adamant that such indulgences would do little to help the party's standing in the capital. As she told the 2012 RTÉ documentary *Crisis: Inside the Cowen Government*, 'I remember looking at that at the time, and maybe looking at some of the people who had gone down to be on the stage, and thinking that's not going to cut it in Dún Laoghaire, that's not going to cut it in Dublin, that's not going to influence the kind of urban voter that we so badly need.'

John McGuinness says the pictures from Offaly were a clear sign that all was not well in his beloved party. 'What transpired after that was this open-back truck down in his constituency, the homecoming, and it just signalled all of the things that were wrong with Fianna Fáil. That blind loyalty, that tribalism that certainly gets you all the numbers and gets you the vibe and the atmosphere that is necessary for good crowded meetings, and all that kind of thing. But it doesn't serve the political system well.'

In May 2008 the public was happy to allow Cowen his honeymoon. Fianna Fáil went up 5% in the polls in a week and 74% of the electorate approved of Cowen. 'About a month after he took over, there was an opinion poll and we were showing very well,' recalls Willie O'Dea. 'The Biffo bounce! Yes, I suppose that's what it was called anyway.'

The lap of honour concluded and the ministers returned to work. Cowen first set about appointing his back-room team. Veteran civil servant Joe Lennon, kept on from Bertie Ahern's administration, became Cowen's chef de cabinet. Another old Bertie man and the taoiseach's speechwriter, the clubbable Brian Murphy, also stayed on, and Professor Peter Clinch of University College Dublin (UCD) became Cowen's chief economic advisor.

They didn't come cheap, these men. At one point Lennon was earning €221,929, Clinch received €181,243 in 2010 and Murphy took home €131,687 per annum.

Cowen had also asked Ahern's government press secretary, Eoghan Ó Neachtain, to stay on. A former army officer from Spiddal, Co. Galway, Ó Neachtain is 6 feet 4 inches in height and tough but engaging. The former ESB communications manager had learned a lot in the crucible of Ahern's final days in power. As the fortunes of the government took a downturn, he was to stoically follow the army officer's tradition of entering the bunker to bring news of another disaster to his political master. The forthright, and sometimes combustible, discussions between Ó Neachtain and his new boss became legend.

To the lucky ones sitting around the Cabinet table, the differences between Ahern and Cowen were immediately evident.

Mary Harney reveals: 'Bertie was very much a consensus person, Brian Cowen was very much the opposite. He's much sharper. When I say sharper I don't mean intellectually sharper. He's a much blunter person. Bertie builds a consensus, reaches agreements. Brian Cowen is more of a "you're for it or you're against it" man. Brian Cowen is not as patient a person, he's a different personality,' she recalls.

Harney concedes that Cowen's more confrontational manner was influenced by events. 'Brian Cowen took over in completely different circumstances, it was almost emergency times ... Bertie was there for the main huge economic success.' Though she expresses firm opinions about the man who became her new boss, she also says, 'I had a very close personal relationship with Brian Cowen and I have a huge regard for him. He's very bright, he's very honest. Honest to a fault.'

The most obvious contrast between Bertie Ahern and Brian Cowen was in their attitudes to media. Ahern had become our first celebrity taoiseach, a natural on television. Cowen was something of a throwback, uncomfortable on television and less accommodating to reporters. From the off, Cowen suffered from a reluctance to engage with the media, according to Harney. 'Perception is reality,' she says. 'He wasn't into doing the media. If you were to ask me what mistakes the government made it was that we didn't have a good communications strategy. And he didn't want to do that.'

Pat Carey felt the taoiseach was too obsessed with detail. 'I wasn't very close to him, and it took me a while to get to the stage to say "Brian will you for fuck's sake" or something like that when he was leaning over Brian Murphy's [Cowen's speech writer] shoulder changing a sentence in a speech again and the bells in the Dáil would have stopped ringing to marshal the numbers.'

The chief whip saw a different man to the much-maligned

public persona. 'You had Brian Cowen, the country solicitor who was obsessive about detail. There is a view out there that Cowen paid no interest to detail. I worked very closely with the guy, I mean the guy would work himself to the bone on the detail. A stickler for the process and procedure ... And I often felt he would have been better if he stood back a bit and addressed the issues more in a big-picture fashion,' Carey remarks.

Cowen's honeymoon as taoiseach was cut short by the humiliating defeat of the Lisbon Treaty referendum on 12 June. That defeat for the government was brought on by an arrogant attitude and a lethargic campaign. The Lisbon Treaty, which would have given Ireland's assent to the establishment of a new European Union (EU) constitution, was defeated by a margin of 53.4% to 46.6%. A total of 752,451 people voted in favour of the treaty and 862,415 voted against. Mary Coughlan, Fine Gael leader Enda Kenny and Bertie Ahern all failed to carry the vote in their own constituencies.

'We were complacent I think. Any of these European referenda, I find, and I've participated in a number of them, you have to be very clear and you have to be very aggressive in your campaign because people really don't understand and a lot of them don't want to take the time to understand,' admits Willie O'Dea.

The 'No' argument, voiced by an eclectic mix of businessman Declan Ganley, singer-turned-politician 'Dana' Rosemary Scallon and the Sinn Féin party, managed to sow doubts over European armies and the losing of vetoes, while the 'Yes' side didn't get out of the traps.

O'Dea says of referendum votes: 'You've a lot of naysayers out there and some people go into the polling booth with the attitude "if in doubt leave it out".' He admits the government expected the electorate to turn up and vote the way it wanted them to. 'We didn't campaign aggressively enough. I think we kind of assumed another building block in the European project would be acceptable and do so much for us, but at that stage all the negatives of Europe had begun to come to the fore.'

O'Dea connects Cowen's Offaly celebrations with the rejection of the treaty. 'The [Lisbon result] must have caused him to realise that lap of honour probably did go on too long, that's what I thought anyway. I thought it would have just been better to just get into it, get on with it, but I didn't think at the time it made a great difference. I suppose in retrospect as you look back on it now, it wasn't a great start. When you're coming in you do need a good start.'

From the outset, Cowen's administration had the hex of the Lisbon loss hanging over it. 'The general feeling was: Jesus, this could be the start of something bad, this could be a sort of turning point,' says O'Dea.

Eamon Ryan also believes there was an inescapable connection between the change of leadership of Fianna Fáil and the perceptible relaxation in the government's campaigning efforts. 'I think it [Cowen's homecoming] was a real mistake ... because we took the eye off the ball on the Lisbon referendum somewhat, and I think for Brian Cowen and for the country and for the government that No vote had very significant repercussions ... And I think to a certain extent any distraction from that [was a mistake] ... you wouldn't fault the guy for going back to his hometown and having a rally or whatever but it should have been just absolute action stations around the referendum and nothing else ... I think that was a real problem for the government – once there was a No vote in it, it did a lot of damage.'

The campaign wasn't helped when Cowen admitted on the airwaves that he had not even read the text of the treaty.

Conor Lenihan says Cowen and the government were simply 'unprepared' to properly contest the referendum. It was a blow to morale that the referendum was 'lost as almost the first act of Brian Cowen's leadership. The problems and travails that affected Bertie from pretty much the point that he was re-elected, right up to the point that he resigned were [also] influential ... There is no doubt that the referendum was lost because the government took its eye off the ball. We were dealing with a round-the-clock crisis about the leader himself, and his difficulties at the tribunal. Certainly that did mean that the government was distracted, there is no point in pretending otherwise.'

The government had surrendered the political initiative to its opponents by the loss of the referendum, which had embarrassed them at a European level. But a far more pressing crisis was emerging. The economy was contracting and the new finance minister was panicked. Just weeks in office, already Brian Lenihan was attempting to prepare his Cabinet colleagues for the need to make dramatic cuts in government spending. Tax revenues were plummeting, the banks were beginning to look very fragile and drastic action was needed. The civil servants at the department that Cowen had just vacated had opened the books for the new minister and the financial predicament he'd inherited was already apparent.

Brian Lenihan had to deal with the worsening financial fortunes. Almost immediately, realising bold action would be needed, he reached out to Ray MacSharry, whose ruthless cutting of spending between 1987 and 1989 when he was finance minister earned him the nickname 'Mac the Knife'. MacSharry had sent a note of congratulation to Lenihan on his appointment, and says that the new minister was quick to pick up the phone and seek a meeting. 'He was keen not to do it so I would be seen around the department, given my record and my time there,' MacSharry reveals. 'He said, "Let's meet", so it was arranged that we would meet in the hotel in Enfield. His demeanour was concerned, there is no doubt about that. He was wondering was it possible to turn the corner even at that early juncture.

'There were no officials with either of us, we were on our own. We were there for a number of hours and the nature of the conversation was going through in the minutia of detail what was done in 1987 to 1989 ... Every single sub-head of spending was gone through and Lenihan was very interested in that,' says MacSharry. 'He was interested in that approach and felt that needed to be done again.

'That is the issue, he was trying to bring the country [along] as early as 2008 but it didn't happen until 2010. That was the problem. If you look at the hard decisions they took, they were all Lenihan's.'

MacSharry had tried to warn Charlie McCreevy and Brian Cowen when they were in Finance about spending recklessly from the temporary taxes generated by the property boom, but to no avail. 'I had spoken to McCreevy about how you cannot continue to spend revenue that you are not sure is going to be there in two, three or five years' time.' But because such warnings had been ignored, Lenihan now had to consider drastic action. 'Lenihan wanted to act and act swiftly in 2008.'

At first Lenihan's inner circle of political advisors was small at Finance. There was Cathy Herbert, the former RTÉ journalist who had been his special advisor at the Department of Justice. The Department of Finance already had two senior civil servants, Eoin Dorgan and Brian Meenan, who acted as his press officers throughout the crisis.

In those early months Conor Lenihan, the minister of state at the Department of Justice, was also close at hand. Brian Lenihan's younger brother became a *de facto* special advisor and a go-between with key members of the press and backbenchers. Like Brian, a former Belvedere College SJ pupil, Conor was well educated and had a razor-sharp political sense. A former political correspondent, he was well liked by sections of the media as well as party colleagues. He was also outspoken and unconventional but, for Brian, he was blood and so could be relied on.

Cabinet documents obtained under Freedom of Information (FOI) show the dispiriting information that Brian Lenihan was required to bring to Cabinet in those early weeks. The memos illustrate that Lenihan was aware of how quickly the budgetary situation was deteriorating in June 2008, 'particularly in terms of tax revenue', says Conor. He says that Brian quickly became distrustful of Department of Finance advice and felt the civil servants were too conservative for what was needed. Nevertheless Brian had to work closely with these civil servants.

On 13 June David Doyle, the secretary-general of the Department of Finance, under the heading 'Office of the Minister for Finance', wrote a memo to Lenihan entitled: 'Memorandum for Government Economic and Budgetary Strategy 2009–2011'. It was stamped 'Secret'. Doyle's note requested that the government be briefed that: 'The serious deterioration in the Public Finances in 2008, due to an emerging and severe tax shortfall in tax receipts of around €3 billion, will give rise to an estimated General Government Deficit (GGD) of close to 3% of GDP in 2008 … The projected deficit in 2009 to 2011 will exceed 3% unless stringent public spending adjustments are made now for 2008 and again in 2009, and/or taxes are raised significantly.'

To emphasise that he wasn't engaging in civil service scaremongering, Doyle, in his own hand, wrote to Lenihan in the margin: 'I recommend that this memo be circulated to Cabinet at first possible opportunity. Next Tuesday. You will need to discuss this with the taoiseach if possible. This memo presents the "diagnosis", a subsequent memo needs to present the "medicine".'

Brian Lenihan was up against some very experienced Cabinet ministers in the intense negotiations that followed such an apocalyptic memo. Conor Lenihan and others close to Brian say the rest of the Cabinet, including the taoiseach and the tánaiste, did not grasp the gravity of the situation. They were inclined to think that Lenihan's dire warnings were part of the poker game that goes on in advance of budget negotiations. 'I had a lot of discussions with Brian around this,' says Conor. 'And of course, at that point in time, a lot of then serving ministers were fighting these cuts in a very robust manner.'

Conor says that his brother thought there was a 'time lag' between the minister for finance's realisation of what action needed to be taken and the understanding hitting home to the taoiseach and the tánaiste. The minister for finance and the taoiseach, even at this early stage, differed in their 'perception of what was required and what was actually required. And I think that was one of the major sources of frustration for my brother as he carried out his role as minister for finance. In my discussions with him it was fairly clear that he felt that a lot of the ministers around the table didn't fully understand the huge impact this global downturn was having on Ireland,' says Conor. 'When one combined the global impact with the disappearance of the exchequer revenues that were derived from the construction sector, the speed with which the crisis was worsening … It meant that there was an extraordinary challenge at the exchequer level to rein back spending. A lot of the line ministers weren't aware of this.'

The confidential memo shows the Department of Finance painting a gloomy picture of what lay ahead. 'A combination of at least [€2 billion] in spending reductions below the existing levels and/or additional tax measures will be required in 2009 to stay below a 3% deficit if provision is to be made for even a very moderate package of Social Welfare increases and the bare minimum of pay increases under Towards 2016,' says the document that was presented to Cabinet. 'Towards 2016' was the name of the latest social partnership agreement, which was a process of power-sharing between the government, unions and employers, to examine pay – to later cause strife as the Croke Park Agreement.

It was difficult for politicians, who had become accustomed to seemingly limitless funds, to accept dire warnings of economic misfortunes to come, particularly when the memo in which they were written also argued for social welfare and public service pay increases. According to FOI documents, Doyle wrote in June, under the heading 'Minister for Finance Recommendation': 'The Minister considers that his next Budget must for both domestic and international considerations target a significant and sustained improvement in the public finances.'

The Department of Finance briefings continued to assume that there would be increases in certain areas. The troubling forecasts for 2009 were calculated, wrote Doyle, 'allowing for an extremely limited budget day package of: A social welfare package providing increases in line with the CPI forecast (2.5% in 2009). This would cost €466 million in 2009 (€506 million in a full year), €897 million in 2010 and €1,347 million in 2011. A pay settlement providing the same magnitude of 2.5% per annum under social partnership, with the 2009 element in two phases.' The memo also spoke of an income tax credit package which would cost the exchequer €365 million. The concern was evident, but still these were not the blandishments of a department which believed its finances were careering towards catastrophe.

Although Lenihan was issuing warnings, Cowen's closest advisors said that the minister for finance was misrepresenting the financial problems at Cabinet. He would keep data back until the last minute, they claimed, and present it without giving due notice to the taoiseach and others. Cowen would then be at a distinct disadvantage in Cabinet. 'I think Lenihan was fucking so cute … you know that kind of way?' says one source, a civil servant who worked at the Department of the Taoiseach throughout the years of this government. 'Lenihan's people even tried to bring in things to Cabinet that Peter Clinch, who was the economic advisor [to Cowen], wanted to look at first.'

This was to become a central issue of contention between the two rival courts – the Department of the Taoiseach and the Department of Finance.

'Lenihan was bringing things to Cabinet that no one would see, you'd have the Cabinet papers beforehand, and he was arriving in with stuff at the last minute,' the source reveals. 'He [Clinch] tried to get a situation where they had to give information in advance so he could then brief the taoiseach on the economic import of all of this kind of stuff. But no, they kept insisting that he'd bring it in at the last minute.'

Although there was tension, Cowen and Lenihan did not have open rows about the suppression of information from the taoiseach: 'No, no, I didn't experience that, no, they were too cute for that,' the source says.

On 17 June Lenihan presented the stark economic data and Doyle's memo to Cabinet, showing slowdowns everywhere. Since Bear Stearns had collapsed in the United States that spring, it was clear something was going seriously wrong in the international banking system. Cowen had been informed in a phone call from Seán FitzPatrick, the chairman of Anglo Irish Bank, while away in Malaysia on St Patrick's Day, of problems with Anglo shares. Cowen had discussed the issue with the Financial Regulator and Lenihan was briefed by the Department of Finance about problems in Anglo.

But concern about the Irish banking system was confined to a small group of government people. The general public had little idea there was a crisis looming until Lenihan spoke to reporters at a conference of Europe's construction leaders in Dublin Castle on 20 June. 'We have had a building boom going on in Ireland in the 1990s and I had the misfortune to become minister for finance a few weeks ago as the building boom is coming to a shuddering end,' he declared.

All hell broke loose. In response to Lenihan, Fine Gael's finance spokesman Richard Bruton asked: 'Where has he been for the last six months? Throughout that period all the indicators have pointed towards a collapse in the construction industry … It's a bit late for Minister Lenihan to wake up and smell the coffee, particularly when he is supposed to be maintaining vigilance on the economy.'

In government, the scale of the economic morass was beginning to dawn on ministers. Eamon Ryan remembers a key conversation with a top official who left him in no doubt as to how bad things were. 'The Revenue figures in that period [summer 2008] … were shocking, they just showed the fall off the cliff. I remember coming out of a meeting around about that time with a top civil servant who said, "The country's fucked. It's going down the tubes", because he saw the Revenue figures,' Ryan recalls.

Lenihan had to take affirmative action. In July he announced an unprecedented mini-budget to address the crisis. 'At that stage it was July, it was fairly clear we were facing into an economic crisis, the scale of it maybe we didn't understand but no one could but see it as a crisis. That's why there's an emergency budget, like how often do you have a budget in July?' exclaims Ryan.

On 8 July came confirmation for the unsuspecting majority of the public that Ireland had entered a new economic phase – a state it had not been familiar with since the early 1990s. Lenihan introduced a series of cutbacks to reduce public expenditure by €440 million by the end of 2008 and by a further €1 billion in 2009. The measures included a 3% cut in the public service, a voluntary redundancy scheme in the Health Service Executive (HSE) and other public agencies, and the proposed abolition of some state agencies.

Citing a projected shortfall of €3 billion in tax revenue for 2008 and an 11% rise in expenditure in the first half of the year, Lenihan said there was additional pressure on the public finances due to the rise in unemployment. He warned of a 'demanding' fiscal position in 2009, and said the situation facing the government the following year would be more difficult 'if we do not act now'.

The government postponed pay increases due in September for ministers, parliamentary office holders, judges and senior civil and public servants. But the instruction to government departments, state agencies and local authorities to reduce their payroll bill by 3% by the end of 2009 did not apply to the Departments of Health and Education, whose pay budgets were – and still are – the largest in the public sector.

Lenihan declined to quantify the level of job losses as a result of this measure, and he did not put a figure on specific savings that could be achieved through restrictions on overtime, recruitment and replacement of departing staff. He also spoke of a targeted scheme to reduce surplus staff in the HSE as soon as possible. There would be at least a 50% cut on external consultancies;

advertising and public relations would be significantly reduced for the remainder of 2008, and there would be further cuts in 2009.

Unspecified savings were to be made through an efficiency review initiated by Cowen before he left the Department of Finance to become taoiseach. The acquisition of office accommodation for the failed attempt to move government departments out of Dublin was put on hold. There was also an announcement of a €45 million cut to some €900 million in the government contribution for overseas development aid. Capital investment would remain a top priority for the government, and Lenihan said there were no plans to shelve any major projects.

Lenihan's family believe that from the very beginning of the crisis, in these crucial weeks, the rival camps were forming. Conor Lenihan says that the first fissures in unity at the top began to show as early as July 2008. 'I think many of them didn't fully understand the enormity of the deterioration in the exchequer finances.'

Yet Willie O'Dea insists that there was an understanding at this point that trouble was coming. Lenihan told his Cabinet colleagues that deep cuts should be made 'straight away, as soon as possible'. O'Dea accepts there was some opposition to the cuts in Cabinet. 'That was argued around the Cabinet table,' says O'Dea. 'Some people supported my view, some supported the other view, and ultimately the majority favoured the €440 million cuts … if you cut deeper or cut as deep as you have to at the start, it means you don't have to do it a second time. And the country has a longer period to recover.'

According to Conor Lenihan, Cowen's appointing of his brother to Finance was deliberate, as Brian Lenihan was not beholden to the financial decisions that went before, which could in theory make his job of cutting easier. 'Brian Cowen knew that difficult times were going to have to be entertained and difficult decisions were going to have to be made. The feeling was, given that times were going to be a little bit more difficult and challenging, that it would have been better to have Brian Lenihan in as minister for finance precisely because he didn't owe anything to the existing set of obligations and informal agreements that exist around a Cabinet table … In effect he was less compromised when it came to inflicting difficult medicine or cutbacks of one kind or another in that he owed nothing in terms of favours to the previous system.'

Despite having been a TD since 1996, and a member of an impeccably well-connected Fianna Fáil dynasty, Brian Lenihan had not made Cabinet until Bertie Ahern formed his last administration. He became minister for justice in 2007 and going into the crisis had only a year's experience as a front rank minister behind him. Cowen had been in and out of the Cabinet since 1992 and had a distinct advantage over his Cabinet colleagues. Far from misguidedly putting an inexperienced minister into a pivotal position, Cowen had moved Lenihan into Finance as the right man to introduce the politically toxic cuts he knew were necessary.

'In my view Brian Cowen exercised great judgement in putting him in because it is very difficult to come in if you've worked with colleagues over years on particular spending programmes to then start cutting those programmes,' says Conor Lenihan. Still, now that the time had come to cut, those close to Brian Lenihan believe that Cowen shrank from the more politically damaging requirements. 'Well I think at times there were tensions around the table from the very earliest days, between my brother and the rest of the Cabinet. And also with the taoiseach and the tánaiste as well … Frankly my brother, Brian, felt that neither Cowen nor Coughlan were fully aware of the extent of the crisis.'

As much as he may have wanted to, the financial storm clouds meant Cowen would no longer be able to do it 'His Way'.

2

NEW BOSS

In mid-July Brian Cowen flew to the United States on his first major trip abroad as taoiseach. He gave no sense to onlookers that the country he now led was nearing financial disaster. It was the first real glimpse of what life under Cowen was going to be like, and comparisons with Bertie Ahern could not be avoided. Ahern was an intelligent and diligent taoiseach – but obsessed with his image. He always looked good on television, and was as comfortable among assorted luminaries as he was among foreign statesman, backbenchers and voters while performing, for over a decade, as the unchallenged Irish political star. Cowen had little or no time for the vicissitudes of modern public relations. His priorities did not involve appearing slick, media friendly, healthy, in shape or a good communicator. He believed that people would be satisfied with the substance of what he would say.

In New York city, among the beautiful people, Cowen attended a reception for members of the touring Abbey and Gate theatres at the residence of Niall Burgess, the Irish consul general to New York. On the 52nd floor of the two-storey penthouse apartment overlooking an art deco masterpiece – the Chrysler Building – the Offaly taoiseach could have been forgiven for betraying a few pangs of inadequacy. When his entourage stepped into the room full of thespians, there was a collective gasp of star-struck awe as all eyes settled on 6 foot 4 inch Liam Neeson and his statuesque wife, Natasha Richardson. Distinguished actors Barry McGovern, Stephen Rea and Milo O'Shea, and Riverdance star Jean Butler added to the glamour. Cowen was asked to stand in for a photo with the sophisticated set. One of his aides meanwhile scurried to procure Neeson's autograph, allegedly for a female relative at home.

Cowen gave an impromptu press conference from the panoramic balcony. The taoiseach can give half a dozen of these small press conferences a day – they are called 'doorsteps' by media and politicians, and amount to impromptu interviews used for broadcast bulletins and soundbites. This was one of the more unusual locations for a doorstep.

By the time Cowen arrived at his next event, a Wall Street business leaders' dinner that night, he was sporting a new and crude haircut. The taoiseach had visited a random local barber near his hotel, Fitzpatrick's, on Lexington Avenue. Cowen wasn't oblivious to his image. Yet it was becoming clear on this trip that there would be less focus on appearances with this leader than there was with Ahern. Cowen accepts that he didn't do his best when it came to public relations, or in that description so prevalent in political discourse, communications. But his approach to his image was not without premeditation. 'I was trying to be authentic, being myself … I was doing my job but … not being this figure that's putting up a face that is not him at all. Do you know what I mean?'

Ahern had in many ways revolutionised the position Cowen now occupied, and the taoiseach was under constant, celebrity-level scrutiny. From the day he took office, Cowen's personal appearance and lifestyle became a topic of much media attention. Many of the politicians we spoke to repeated two words when describing Cowen – 'intelligent' and 'shy'. However, of himself, Cowen says he is 'gregarious'. He gets to the heart of the matter when asked about his relationship with the media and their portrayal of him. 'They didn't know me at all.'

Aside from his much-criticised personal presentation and manner, the truth is Cowen is a complex figure. What could have been endearing and even reassuring idiosyncrasies in good times were soon warped into flaws and failings in the white heat of an unprecedented crisis. Because of his difficult relationship with the media, Cowen became the victim of bitter attacks from his political enemies and political commentators.

Often on overseas trips, the press travel with the taoiseach's entourage and have unique access to the leader. The New York group, which included one of the authors of this book, John Lee, had moved around according to the taoiseach's meetings all day and there was no question of anyone touching a drop of alcohol. Cowen had given a brief speech to end his day's work at around 5 p.m. at the Irish Consulate on Park Avenue. As he stepped down from the rostrum, he loosened his tie, put his hand through his hair and was handed a bottle of Heineken. He immediately looked a little too relaxed. With talk of his personal style already out in the ether, there was murmuring in the room about this little scene, though most agreed it wouldn't have been commented on with Ahern.

Cowen was already being treated differently from Ahern and he knew it. 'At the end of the day, there is no doubt I'm a gregarious type of fella, you know what I mean … if I have a long day or a hard day I relax by talking about other things. I sit down and have a couple of pints with a couple of people. I mean Bert [Ahern] would have done that and there wasn't anything about it, but Brian Cowen was having a drink – then, suddenly, it became a big issue.'

There are a number of reasons Cowen was discriminated against when it came to the issue of socialising. Rumours circulated in the intersecting worlds of politics and journalism that he zealously enjoyed a drink. Journalists, to their discredit, enhanced these rumours and sometimes deftly wound them into coverage. Political enemies who observed Cowen socialising exacerbated the rumours.

It was not in Cowen's favour that his 'local' in Dublin was the opposition-roaming Dáil bar. His immediate predecessor, Bertie Ahern, was rarely seen in the Dáil bar, preferring to travel the two miles to his Drumcondra neighbourhood to join friends in Fagan's, Kennedy's or the Goose Tavern. The leader before Ahern, Charlie Haughey, would not miss an opportunity to quaff 1967 Château d'Yquem with his mistress and to fraternise with back-benchers over beer. And yet Haughey, a big drinker, was rarely seen in public with a drink in his hand. Albert Reynolds was a teetotaller. Cowen's three immediate predecessors understood the value of distance for a leader. Yet they also understood the value, in a community-based, family-driven party like Fianna Fáil, of staying close to and identifying with the troops. It is a notoriously difficult balancing act.

There isn't always logic attached to press coverage, which is decided on by human beings susceptible to the prejudices and failings common to all. Enda Kenny, for instance, has not been subjected to the harassment that Cowen was in his time as taoiseach. Cowen, when it came to his treatment in the press, was unlucky, as he was to be in many aspects of his premiership.

During the trip to New York, Cowen also met then mayor Michael Bloomberg, a legendary business magnate. He visited with 'Masters of the Universe' on Wall Street and met enough financial wizards to get a comprehensive briefing on the global financial and banking landscape. But he was given no sense of the crisis brewing in Manhattan at Lehman's and other finance houses, nor did he show that he detected any.

Throughout the trip, he seemed preoccupied by events at home. Cowen made it known he was 'furious' at statements by the French president, Nicolas Sarkozy, about his belief that Ireland should run a second referendum to pass the Lisbon Treaty. Back in Dublin, Cowen met Sarkozy at Government Buildings, yet all seemed cordial between the two, with Sarkozy planting kisses on both of Cowen's cheeks.

While pressure was put on the government by foreign heads of state in public, behind the scenes pressure was also being exerted by the banks for the state to do something about their situation. Following the St Patrick's Day fall in the value of Irish bank shares, senior government officials and advisors were lobbied by banking figures to introduce some form of state support or guarantee to stave off further attacks on the Irish banks. When financial share dealers become aware that a sector is weak they will sell shares, and the sale of a large volume of shares diminishes their value. Irish bankers believed an injection of government cash would restore confidence in Irish banks on international share markets.

Kevin Cardiff, who was then second secretary at the Department of Finance, said the extensive lobbying of senior government figures by bankers and businesspeople for some form of guarantee began in March 2008. Cowen has also confirmed that there were discussions in April and May about a guarantee. Indeed, according to Cardiff's contemporaneous notes, at the end of April 2008 Anglo Irish Bank chairman Seán FitzPatrick told the Central Bank governor, John Hurley, that there should be a guarantee. A few days later, somebody with the initials DD did the same, according to Cardiff's notes. 'There's two people it could be in my mind, but it's not fair [to speculate],' he told the Banking Inquiry in 2015. Notable figures in the financial world at the time included David Drumm, the chief executive of Anglo

Irish Bank, and the financier Dermot Desmond, who did lobby for a guarantee.

Charlie McCreevy, the EU commissioner, also suggested a guarantee was needed. In July Davy Stockbrokers did the same. That same month David Drumm also informed the Financial Regulator that he would negotiate with ten large Anglo customers to purchase businessman Seán Quinn's shareholdings in the bank in an effort to reduce its exposure.

Then, on 28 July 2008, Cowen played golf and had dinner with Seán FitzPatrick. The dinner later fuelled unsubstantiated rumours that senior government figures were personally close to bankers. The meeting became a source of significant public controversy when revealed in the newspapers. The game had been organised by Fintan Drury, Cowen's friend, who had resigned as a director of Anglo a month earlier. After the game at the Druids Heath (a fashionable, if less prestigious course than the other one at the complex, Druids Glen, the former Irish Open venue) there was an unscheduled dinner. FitzPatrick has refused to say what was discussed. Cowen insists it did not relate to the developing crisis in Anglo but covered 'the world, Ireland, the economy. It was absolutely nothing to do with Seán Quinn or with Anglo Irish Bank or anything like that.'

Gary McCann, former chairman of Smurfit Kappa, and Alan Gray, Cowen's friend and a leading economist and director with Indecon Consultants, were also there. Gray was a Cowen-appointed member of the Central Bank board. It is hard to believe that matters of high finance did not arise either on the golf course or over dinner. While Cowen rejects the claim that anything sinister took place that day, he later stood accused of sins of omission for not disclosing it.

By the end of July the Irish banks and the Irish public finances were in deep trouble and needed decisive action. Yet, despite the gathering storm clouds, Cowen and his ministers headed off on their summer holidays, seemingly oblivious, or unwilling, to confront the maelstrom coming their way.

Cowen's summer break began in earnest at the end of July, leaving him open to criticism. Mary O'Rourke says that the taoiseach 'needed his holidays' but complains 'we never heard from Brian Cowen for five weeks. So we had lost Lisbon, he was our new leader, but where was he? What was he saying, doing and thinking? We didn't know.'

She contrasts this with Brian Lenihan's approach. 'Brian was all the time head-down working. I think he and the family only went to Ballyconneely for a very short time. He had a lot to master and a lot to do. And the bad news was breaking not on a daily basis but on an hourly basis … he got very aware very quickly that things were very bad.'

Ballyconneely, outside Clifden in Connemara, was where Brian Cowen and Brian Lenihan, whose lives had so many parallels, routinely spent their August holidays with their families. It was here Cowen experienced the new levels of scrutiny that came with being taoiseach. That summer the family stopped off at the Galway Races on the way to Ballyconneely. It was the first year that there was no 'Galway Tent', as Fianna Fáil's infamous Ballybrit Suite marquee had come to be known. This was a fundraising event held every year at the Galway Races. During the boom, the Tent took on legendary status as a hub in which politicians, developers and bankers interacted. Politically, enemies of Fianna Fáil in the Dáil used the Tent to attack Cowen and company for the 'axis of collusion' that caused the country's downfall. In one of his first and most astute moves, Cowen had abolished the annual corporate day out for those developers, businesspeople and hangers-on who wanted to get close to Bertie Ahern and his financier friend Des Richardson.

Cowen and his wife, Mary, kept a mobile home in a caravan park overlooking the Atlantic. Though hardly Camp David, it has the most enviable views of a setting western sun and was strategically located beside the links of Connemara Golf Club. Cowen's two young daughters could also enjoy a seaside holiday. The mobile home had been a haven for the family for years. Yet journalists were to find, to their surprise, that mundane assignments to see what the taoiseach was up to on his holidays revealed a shockingly low level of security that allowed them to drive right up to his mobile home. He was interviewed there in August by Niamh Horan, a *Sunday Independent* journalist, as a number of media commentators asked whether, with what was then called the 'credit crunch' tightening and pay talks collapsing, he should be on holiday at all.

Again, Cowen was being unfairly judged, as he had by mid-summer instituted a secret team of officials at the Department of Finance, including Kevin Cardiff, which was working on a contingency plan in case the banking system collapsed. Cardiff says, 'We were afraid that at any point the knowledge there was a team working on a banking rescue might trigger a run.'

Cardiff's preparation for a potential banking collapse included a carefully constructed simulation exercise in which the Department of Finance, the Central Bank of Ireland and the Financial Regulator pretended one Irish bank was in trouble. 'Those parties playing the Central Bank/Financial Regulator [recommended] that the government should provide a guarantee,' Cardiff recalls. 'Those playing the government were more reluctant to rely on the transfer of risks to government. One key lesson, therefore, was that one should not jump too quickly for a guarantee approach and should insist on a broader consideration of options. There was a real consciousness of the necessity to avoid knee-jerk guarantee responses.'

In early September financier Dermot Desmond rang Central Bank governor John Hurley about a guarantee and said, 'Look, I'm in this market, I see things happening. I think you might need to consider this guarantee thing.' Later in the month, a guarantee was raised by Gillian Bowler, chairwoman of Irish Life & Permanent, and, separately, by Brian Goggin, the chief executive of Bank of Ireland, with senior government officials.

Fears of a bank run, which had happened with Northern Rock in Britain the year before, stalked the government. Whereas Cowen was handling a lot of the low-key communication with the banks himself, Brian Lenihan was, as ever, more conscious of how matters looked to the public. He got Conor Lenihan to conduct some behind-the-scenes work. 'I communicated with people from all the banks,' says Conor. 'At that particular point in time there was an issue about the brother even meeting people from a senior level from certain banks because that would start further rumours and reports of catastrophe *et cetera* ... I was doing a lot of work for Brian, meeting members of the banking community, senior executives, and people who wanted to help out, including businessmen and people from the investment community. And also the international financial community, who wanted to be of assistance to Ireland.'

Brian Lenihan, as well as being suspicious of his officials at the Department of Finance, was developing a cynicism towards the information coming out of the banks. 'And a lot of people within the banking structures of Ireland were very suspicious, even at director level, of what their own executives were telling them in relation to the true state of the bank's balance sheet,' says Conor. The banks were telling the government in official communications that 'there wasn't an issue or a difficulty'. The Lenihans' fears about and mistrust of the banks would be justified.

Conor Lenihan says that he and his brother lifted the lid on a deeply dysfunctional banking sector during those summer months, when they discovered that even board members at banks were concerned that they weren't getting the full picture from their own banks in terms of the balance sheet situation. In a certain sector of lending, the banks didn't seem to have a holistic understanding of what was going on. The board members said they were not getting a clear view of 'the lending exposure of the bank to the property sector'.

'In fact we knew from words and information that were being communicated to me personally and to the minister for finance, Brian Lenihan, privately, that there was a great deal of unease in these banks,' says Conor.

The attitude of the Lenihans was that the banking sector as a whole had gotten itself into trouble. 'There was a tendency among bankers to blame Anglo Irish Bank for everything. The more established banks wanted to focus on the situation at Anglo, rather than looking at the situation at their own bank … a number of the banks decided that Anglo should be closed. But we didn't believe that was a solution. Nobody believed that the problem was confined to Anglo,' he says.

There was enhanced concern about international and national finances as it became clear that the European Union was slipping towards recession. On 3 September Lenihan brought an extensive memo (available under the Freedom of Information Act) to Cabinet. It outlined a forbidding new fiscal and economic position. According to the document, which is stamped 'Secret', 'conditions in the economy have deteriorated sharply over the summer and the position of the public finances has worsened considerably'. In handwriting at the top of the cover sheet it says, 'sent to Minister 30 August. Discussed between Minister and Taoiseach 30 August', which indicates close co-operation between Lenihan and Cowen at this stage.

Lenihan, in a document entitled 'Speaking points for Government meeting, 3 September 2008', outlines a chilling scenario. 'In July the government adopted measures to make savings of €440 million in 2008 and €1 billion in 2009. This was based on the assumption of a tax shortfall of €3 billion for the year and GDP growth of 1.25% in 2008, with growth averaging 3.5% over 2009–2011 period … these assumptions are no longer realistic.'

Lenihan's briefing note continues: 'At the end of June, Exchequer tax receipts were some €1.45 billion behind target. Tax receipts in July and August were €1.3 billion below profile for those two months alone … At this stage it is now expected that the tax shortfall will be at least €5 billion this year and it could be higher.'

It was at this 3 September meeting that Lenihan proposed moving the biggest showpiece of the government's year. 'Given the scale of the situation and the need for a co-ordinated government response, I am proposing that Budget Day be brought forward to Tuesday, 14 October 2008.' He went on to propose a series of additional cost-saving measures and concluded his address by saying, 'If action is not taken now on the spending side, wide-scale sustained and substantial tax increases are inevitable.'

There had been no official public statements of any substance from the government on the banks, but growing speculation was creeping into the newspapers. On 7 September the *Mail on Sunday* ran a splash story on the front page with the headline: 'Cowen to Bail out Banks'. The story had been leaked by the Department of Finance to John Lee in an attempt to quell the jitters of the wider population. As a whole the Irish nation had not yet woken up to the new financial storms engulfing the country, but for the government it was only a matter of time, and leaking to the media was one way of softening up the people.

With the Department of Finance, Central Bank and Financial Regulator engaged in war games, preparing for financial Armageddon, Fianna Fáil did what it then did best – it convened for pints and a sing-song. The annual Fianna Fáil parliamentary party meeting at a plush rural hotel was scheduled for 15 September 2008 and proved to be the opening ceremony for a hellish Dáil session ahead.

The entire Fianna Fáil parliamentary party of over a hundred TDs, senators and MEPs headed for the Clayton Hotel in Galway, accompanied by journalists and a few handlers. Crossing the country in a rush, Brian Cowen's black Mercedes E240 was clocked doing 106km in an 80km zone near the Galway village of Kilreekil. He was hurrying to make an 11 a.m. photo call.

As the group was preparing for dinner that evening, news was breaking on CNN and Sky News from New York that financial services firm Lehman Brothers had filed for Chapter 11 bankruptcy protection that day. The filing remains the largest bankruptcy in US history, with Lehman's holding over $600 billion in assets.

As the financial world struggled to understand the ramifications, Cowen and Lenihan didn't see the need to avoid a social get-together that evening after the workshops and talks. This was Cowen's first 'think-in' as leader and there was no outbreak of the carousing and heavy drinking that had marked such events in the past. The swirling rumours and tangible concerns about the financial system had affected the mood of proceedings.

At the event, millionaire TD Ned O'Keeffe warned that bank

runs were imminent. 'Have you any bank shares, John?' O'Keeffe asked Lee in his notoriously impenetrable Cork accent. 'If you do, sell them. We'll be queuing at soup kitchens soon.' As always with O'Keeffe, it was difficult to determine whether he was being serious or not.

After dinner the 120 guests sat and watched as a homespun, traditional hooley unfolded in the main ballroom of the Clayton. It couldn't have been in greater contrast to the antics of the champagne-quaffing, faux sophisticates who had inhabited, up until the previous year, the Galway Tent just a few hundred yards away at Ballybrit Racecourse. Mícheál Ó Muircheartaigh, former commentator of the GAA, gave the keynote speech. On the stage was a prestigious traditional super group featuring singer Eleanor Shanley and accordion player Sharon Shannon. Shanley gave a particularly rousing rendition of 'Raglan Road'.

But the main act was the taoiseach himself – he crooned Percy French's much-loved ballad 'The Mountains of Mourne'. As Wall Street was reeling from its impending financial collapse, it was appropriate that the taoiseach should sing the lyric 'gangs of them digging for gold in the streets'. Cowen's audience of TDs and senators joined in to sing about the Irish lad who heads to London to find his fortune. There was a chorus of willing accompanists for the heartfelt line: 'But for all that I found there I might as well be/Where the Mountains of Mourne sweep down to the sea.'

Joining in was Fianna Fáil TD Beverley Flynn, attending her first parliamentary party get-together in many years. Cowen had readmitted the daughter of former EU commissioner Pádraig Flynn to the parliamentary party after a suspension due to allegations of the role she played in the National Irish Bank scandal in the 1990s.

As TDs spread out to the various bars, Brian Lenihan mingled in the main bar with a group of journalists. The finance minister enjoyed glasses of red wine and seemed utterly unperturbed by what was going on in the United States. He remained socialising until after 3 a.m.

Dara Calleary had been elected to the Dáil for the Mayo constituency in 2007. Son of former Mayo TD Seán Calleary, Dara was promoted to junior minister the following year. He, like many others, was taken aback at the relaxed demeanour of the two Brians. 'If you want to bring it back to just September, the day Lehman's went, we were having our think-in in Galway, the first think-in,' recalls Calleary. 'And one thing that jarred me and jars me to this day was waking up on a Monday morning, and Lehman's was going, and on a Tuesday morning the various ministers left the parliamentary party meeting to go back and do a deal on social partnership. What the fuck!'

Social partnership had originated in the late 1980s, bringing government, trade unions and employers together in a bid to avoid industrial unrest. Highly successful in its early days, it became increasingly controversial as it sought to award pay increases to employees at a time when the country's finances were in freefall. Brian Lenihan, too, was privately sceptical of the merit of looking at pay increases to state employees at such a delicate time, but held his fire.

The TV images of New York bankers leaving offices with boxes of belongings were a wake-up call to everyone who watched them. Calleary felt that the convivial atmosphere in Galway was in stark contrast to the New York events. 'But it just struck me as unusual given everybody understood Lehman's was a world thing, and we were going to sign ourselves into something [social partnership] for two or three years,' he says. 'You know it shows the instability of the time. Lehman's going and the impact that had, Northern Rock going and the impact this had, absolutely fed into the bank guarantee ... We did not want to be the country that woke up, and next day people could literally not get their money. And we did not want to be the country that recused on its banks.'

Yet Cowen and Lenihan thought it essential to work hard on keeping an air of normality. As they showed over the coming two-and-a-half years, neither man was given to publicly displaying evidence of the effects of pressure.

At this time Michael Somers, chief executive of the National Treasury Management Agency (NTMA), told the secretary of the Department of Finance, Kevin Cardiff, that a blanket guarantee 'might have an adverse [effect] ... it might look bad in the market'.

The perilous state of Ireland's finances, which had been kept, to a degree, among the financial and political classes, was about to emerge into the open via that national discussion forum – RTÉ radio's *Liveline*. On Thursday 18 September Ireland almost experienced a bank run triggered by this radio talk show.

With its daily invitation to 'Talk to Joe', Joe Duffy's *Liveline* is considered eerily precise when gauging the mood of the masses. *Liveline* began its programme that Thursday with an employee of An Post extolling its security for savers. However, it quickly began to give panicked callers free rein to express their lack of confidence in the banking system. Several callers told of how they had withdrawn their money from banks, some of which were identified, and were either carrying it around on their person, or considering keeping it 'under the mattress', or even burying it in their garden. Seemingly many were oblivious to issues of personal security. Duffy asked one woman what it felt like carrying over

€70,000 'down the street', and another man how he would feel carrying his savings with him 'on the bus'.

At one stage, Duffy sought to editorialise, offering his opinion on the stability of the banking system. 'I think people will not believe them,' he said, if the Irish banks tried to assure customers that they were stable. Duffy also suggested that were the government to raise the deposit guarantee limit it would be seen as a 'panic' measure. Up to this point, the government guaranteed all deposits of up to €20,000 held in domestic banks.

Seemingly appalled that ordinary people might actually be aware of the factual predicament of their banks, Brian Lenihan contacted the national broadcaster. He rang the director-general of RTÉ that day to express his outrage at *Liveline* causing fears which might lead to a run on the banks. Officials in his department had told Lenihan that the Financial Regulator and banks across the country were being 'inundated' with telephone calls from customers alarmed that they were about to lose their savings.

Mary Harney recalls an incident in her local bank branch in Clonskeagh in Dublin. 'After that day my husband, Brian, went into our bank, which is at the top of the road, AIB in Clonskeagh, and he remembers the bank manager crying, a woman saying to him "everybody is in here looking for their money".

'I remember Brian telling me that evening "the bank manager is under terrible pressure".' Harney said she could tell something serious was happening in the banks. 'I had a feeling in those two weeks that things were really, really serious. I knew of people who were telling me that they were going to banks to take their money out. I knew of one reasonably well-off friend who was hammering down the door and they were told they had to give a week's notice.'

Significant sums were removed from Irish banks over the

following days and an estimated €50 million was lodged in An Post's state-guaranteed savings scheme in just one 24-hour period.

RTÉ publicly sought to defend Duffy and the *Liveline* team, stating that the programme 'fulfils a legitimate function' in allowing 'ordinary people' to express their views. Lenihan made public his concern about the programme on Friday morning when RTÉ's then economics editor, George Lee, interviewed him. He insisted that deposits were not in any danger and said that people should not be going to banks to shift their deposit accounts 'on the basis of unfounded allegations made on radio programmes'.

Lenihan's strategy – dealing with the emerging banking crisis behind the scenes while publicly maintaining confidence – had been blown apart. That Saturday, 20 September, it was announced via the Department of Finance's website that the government would guarantee all deposits in Ireland up to €100,000, increasing significantly the existing €20,000 state guarantee on private bank deposits. This told the world that Irish banks were in real trouble.

According to Éamon Ó Cuiv, who explains the crucial events of those weeks in September in his familiar, homespun style, it was the rapid failure of this initial measure that made it clear to the government that a larger one would be required. 'Things were fairly reassured with the €20,000 guarantee and we didn't face any serious trouble until the famous Joe Duffy incident, where people were running down to the bank, taking it out, and putting it into the post office.

'And everyone thought that the big risk was that domestic deposits would fly out of the banks and that this would cause, as it would in any bank no matter how solvent it was, a major liquidity crisis … Without a murmur from anybody, we raised that guarantee to 100 grand … Okay so there was a little bandage that stopped the blood from flowing out, the blood being the money. And that seemed to be holding nice and we didn't seem to be getting a Northern Rock situation. Until the bandage started to leak blood seriously and there was the potential that it would burst.'

The €100,000 deposit guarantee gave the government just ten days breathing room. 'Now that guarantee only lasted a week and the run was coming again,' says Ó Cuiv. 'The banks were warning us that people were going to be queuing up outside the banks – queuing for their money.' He believes wholesale runs on the banks, with customers withdrawing all their money, recalling traumatic images of the United States and Germany in the 1930s, was a distinct possibility in Ireland in September 2008.

'It was the high-street banks, particularly AIB bank, had the run on it. What I call the Joe Duffy run,' he says. As the week progressed, it became clear to him and the other ministers that the €100,000 deposit guarantee had already exposed the state to the extent of €80 billion. €80 billion it didn't have. The Cabinet was slowly coming to understand that Ireland might be bust.

Eamon Ryan, too, says they were confronted with a bank run. 'Look at the television at the time, I mean it was scary … it wasn't as if we weren't absolutely fixated on the economic situation – it was clear for everyone that this [bank run] was unprecedented.

'I mean you got An Post, there's a run on the banks, there's a run on the banks! Do you know what a run on the banks is like, how much is going today? Billions. And when that's happening, that's not small,' Ryan recalls in an animated fashion.

Cowen, Lenihan, Kevin Cardiff and others in authority were discussing a guarantee in some shape or form as September progressed, and as Ó Cuiv points out, the deposit guarantee had already exposed the state beyond its means.

Conor Lenihan continued to act as his brother's unofficial go-between with the banks. 'I was very active meeting banking people from all of the banks in the run in to the guarantee. Sometimes these were official, as in people who had an official role to represent the bank with the government, and in some cases it was unofficial ... People from the bank who wanted to make unofficial contact with the government without their own board or their own senior executives knowing about that contact did so through me.'

The Central Bank was the government's means of communication with the European Central Bank (ECB) and its president, Jean-Claude Trichet. 'In fact John Hurley did fantastic work in this phase for the government and the country because John Hurley was not in good health,' says Conor. 'At the request of my brother he agreed to stay on longer in the job, despite his own personal health, because he was an extremely good friend of Trichet's. John Hurley spent most of the period of the crisis virtually living in Frankfurt, liaising with Trichet ... He would dine pretty much weekly with Trichet in Frankfurt during this period ... He was the subject of very unfair commentary about his position as Central Bank governor but he was very valuable in terms of his relationship with the ECB.'

Despite the mounting crisis, for the week of Monday 22 to Friday 26 September Brian Lenihan's diary was filled with budget meetings with ministers and officials. Meetings continued between officials and the banks. Conor continued to represent Brian with the banks. 'Obviously the situation was worsening, you had all of the banks ... getting very agitated, there was a series of meetings, informal, formal, between the Department of Finance and their senior executives.'

Brian Lenihan's diary says that on Saturday 27 September

his afternoon appointment was '1 p.m. Gowran Park Race Day, Gowran Park.' Lenihan later claimed that at this time he received a warning from Jean-Claude Trichet telling him to 'save' Irish banks. The exact circumstances of what was said, and when, have, despite the Banking Inquiry, never been fully established. In an interview for the RTÉ One documentary *Freefall*, which was broadcast in September 2010, Lenihan said, 'Mr Trichet rang me, and hadn't been able to get through to me. I was at a racecourse in County Kilkenny at a Fianna Fáil event on the Saturday. So I caught up with Mr Trichet's message the following day, which was that "you must save your banks at all costs".'

However, Trichet has denied that he phoned Lenihan in the days before the bank guarantee to insist that the Irish government save its banks at all costs. When asked about the late finance minister's statement, Trichet told members of the Banking Inquiry that there was 'no message to Brian, no message to the government of Ireland'. In an interview with Danny McConnell, published in the *Sunday Independent* in September 2013, Trichet denied repeatedly that Ireland was singled out by the ECB to be punished: 'we had the same message to all countries. Because they all had enormous banking difficulties. Whether Germany, Belgium, Ireland France … same message. The message was for all of them – when you take any decision, take into account all dimensions of these decisions, including the systemic aspects of these decisions.'

In a new twist to this story, Kilkenny TD and former junior minister John McGuinness, who was already becoming close to Lenihan, was with him for most of the day at Gowran Park. He gives his insight into what happened. 'I remember being at a fundraising meeting in Gowran, a horse-racing meeting, and we were standing outside on the balcony discussing anything and everything, in general conversation, and Brian Lenihan was beside me and he was called away to take a phone call … and when he came back, after some time, I remember him being ashen-faced. And he looked at me with those big wide eyes and he said, "John we're in real trouble." It was from Trichet; he did phone him that day. It was on his mobile phone that he called him – I was standing beside him.'

McGuinness was asked whether there was any discussion of what had been said. 'No. But everyone knew how serious that phone call was. Because Brian Lenihan was not the happy-go-lucky Brian Lenihan after that call as he was before it. He just quickly finished what he was doing and left.'

The following day, Sunday 28 September, officials from the department had a lengthy meeting with the NTMA at which they were 'working out the options'. There was no sense of urgency or imminent need for action on the banks. Lenihan and his top officials had detailed meetings with the Central Bank governor and the Financial Regulator. Cowen told us: 'We had discussed it on the Sunday. We didn't expect the thing to hit on the Monday.'

Éamon Ó Cuiv believes that the state was already in over its head at this stage. 'You see everybody forgets, we had already gone for broke in reality by putting the €100,000 guarantee in. I've been given varying estimates, between €50 and €80 billion … So if everybody went to the banks we didn't have enough cash anyway, nobody had €80 billion on hand and there was no emergency liquidity available from the ECB. So in fact at that stage if there really was a run on the banks you're out of your depth anyway.'

Willie O'Dea did not believe that he was given sufficient information at the Sunday Cabinet meeting or any other before the blanket guarantee that was imposed in the early hours of the following Tuesday. 'Well we had a rough agreement about the figures, [but] there was no agreement to my knowledge about a course of action, particularly about the guarantee … I mean if we'd agreed, in principle even, to something as big as that, sure that would have stuck in my mind …'.

3

FLYING AHEAD OF THE SUN

After Lehman's, a flight of deposits had occurred in the six main Irish banks. By Monday 29 September they were in deep trouble. And one, Anglo Irish Bank, was on the verge of collapse. At 3 p.m. that day, Anglo chief executive David Drumm and chairman Seán FitzPatrick arrived unannounced at the offices of economist Alan Gray. Their maverick bank was finally running out of cash and it threatened to bring down the rest of the financial system. They needed help.

A friend of Brian Cowen, Gray was approached by Drumm and FitzPatrick in the faint hope that he could help. Gray had rebuffed a similar appeal from FitzPatrick earlier in September, so their decision to arrive uninvited at Gray's office on Dublin's Fitzwilliam Place was a clear sign of despondency. Drumm and FitzPatrick were armed with the information that their bank would be unable to open the following day unless some major intervention took place.

Gray had advised a number of Irish governments, had been appointed to the board of the Central Bank by Cowen and had met Cowen and FitzPatrick at the 'Anglo dinner' at Druids Glen in July. FitzPatrick had called to Gray's office shortly afterwards. He told the economist that the Irish banking sector, in particular Anglo Irish Bank, was experiencing liquidity difficulties. 'I indicated that this was well known in the market,' Gray recalls, 'and recommended that the appropriate channel to discuss this was for Anglo Irish Bank to contact officials in the Central Bank.

Mr FitzPatrick revealed that they were already informed and the meeting concluded after a number of minutes.'

However, like a spurned lover who just won't take no for an answer, FitzPatrick returned. 'To my surprise, late in September, most likely on the 29th, Mr FitzPatrick and Mr Drumm arrived unexpectedly at my office.

'I did not know Mr FitzPatrick prior to meeting him on 28 July, and I had never met Mr Drumm. At the meeting they expressed their view that due to the crisis in the international financial markets, Anglo was experiencing extremely severe liquidity difficulties – a fact which was of no surprise to me as this was by now well known in the financial markets.' Gray continues: 'The discussion at this brief meeting centred on Mr FitzPatrick and Mr Drumm outlining that the crisis in banking wasn't just an Anglo Irish Bank problem but a problem in banking as a whole.'

It is not clear what they wanted Gray to do, but it can be assumed that they hoped he could use his influence with the government. However, Gray said this wish was certainly not articulated. Within ten minutes they were gone elsewhere on their mission to save their bank.

FitzPatrick also contacted Richard Burrows, the chairman of Bank of Ireland, that day with an urgent request for a meeting. With their bank only hours away from running out of cash, and knowing they needed a drastic intervention, they sought to plead their case. Burrows, Bank of Ireland chief executive Brian Goggin, FitzPatrick and Drumm met in the boardroom of the bank's head office on Baggot Street at lunchtime. Burrows and Goggin were not in a giving mood and the meeting was short and to the point. Burrows said, 'Mr FitzPatrick claimed that Anglo Irish Bank had a significant credit facility which was to fall due the following day and that it was not in a position to repay this facility or to roll it over. I cannot, at this stage, recall the size of this facility but I remember that it was significant. Mr FitzPatrick asked if Bank of Ireland would be interested in buying Anglo Irish Bank or any part of it.'

Burrows declined and the Anglo pair resumed their fruitless odyssey, with FitzPatrick stating at the end of this brief meeting that he was going to contact Allied Irish Bank (AIB). Dermot Gleeson, then chairman of AIB and a former attorney-general, took a call from FitzPatrick but refused to meet him.

Over at Merrion Street, in the Department of Finance, Brian Lenihan was, by early afternoon, acutely aware that Irish banks were haemorrhaging money. Lenihan put his brother, Conor, on standby as there were momentous things happening on the markets and he felt he might need family support.

'I came into the Dáil to meet him on the afternoon of the guarantee. I had given up on the possibility of doing constituency work. He asked me to come in because they were heading towards a decision on some fairly serious issues so he wanted me available,' Conor recalls. 'I went over to his department to talk directly to him … just after teatime, six or seven o'clock. Things were going to develop that evening.'

Conor spent much of the night waiting anxiously in the Merrion Hotel across the road from the Department of Finance. He was in contact with Brian throughout the evening and was one of a number of Lenihan allies asked to stay near to Merrion Street that night for potential support.

There had been more international banking casualties that day: Hypo Real Estate in Germany, Fortis Bank in Belgium and Bradford & Bingley in the UK were all rescued.

'Money continued to leave the system and the rate run increased to such an alarming degree that arrangements were made for a meeting to take place at the Department of An Taoiseach after the close of business to review the situation,' Cowen reveals. The taoiseach, along with his finance minister and key officials, gathered at 6.15 p.m. in Government Buildings to decipher the scale of the crisis now facing them. 'This took place in the meeting room adjacent to the taoiseach's personal office,' Cowen explains. 'It is worth remembering that over the course of that evening, while I remained in this meeting room, some people left the room for the purpose of consultation, information gathering or to undertake some technical work. All major decisions were taken in the taoiseach's meeting room.'

In the main meeting room that evening were: Cowen, Lenihan, Attorney-General Paul Gallagher, Secretary-General of the Department of Finance David Doyle, Assistant Secretary of the Department of Finance Kevin Cardiff, Governor of the Central Bank John Hurley, Deputy Governor of the Central Bank Tony Grimes, Chairman of the Financial Regulator Jim Farrell, Chief Executive of the Financial Regulator Patrick Neary and Eugene McCague from Arthur Cox & Co. solicitors. Secretary-General of the Department of the Taoiseach Dermot McCarthy joined the meeting after it began, as did another Department of Finance official, William Beausang. Eoghan Ó Neachtain and the taoiseach's chef de cabinet, Joe Lennon, came in and out throughout the evening. Cowen chaired the meeting – he did not take notes.

Very few realised the magnitude of what was being discussed, with many bamboozled by the numbers involved. From the beginning, the media and the public found it difficult to comprehend that a decision of this gravity, one that ultimately was blamed for bankrupting the country, could be taken in such a short space of time and by so few people. Ultimately one man – Cowen – was held responsible for it.

The meeting ran into the night, the Cabinet wasn't called into Government Buildings, Anglo Irish Bank was centrally involved in the discussions – for these and many other reasons the conspiracy theories spiralled. The primary theory was that the guarantee was a taxpayer-funded ready-up by Fianna Fáil to rescue the party's developer friends who had borrowed recklessly with the willing help of cavalier bankers, as later claimed in the Dáil by Labour Party leader Eamon Gilmore. And, yet, after a Banking Inquiry and countless post-guarantee proposals of alternative action, nobody has categorically proven that these men did anything but their best that night. Nor has it been definitively agreed what else should have been done.

Cowen recalls: 'Governor Hurley outlined what had been happening during the course of the day regarding the lending institutions. He referred to a situation which had developed at Anglo where it had lost €2 billion in deposits that day and they expected the rate [of deposit losses] to continue the next day. Before Monday, the [consensus] opinion was that Anglo would have sufficient funds during the course of that week. This was now not going to happen. The issue was going to have to be addressed immediately.' Hurley adds that bank shares were down in the market and Anglo Irish Bank had run out of cash.

Kevin Cardiff felt from early on that night that Cowen favoured a broad guarantee, which was estimated to cover liabilities and deposits totalling €440 billion. 'He [Cowen] started the meeting along the lines of "look lads, we need a good broad solution that has a real chance of changing the trend, of doing one big job that will be somewhat comprehensive". And it became quite clear in his discussion that what he had in mind was quite a broad guarantee.' Cowen, however, contends that he had not made up his mind and that he sought opinions from the room.

Chief Executive of the Financial Regulator Pat Neary spoke of the need for the introduction of a guarantee to be considered in view of the serious situation which had developed across the financial system. Cowen asked John Hurley to give a view of the ECB's position. Hurley had been in touch with the president of the ECB, Jean-Claude Trichet, over the weekend and confirmed to the meeting that there was no euro-wide initiative in the offing. Just as other countries had to take decisions about their own banks, the Irish government had to act alone.

'It was clear that we were on our own, we would have to deal with this at a national level,' says Cowen.

So, while the government had to act alone, the difficulty was that the ECB – of which Hurley was a member of the governing council – was insistent that no European bank was to be allowed to fail because of the contagion effects. In other words, there could be no 'Lehman Brothers-type event' in the euro area.

'The governor made the point that we would have one go at addressing this, and if it did not work, we may not get a second chance to revisit it, as confidence would be gone. Where a first initiative may be deemed inadequate by the market, putting forward a second course of action could then completely undermine our credibility. His outlining of the seriousness of the situation had an immediate impact on all present,' Cowen insists.

In a wholly unsatisfactory contribution to the Banking Inquiry, Trichet confirmed that central bankers across Europe were telling their governments: 'Don't do a Lehman Brothers.' It was also at the Banking Inquiry that Trichet denied that he phoned Brian Lenihan three days before the bank guarantee to insist that the Irish government save its banks at all costs.

Events moved rapidly on Monday evening, and it is now clear

that many members of the Cabinet weren't consulted sufficiently. Willie O'Dea maintains that ministers were totally in the dark as to what was going on and that he received no contact: 'I know I got no contact whatever.'

Mary Harney was contacted: 'Brian Lenihan rang me about 9 p.m. But because my husband and I had shares in Bank of Ireland I couldn't be involved in any decision. I had told him that previously and I said I will support whatever decision yourself and the taoiseach arrive at.'

She has a great deal of sympathy for what Cowen and Lenihan were confronted with that night. 'First of all, the decision was being made very rapidly, because the next morning there wasn't going to be any money in the ATMs. The information on which the decision was made was very scant. There was no awareness that the banks were in such serious trouble. And that the lending was so reckless, we didn't have the freedom to leave anybody out [of the guarantee]. The reality is, with the ECB, we didn't have the freedom,' says Harney.

As the evening progressed, and as the scale of the crisis was becoming clear, a difference of opinion emerged between the taoiseach and the finance minister as to what to do. 'Lenihan indicated that he felt part of the solution would be the nationalisation of Anglo. I did not think that nationalisation should be the first course of action and I said so,' Cowen insists.

The former governor of the Central Bank, Patrick Honohan, has said that Cowen took a unilateral stance. Lenihan argued strongly for the immediate nationalisation of both Anglo and Irish Nationwide Building Society – but 'he was overruled on the night'. At the Banking Inquiry, Honohan was asked by Fine Gael senator Michael Darcy who could have overruled the minister for finance. 'The taoiseach and the attorney-general were present.

They are the only other political people who were present on the day,' Honohan responded.

Conor Lenihan concurs with Honohan. 'When Professor Honohan made that particular statement to the Dáil committee, I said that Professor Honohan's recollection is correct. And I said that at the time and I still repeat that today. Yes, my brother's view was that Anglo and Irish Nationwide should have been taken immediately into public ownership rather than left out there.'

Cowen didn't see nationalisation as a confidence-building measure, given the volatility in the markets – he was concerned that it would create an expectation that other nationalisations would follow. And, he felt, nationalising a bank meant taking all of the assets and liabilities onto the state's books there and then, which was, in effect, an open-ended guarantee. He believed the guarantee choice looked like a safer option if it was time limited.

Pat Neary, the chief executive of the Financial Regulator, confirmed to the meeting in Government Buildings that all the institutions had sufficient capital and were solvent.

Cowen is adamant of one thing. 'Allowing Anglo to fail was simply not an option on the night. It would have had implications for the whole system.'

One source, an official who was in Government Buildings and involved that night, characterises Cowen as being 'in charge' and Lenihan as 'indecisive': 'Lenihan was no leader of men that night. People often speak of Lenihan's strengths as a barrister but his weaknesses came to the fore that night. Realising a decision was needed and coming from the deliberative and nuanced world of the Law Library, ultimately he couldn't make his mind up. It was infuriating.'

A second source is even more critical of Lenihan. 'He later sought to be a leader of his party but his performance that night was pathetic. Certainly not a leader of men.'

The comments from those inside this entirely male environment reveal just how frenzied and pressurised the atmosphere was on the night of the guarantee. It must be noted that the decision took place in the absence of the tánaiste, Mary Coughlan.

As taoiseach, Cowen was the highest-ranking politician, and he was immeasurably more experienced than Lenihan as a Cabinet minister. Ultimately both men understood that it was Cowen who would have to take responsibility for the decision that was made. Cowen had a more abrupt style than Lenihan, so it was natural that he would appear to those present as the boss.

Just after 9.30 p.m. Cowen and Lenihan were informed that the chairmen and CEOs of AIB and Bank of Ireland were looking to meet with them. To Cowen, they were not the people he most wanted to see at this time: 'I didn't go get them. They asked to come in.'

Richard Burrows, chairman of Bank of Ireland, and his CEO, Brian Goggin, along with AIB's chairman, Dermot Gleeson, and his CEO, Eugene Sheehy, were shown in to meet the taoiseach and finance minister and many of the senior officials. Burrows recalls: 'Following my return from my meeting [that afternoon] with Mr Hurley, I spoke with Mr Goggin. We were both concerned about Anglo Irish Bank's position and the risk of collateral damage to Bank of Ireland. We decided that we should seek an urgent meeting with the government to update them on the situation. We both felt that AIB would share a similar view to our own, so I called the then chairman of AIB, Dermot Gleeson.'

However, the data that the government was working on had irrefutably revealed the trouble that the system was in at this stage. Cowen adjourned the meeting before the bankers could be admitted. 'During this break, I decided to get an external view. Mr Alan Gray, an economist and a Central Bank board member, was someone whose views I respected. I phoned him and asked him what he thought of a guarantee option being used,' he reveals. 'Mr Gray emphasised that providing a guarantee would obviously give an advantage to those institutions to which it would apply vis-à-vis competitors, since they would have the backing of the Irish government. It would be important to be seen to charge a proper fee for the value of that guarantee to those institutions that got the benefit of it.' Gray, who was not paid for his advice, also stressed to Cowen that a guarantee should be strictly time limited. To Gray, the idea of a guarantee had been floating around for some time and in this discussion he focused on the issue of the importance of considering compliance with EU state aid.

Cowen and Lenihan then went to the taoiseach's private office and had what Cowen describes as a calm and non-confrontational conversation. According to Cowen, Lenihan was still backing the nationalisation of Anglo, while Cowen wanted the time-limited guarantee. The discussion continued in the main room with the others. Kevin Cardiff does not recall Cowen, as has been reported, shouting, 'We are not fucking nationalising Anglo' and thumping the table. 'It would be a lie to say that I never heard the taoiseach use the f-word, but I don't remember that specific turn of phrase. I don't think that happened, I don't think it happened in that way,' Cardiff recollected at the Banking Inquiry.

As things were still very fluid, Cardiff, who supported the idea of nationalisation, told Cowen that, if that was to be the decision, he would need a few hours to prepare. 'It must have been nearly midnight when I said to him, "Look, if we're doing a nationalisation, I need a few hours to get it ready – a few months would be great, but I need a few hours."'

Having been made to wait for a long time, the bankers were eventually given a hearing. When they were brought in to meet the taoiseach, it was clear from their contributions that Bank of Ireland and AIB wanted a guarantee for themselves and wanted Anglo and Irish Nationwide dealt with differently. Cowen and Lenihan listened to them. 'I did not comment on the presentations made by the banks. We would consider their views but they were not going to be participants in any decisions. They then left the meeting [having been dismissed]. It was clear the banks were running out of cash and depending on the run rate, it could now be days rather than weeks,' recalls Cowen. 'This reaffirmed my view that something comprehensive would have to be done.'

With the bankers dismissed, Cowen, Lenihan and their officials continued to debate the nationalisation and guarantee options. 'If we decided we were to go with the guarantee option, then it would be limited to two years,' says Cowen. 'Eventually, I put it to the table that it seemed to me that a full guarantee option provided the best prospect of addressing the urgent liquidity problem and of sending a clear message that Ireland was standing behind the financial system, which would be understood by the markets. It is my recollection that I then asked everyone could we run with a guarantee-only approach in principle. There was agreement on that. Further details would now have to be worked out.'

With agreement in principle, the government needed to make some contingency arrangements, in case the announcement did not work and Anglo needed some support the next day. The bank representatives from AIB and Bank of Ireland, who were camped in separate rooms in Government Buildings, were brought back into the meeting and the issue of liquidity support for Anglo was raised with them. Burrows agreed to provide €5 billion if the government would guarantee that Bank of Ireland would get its money back. Gleeson recalls that he agreed to provide €5 billion but he claims he was of the belief 'that an orderly dealing with Anglo would occur the following weekend'. In layman's terms, Gleeson understood Anglo was to be wound up and liquidated.

When the bankers finally departed for home, Cowen, Lenihan and the officials began working out the exact details of the plan. They addressed the issue of bondholders and whether they would or wouldn't be covered. Decisions were being made at rapid speed at this time, and issues that were to cause long-term political damage were dealt with in a seemingly slapdash manner. Yet the matters were dealt with – and it was foreseen that bondholders would be problematic.

Those at the meeting concluded that if they decided to impose losses on, or 'burn', bondholders, it would further drain the system of confidence and drive away those willing to borrow Irish debt. Cowen discussed the matter with John Hurley and it was agreed that it was best, on balance, to include junior bondholders in addition to senior bondholders, as they were a very small percentage of the total securities that were covered. Lenihan reminded Cowen later on that he was absent when the decision to include junior bondholders was taken.

Mary Harney agrees with Cowen that there was no leeway on this issue, and that there was something of a misconception about who constituted bondholders. 'We didn't have the freedom to exclude anyone. Some of those bondholders were credit unions in Ireland; they weren't all alien, foreign people,' she maintains.

Legislation now had to be drafted to put the decision into law.

The bankers had brought in a draft wording of a guarantee, which was barely a page in length. Cardiff didn't like it and said: 'Look, Taoiseach, there are turns of phrase in this short draft that to me mean that if we use it, we will end up giving a guarantee that is even wider than the one being discussed. They'll be laughing at us.' With Cowen's approval, Cardiff went away to redraft a more acceptable version of the guarantee.

This was to be a government decision, one that would have to be defended by all members of the Cabinet. The ratification of the Cowen and Lenihan judgement had now to be put to ministers, many of whom were tucked up in their beds. So the decision was made by means of an 'incorporeal' Cabinet meeting, whereby ministers were individually contacted by phone, had the guarantee run by them and were asked for their assent. Ministers had been contacted one by one between seven and nine that evening by an official of the government secretariat to tell them to expect a call, at any hour, to discuss a banking decision.

The politicians at the centre of the maelstrom still disagree about this most controversial political act – the decision to get Cabinet assent by phone. Éamon Ó Cuiv feels it was a mistake not to call the Cabinet to Dublin for a face-to-face discussion in Government Buildings. 'I was just going in to a meeting in Galway, and I got a phone call,' he says. As that call had come early enough in the evening, Ó Cuiv feels ministers could have got to Dublin, as he did later on.

When in Dublin, Ó Cuiv stayed in his mother's house, not far from the city centre. 'I came out and sat in the car. I came to Dublin and I was in two minds whether to head to Merrion Street or just go out and wait for the call,' he says. 'The thing was imploding, we had to do something, and the only thing to do was to widen the guarantee. And I had no issue with that in the sure and certain knowledge that it was a Monday night, and there was a Cabinet meeting at 10.30 a.m.'

Whatever doubts Ó Cuiv had, he was somewhat pacified by this knowledge that the Cabinet was due to meet the following morning. He also points out that there was no legislation passed that night. 'They could not make any detailed decisions without a detailed memorandum. All we were doing was issuing a statement saying that they were effectively going to guarantee the banks.' Still, he says, the Cabinet should have been hauled in. 'In hindsight, for the reassurance of the public, we should all have collected in Government Buildings.'

Cowen, describing his version from the epicentre of events, is typically matter of fact. 'Ministers were contacted and the decision was confirmed,' he told the authors. 'Some ministers were away, you wouldn't need to have them all there. But if it was half twelve when we rang them and you say be here for six, I'm sure they would have got there ... We discussed this yesterday [Sunday], this is what we have to do. This man, the minister for finance has to be up at six or half five ringing around people, preparing his statement, getting everything ready for 7 a.m. If he is at a Cabinet meeting between six and seven, is that stopping him from what he has to do, which is a big thing? You just sort of come to a judgement, we were meeting at 10.30 a.m. anyway.'

Cowen has characterised the evening and early morning in reasoned tones, but he betrays something of the atmosphere on Merrion Street during those hours. 'The whole thing went crazy, that day was a crazy day for Ireland.'

A few minutes after midnight, Billy Kelleher, the junior trade and enterprise minister, had received a surprise directive from an official in Government Buildings, which was to lead to some rather surreal conversations with Brian Lenihan. 'I got a phone call at some stage on the Monday – very late, late Monday night – asking me to come to Dublin,' Kelleher reveals. Clipped civil service tones told him 'to be in Dublin early in the morning and to be out around Government Buildings the following morning, that Minister Lenihan would brief me about something that might be happening that could be of relevance because I had an economic portfolio.' Having been given his orders, Kelleher was vaguely aware that this was a financial emergency as he set off shortly after 4 a.m.

Eoghan Ó Neachtain had tried ringing John Downing, his Green Party counterpart, because he couldn't get John Gormley. The Green Party leader and minister for the environment, heritage and local government had to be awoken by gardaí from Ringsend station knocking on his door after he failed to answer his phone. He was a man who liked to head for bed early and his phone was turned off.

Mary Harney was happy to go along with, and trust, the men – and they were all men – in the room that night. She had been around for many emergencies since the Charlie Haughey years. 'People say now there should have been a Cabinet meeting called. But if you're dealing with the sort of emergency that was emerging, and you have meetings that were going on to two or three in the morning, it's easy to see why certain protocols can be overlooked in the overall interest,' she says. 'I don't believe that a Cabinet decision would have come to any different conclusions and I think people would have gone with what the line minister and the taoiseach were recommending on the night.' She would have had no truck with the optics of that night. 'Sometimes the procedures had to take second place to the overall decision in the national interest.'

In contrast, Willie O'Dea is adamant that the Cabinet should have come in. 'I was 140 miles away in Limerick. I got a call, there was no debate. I would have welcomed discussion at Cabinet, but I was told this had to be done before the markets opened.'

He continues, 'It reminded me of stories of a cabinet meeting during the American Civil War. Abraham Lincoln was forging some very controversial policies to which the cabinet was opposed, but at the end of the meeting he said, "Look this meeting is at a close. All in favour put up your hand and all against put up your hand." Of course, all the hands went up and Lincoln says, "The aye's have it!"'

Mary Hanafin gave her view to the RTÉ documentary *Crisis: Inside the Cowen Government*: 'That decision should not have been taken at a quarter to two in the morning.'

Minister for Foreign Affairs Micheál Martin was in New York at the autumn United Nations convention. He doesn't see that the decision was a bad one. 'I can't say that bore on my mind,' claims Martin, who was flying home on the Monday night from New York, which is five hours behind Dublin time. 'I just got the incorporeal phone call, before I got on the plane, and I was told there would be a meeting the following day but nonetheless your permission is sought to do the bank guarantee. It was an official from the Department of An Taoiseach ... It was broad daylight, I think I was eating at the time, we were due to get the plane back,' Martin recalls.

A civil service source at the Department of the Taoiseach reveals events from the official side. 'Dermot McCarthy and his team then went and briefed the ministers [by phone]. Brian Lenihan and Brian Cowen would have spoken to those who requested to [speak to] them. I couldn't say they spoke to all of them.' Cowen then sent Lenihan home to get a couple of hours rest because he had a very busy schedule to resume. The markets would open at 7 a.m. 'I remember Brian Cowen, who was leaving and going to stay in Farmleigh, saying to Brian Lenihan "Well, the decision is made now, it's up to you to sell it now, Brian."'

Cowen left Government Buildings around 3.30 a.m.

All night Eoghan Ó Neachtain and Joe Lennon drafted and

redrafted a press release. The two men went in and out of the main room to collect further drafts of a press release for the approval of Dermot McCarthy. They sat at a computer in Lennon's office. Along with Eoin Dorgan, Lenihan's press officer in the Department of Finance, they worked the release into shape.

Shortly before 5 a.m. David Murphy of RTÉ was contacted by Dorgan, who had tried, unsuccessfully, to reach George Lee the night before. Murphy was briefed for a news report on RTÉ Radio 1's *Morning Ireland* programme at 7 a.m., just as the markets opened. He was also offered an interview with Lenihan for his report.

Lenihan returned to work from his home in Strawberry Beds, Castleknock at 6 a.m. and began calling some of his European colleagues to inform them of the Irish government's decision. As he arrived back into his department on Merrion Street, Billy Kelleher was waiting in his car across the road. 'I was outside the Merrion Hotel on the Tuesday morning at 6.10 a.m.,' Kelleher reveals. He sat in his car, in the weak dawn light, waiting, and Lenihan eventually called him at around 7 a.m.

'Brian Lenihan rang me himself ... He told me that there was an incorporeal meeting that night and that there was a press statement going out and he just outlined briefly that there was going to be an overarching guarantee and the broad detail about how they were to stop a run on the banks,' Kelleher says. 'He wanted me to be briefed along with ministers in the other economic departments so that [we would be informed] if there was any need for us to go anywhere to explain the guarantee or if there was any press or media to be done.'

That wasn't all, however – Lenihan had also hatched a plan to send Kelleher to the United States. 'He was explaining that we should be ready to travel because we might have to get ahead of the markets to explain.' Kelleher recalls, with a smile, Lenihan exclaiming with a flourish: 'We need you to fly ahead of the sun!'

Given the five-hour time difference between Dublin and New York, the international financial capital, Lenihan clearly envisaged Kelleher taking the government jet, landing at JFK and hitting the boardrooms and TV stations in New York to tell the opinion makers of the great financial coup that had been pulled off in Ireland. 'He wanted to be ahead of the markets anyway,' Kelleher recalls, 'so that [we would be ready] if the markets opened and if there was a requirement for people to be available for whatever reasons, either travelling ourselves or being available to do interviews for news stations in advance of markets opening around the world.

'You would have had New York a number of hours later, so the idea was that you were going to try to address the European markets first … [and it was the reason] the press release went out early in the morning in advance of the markets opening,' says Kelleher. He went to the Department of Finance, where he was briefed by officials on the night's events. 'They spoke about the bank guarantee, why it was necessary, the import of it and I got quite a briefing on that.'

All this occurred before a scheduled 10.30 a.m. full Cabinet meeting.

Sadly for Kelleher, and perhaps for New York financiers and TV audiences, the charming minister of state wasn't called upon to assume Lenihan's proposed role of jet-age town crier.

Pat Carey, as chief whip, also sat as a minister at Cabinet, albeit without voting rights. He was, to his surprise, not consulted the night before. 'This famous incorporeal meeting, I wasn't consulted, the whip wasn't consulted,' admits Carey. 'Only very shortly afterwards, maybe 7 a.m.' Despite this he was to play a central role that morning in the organisation of Dáil logistics. Carey and his office had been on standby to bring in emergency legislation since the start of September. 'It is highly likely that it was pencilled in that we would have an early morning meeting. I think we were anxious to be in before the markets opened ... There was a huge flurry of activity before 8 a.m., maybe even before 7 a.m. Lenihan was here, there and everywhere; he'd come back having had a conversation in French with Christine Lagarde, a conversation in Portuguese with Barroso, the primate of England on the line ... it could have been anybody,' Carey adds.

As the nation awoke, unaware of the night's drama, Lenihan addressed a press conference, announcing to the country and to the world that Ireland had taken this drastic step to safeguard the Irish banking sector. The Irish media quickly sought to get a handle on what exactly the guarantee meant, while the European media immediately gave a far more sceptical verdict on Ireland's unilateral move.

Lenihan thought it important to contact Europe's senior politicians personally. Christine Lagarde, then France's finance minister, was furious with Ireland for taking such a massive decision without any warning, as was the British chancellor of the exchequer, Alastair Darling. And Darling had good reason. Britain, in particular, was to see a flight of capital in the coming weeks as Ireland's banks were, for a time, seen as a safe haven. It fell to Cowen to contact the British prime minister, Gordon Brown, another no-nonsense politician whom he knew well from their days at their respective finance ministries.

'I spoke to Gordon, yeah, and that was okay,' the former taoiseach insists, though it was clear at the time that Brown was anything but okay with it. 'They [the British] were wondering why we did what we did but they were throwing money in [to their banks] and not announcing it at all, throwing big money in. They weren't even announcing it to their own people … but everyone was looking after their own interest and that was the problem because there wasn't a European agreement at that level to address this issue.'

Cowen forcefully tells us that it was not incumbent upon him to contact anyone, least of all the British, to somehow ask for their permission to guarantee our banks. 'That was the problem. It had been decided in a treaty that every national regulator would regulate their own banks,' he says. 'From our point of view, we had to do what we had to do. We were told we were on our own, the EU knew this was coming … then they start saying, "Why didn't you ring this fella and that fella?" But we were an elected government,' says Cowen. 'Why should we be expected to ask a fella who is not answerable to anyone over in Europe what I can and can't do in a situation where my Central Bank governor, who is a member of the ECB board, is telling me "You have to make a big decision tonight"? … So it comes down to your own authority. I saw it as a duty of the government to make that decision, a duty for Ireland to make, it was not for someone else outside to say, "Should you do that?"'

The British government had intervened to help its banks, giving them huge cash injections with far less fanfare and little vocal criticism. There was certainly no protest from the Irish government. 'You have to do what you have to do and I don't remember any of them ringing me when they had to do what they had to do. With Bradford … when Northern Rock went, did anyone ring me asking me what did I think of this? Of course they didn't. It is their government,' says Cowen.

At 10.30 a.m. on Tuesday the Cabinet met for an extended discussion on the guarantee, before what was to be a rather chaotic beginning to the debate in the Dáil on Tuesday night.

'The Cabinet meeting was a difficult affair, there is no doubt about it,' Pat Carey says with significant understatement. Ministers, who were angry at being sidelined the night before, were brought up to speed as to what exactly had happened.

Willie O'Dea says there was unhappiness but the die had been cast. 'The deal was done and we discussed it. And it was out there; you know it was a different Cabinet meeting when the deal isn't done as compared to when the deal is done. It was a bit of an anti-climax really. A sort of worried resignation.'

Micheál Martin landed from New York and made straight for Government Buildings. 'I arrived in at around 7 a.m. or 8 a.m. in the morning, I had *Morning Ireland* on in the car and went straight into Cabinet.' To his mind, there appeared to be no sense of alarm as Lenihan and Cowen made their presentations. 'The issue was presented fundamentally as an issue of liquidity at the time,' Martin recalls. 'We were told that collateral was there to cover any potential exposure, and there certainly would not have been the sense of the scale of losses that subsequently emerged in relation to the bank [Anglo].'

Ministers did not recall any serious argument against the actions the taoiseach and minister for finance had taken the night before. Many of them had given their assent by phone. Martin claims that there was no apprehension in the Cabinet room that morning. 'At the time it was welcomed in Ireland. Broadly speaking I think the media reaction was positive on the morning of the Cabinet meeting. There was a sense that a decisive meeting had taken place.'

Despite their disagreement the night before, at no time during the Tuesday morning meeting did ministers observe tension between Cowen and Lenihan, only unity. 'There was no sense of that the following morning … there might have been a reference to "some officials wanted nationalisation but we still have the legislation" … there was no sense of argy bargy,' says Martin.

'No, there was absolutely no sense [of a split between the two Brians] the following morning at the meeting and I recall it very clearly,' says O'Dea.

When the Cabinet agrees to change the law, the legislation is then sent to the Dáil to be voted on, which with a government majority is invariably a formality. 'The emergency legislation had been prepared by the AG's [attorney-general's] office,' according to Carey. 'My job turned out to be, when the briefing was given at the Cabinet table, I was to contact the whips of the other parties, for them to get their finance spokespersons over to the department for a briefing from Lenihan and his officials as soon as possible.'

As Carey was leaving the Cabinet room, he reveals, someone came and whisked a draft copy of the guarantee legislation out of his hand. 'I didn't have it long enough, but it struck me that it was an unusual-looking document, because as whip I would be well used to the layout of the Oireachtas print … I thought it was on different-coloured paper, even though I am partially colour-blind, and the font was different. It may just have been a working draft they had in the AG's office, but I still have a nagging thing in the back of my head – that it was something that came from Trichet's office.

'I can't remember precisely, but I think it was Paul [Gallagher, the AG]. I haven't spoken to him about it, and I had it for thirty seconds in my hand,' Carey claims.

That day, amid a growing sense of unease and confusion, the Dáil debate on the bank guarantee was delayed four times. The opposition was furious at being given only fifteen minutes to view the plan before the debate. During his contribution in the Dáil, a weary Cowen strongly defended the move to introduce the guarantee. The Dáil sat until 11.40 p.m. and adjourned until the following morning.

Initially, the guarantee had the desired impact on the stock market as it rallied by 8% by close of business on Tuesday.

Cowen was not in the Dáil when proceedings recommenced on the morning of Wednesday 1 October. He was in France meeting President Sarkozy, and later reported that his new friend supported the move. He was back in time for the final round of the debate, which ran late into the night.

Those who were in Leinster House for the opening days – and nights – of the financial crisis remember a raucous atmosphere. Older TDs were reminded of the heaves against Charlie Haughey in the 1980s. 'There's nothing like the smell of a crisis to get the adrenaline going,' one TD recalls.

There is also nothing like a series of concurrent late-night Dáil sessions to get the beer taps in the Dáil bar going. When you lock 166 mostly middle-aged, mostly men in a building with two private bars, there is bound to be quite a bit of drinking.

Lenihan told the Dáil during the debate: 'There is understandable concern that the exchequer is potentially significantly exposed by this measure. I want to reassure the Irish people that this is not the case. The risk of any potential financial exposure from this decision is significantly mitigated by a very substantial buffer made up of the equity and other risk capital.'

Shortly after 2 a.m. on Thursday, the Dáil overwhelmingly passed the bill, by 124 votes to eighteen, after a number of changes had been made to the legislation. Fine Gael, despite having some concerns, voted en bloc with the government, as did Sinn Féin, while Labour voted against it.

While Fine Gael's finance spokesman Richard Bruton may have understood the significance of the guarantee decision, many others on the Fine Gael front bench, including the dangerously quiet Enda Kenny, were not so solid. Tom Hayes, the party chairman, said his party was prepared to 'trust the government' and supported the deal in the national interest.

Labour was able to assume the high moral ground. Eamon Gilmore, Labour leader, with some urging from his finance spokeswoman, Joan Burton, said too many questions hadn't been answered and it was not acceptable to support something when they were being asked to vote blind. 'What is the full extent of the exposure of the Irish taxpayer?' he asked. 'What will the banks pay for this cover? What will the impact be on the cost of borrowing by the Irish government, with further knock-on consequences for the Irish taxpayer? We did not get satisfactory answers to those questions on Tuesday. We did not get them during the Dáil debate. And we still have not got them – even with the legislation now passed. As I said on Tuesday morning, the Labour Party was not opposed to action being taken to rescue the banking system. Now that the guarantee has been given, I hope it works.'

The legislation was then passed in the Seanad, and Lenihan attended the Upper House until well after 2.30 a.m.

Reaction to the guarantee was decidedly mixed. On radio the next day, Colm McCarthy, UCD economist, said that the government was punishing the prudent banks and rewarding the reckless. 'What the Irish government has done is written a blank cheque for double the country's GNP. No bank has been deemed sufficiently reckless as to be told to go off and fail. Every bank is being treated the same. One of those six banks in my opinion has been very prudent over the years, one wildly imprudent – but both are equally wonderful in the eyes of the government,' he said, referring in the first instance to Bank of Ireland and in the second to Anglo. 'This could cost an awful lot of money. The stock markets are saying the banks have lost an awful lot of their capital and the share prices of the banks are a quarter of what they were a year ago. It is entirely likely that one of the banks could have negative capital.'

Lenihan received two phone calls on Wednesday from his British counterpart, Alistair Darling, who pleaded for the government to think twice. Darling was also to ask the government to take some action to prevent the flow of money that had begun from banks in the UK to Irish banks. Gordon Brown made calls to the president of the European Commission, José Manuel Barroso, expressing his grave displeasure at the Irish action. Pressure was soon brought to bear on Lenihan to extend the guarantee to the foreign banks based in Ireland, to ensure they didn't experience a run. Bank of Scotland, National Irish Bank and Ulster Bank applied for inclusion in the scheme, and Lenihan insisted he would consider all applications.

By late Thursday a relative calm had been restored within government and Leinster House, even if the public mood was one of bemused apprehension.

Cowen watched and waited. He felt the opposition received it well at first, and, of course, Fine Gael had voted for the guarantee, after a long debate. The former taoiseach stresses that Ireland, the public and the media received the bank guarantee with open arms in the autumn of 2008. 'The reaction to it at first was it was a good decision,' he says. 'If you look at the newspapers, if you look at the commentary, they said: "Look, the system has been saved"'. The sin, however, was one of lack of knowledge. For all the brave actions of Cowen and Lenihan that night, they blindly guaranteed banks that were plunging into the abyss. Anglo had sunk to the depths quite a while before, and nobody outside the bank, including the Financial Regulator, the governor of the

Central Bank, the minister for finance and the taoiseach, knew about it.

As Anglo was exposed as an unprecedented financial horror show over the next three months, the mood manifestly darkened. 'The problem was that people started questioning then whether it should have been as broad as it was. All this sort of stuff started,' says Cowen. He believes that the mood turned for a myriad of reasons. 'That you were going from ten years of growth to a very sudden precipitous downturn and people were not making sense of it; why is this happening?'

He also believes that we were insular, and claims that Ireland was only following in practice what other countries were doing. 'Then it [the guarantee] was portrayed as a particularly Irish problem when in fact people now realise that there were guarantee schemes all over Europe, just of different magnitudes and of different types depending on what every government had to do to sort out their problem. So you had this rather insular debate and it was then allowed to feed into this question of, you know, the government have not acted in the national interest, they've acted for sectional interests, they've acted for banks rather than for the country.'

We asked Cowen if he understood in those September days that he had made an irreversible decision. Was it tangible then that he had made a historic judgement? 'I knew it was a big call and it was a call that had to be made,' he admits. And he was nervous, he says. 'You had a lot of worries during that time and subsequently about it, to try to make sure that we got EU approval for it. I knew politically it was putting us in a difficult position, and I knew it wouldn't be a popular decision.'

The initial enthusiasm was later supplanted by trenchant criticism from the opposition benches, as Cowen recalls. 'I remember

Enda Kenny came into the house and started talking about this Fianna Fáil bank and all this sort of stuff, and there was "you were sort of trying to protect the bank" and so on.' Indeed, it was later alleged that Cowen, Lenihan and the whole Fianna Fáil government had acted somehow to protect Anglo Irish Bank.

Cowen has always emphatically denied this. 'All we were doing was trying to protect the economy, and we knew, and I think it's accepted from the Inquiry now, that there's no way it could have been let go,' he says. 'This idea was "Let it go to the wall, what are ye worried about?"

'And there was even an argument [over] whether it was systemic or not. The Honohan report and everyone else has clarified that it was systemic.' Cowen's position was then, and still is, that Anglo would have brought the other banks and the economy down with it. 'So a lot of the political controversy that was generated, which was questioning whether it [Anglo] should be part of a guarantee, or whether it should have been nationalised subsequently, or whether it should have been allowed to go to the wall, or whether it was systemic – there was a political agenda behind that to create the idea of this "axis of collusion" sort of stuff … So the political atmosphere was very frayed and it was very hostile; it was very intense.'

But in the immediate aftermath of that embattled decision on 30 September, Lenihan received an unexpected message of support for the guarantee. 'Congratulations Brian, you did the right thing there,' US Treasury Secretary Hank Paulson told him. Paulson was thrilled that little Ireland had stolen a march on, and infuriated, the British by the audacious move to underwrite €440 billion worth of bank debt. Paulson was still sore at the British refusal to support Lehman's bank a fortnight before, believing their action had precipitated its collapse.

Lenihan, having had little sleep, was apprehensive, but Paulson's phone call calmed him. As Conor Lenihan recalls, 'I came into Brian's office and he said, "I've just had Hank Paulson on, euphoric about my decision." So he was very supportive.' Conor also says that Brian's summary of Paulson's words was along the lines of 'Well done, Brian, you fucked the Brits.'

4

WILL YOU STILL NEED ME ...
WHEN I'M SEVENTY?

The bank guarantee legislation passed quickly through the Oireachtas and into law. The guarantee gave state protection to the six domestic banks, which helped insulate them from the vultures of the international markets. The banking crisis was put in temporary abeyance, but the national finances continued to deteriorate. It was hoped the early budget would have a similarly calming effect. It didn't.

Looking after the elderly had been for decades a foundation of Fianna Fáil policy. Brian Lenihan, in his emergency budget speech on Tuesday 14 October, undid that legacy when he announced to the Dáil that he was abolishing the automatic entitlement to a medical card for those aged over seventy.

That move, Brian Cowen admits, was a major error. 'It was a political mistake no doubt, and it cost us about 10% in the polls, which we never really recovered from.' Within minutes of the speech ending, Fianna Fáil backbench TDs were telling political correspondents that the cut would have to be reversed, as phone calls had already started coming in to constituency offices.

Cowen agrees that a rushed budget process had allowed a huge mistake to slip through. The minister for finance had pushed for the budget to be moved from December to October. 'We had agreed to move the budget back a bit, Lenihan wanted to bring in an earlier budget than usual. I said fine, but it probably narrowed the time for discussion a bit.'

Conor Lenihan says that his brother believed the move would drive home to the public the gravity of affairs. 'They decided to bring forward the budget to underline the seriousness of the situation facing the economy, and you can argue whether that was politically wise or not.'

Pat Carey says the decision to bring forward the budget certainly didn't do anything for confidence in the government. 'It was as if there was an impression they were making it up as they went along, there was no strategic thinking.'

With such draconian reductions in spending required, many unpalatable choices had been on the table. So difficult was the task of choosing where to wield the axe that ministers found themselves in an endless series of meetings.

One of the most contentious measures put forward as a means of saving money was that decision to abolish the automatic entitlement to a medical card for those over seventy. Everyone over the age of seventy had been entitled to free medical, dental and optical treatment. They also received free medicine. The benefit did not discriminate on the basis of income – the budget proposed to change this and introduce a means-tested system of benefits.

Eamon Ryan supported the cut. He saw it as removing a universal entitlement to those people who could afford to do without it. 'It was a social justice issue. Actually the way it was presented, and correctly, was that this was a provision we were giving to those on very high incomes and it actually could be adjusted in a way that allowed you to maintain a level of service. It was seen internally as a way to bring back some progressivity into the nature of the social card services, so that was the impetus.'

Ryan doesn't agree that the cut was a slipshod last-minute addition to the budget – it was thrashed out at Cabinet. 'It's not as if it wasn't discussed. Maybe it should have been discussed more. I don't know how many meetings we had that month running up to the budget, my guess is about ten.' Ryan supported the proposal because 80% of public funding goes to social welfare, health and education. 'So if you're looking at the start of the process where you're going to have to make significant savings, those three areas are the key ones and all three are incredibly sensitive.'

Ministers did realise that the reduced entitlement to medical cards would cause major controversy, but the Cabinet decided to plough on. 'So it's not as if they weren't discussed maybe and I do remember the last kind of meeting where we signed off on it. There was a concern raised within Cabinet. "This thing's gonna blow up," people were astute enough to realise, but it was decided, feck it,' says Ryan.

The subsequent spin was that the government measure was some kind of error, although it is clear from what Ryan says that the Cabinet as a whole was made fully aware of the plan. Mary Harney, as health minister, says that the decision to cut the medical cards was made after discussions with Lenihan. 'The minister for finance and I had a discussion and one of the things that was concerning him was the recurring expenditure. You know, that we were committed to things, bills that were going to get bigger and bigger and bigger.' Harney recalls that Lenihan raised the recurring cost of medical cards. 'What he was interested in was the ongoing exposure of the medical card being available to everybody. That was the issue. But it wasn't easy.

'The issue with over-seventies was that we were giving cards to people who were relatively well off, and we weren't able to extend cards at the bottom. I think the mistake we made was that we should have said, anybody who has the card can keep it,' she says.

Lenihan began his 2008 budget speech to the Dáil just before 4 p.m. with the portentous overture: 'We find ourselves in one of the most difficult and uncertain times in living memory. Turmoil in the financial markets and steep increases in commodity prices have put enormous pressures on economies throughout the world. Here at home we face the most challenging fiscal and economic position in a generation.' In the avalanche of cuts and the popular uprising over the medical cards, it is often forgotten that Lenihan actually increased the state pension by €7 per week for all pensioners, bringing the state contributory pension to €230.30 per week.

About five minutes into the speech, under a section headlined in his script as 'Targeting Resources', he said: 'The government has decided to abolish the automatic entitlement to a medical card for those over seventy who are above the eligibility criteria.' The opposition smelt blood and cries of 'shame, shame' echoed from the opposition benches. Fine Gael TD Michael Ring, a legendary vote-getter in Mayo, with a unique intuition for the electorate's concerns, spotted the problem immediately and shouted across the Dáil Chamber: 'That is an attack on the elderly!' Fianna Fáil TDs heard this heckle and it resonated, causing them to sit uncomfortably as the grim news was aired.

Lenihan tried at the end of his speech to rouse a sense of a national effort at a time of crisis. 'It is, a Cheann Comhairle, no less than a call to patriotic action,' he said, to hearty applause from the benches behind him.

But within minutes of the speech ending, the mood among Fianna Fáil backbench TDs changed. They were now telling political correspondents that the cut would have to be reversed, as the aforementioned phone calls had already started coming into their constituency offices from elderly people distressed at the news. 'I remember literally meeting a couple of Fianna Fáil backbenchers who were in full retreat; they were heading for Government Buildings and once that starts it is very hard to stop. A physical sense that they're running, they're running back up the corridor and once that starts, it's very hard to stop it,' Eamon Ryan recalls.

By the following day the proposal had provoked a wave of virtually unprecedented fear and anger from lobby groups, the public and the opposition, who accused the government of mugging the elderly.

Overnight, Fianna Fail's reputation as defenders of the elderly was destroyed. Even before Charlie Haughey's introduction of the free travel pass for pensioners, Fianna Fáil had always prioritised older citizens through medical care access, pensions and such benefits. 'Fianna Fáil had huge support from older people, because down through the years, from the time of [Éamon] de Valera, they relied heavily on Fianna Fáil, they knew that they were safe with Fianna Fáil. And for Fianna Fáil to betray them the way that they did was shocking,' says John McGuinness. Two days after the budget, an estimated 15,000 elderly people marched on Leinster House in protest. It was a watershed moment for Fianna Fáil.

Images of Cowen's close friend and constituency colleague John Moloney, the junior health minister, being booed off stage by elderly protestors in St Andrew's church, scared many Fianna Fáil TDs. 'It was just shocking to look back on it and see the anger that was there in that church against the party,' adds McGuinness. 'It was a hugely damaging event that Fianna Fáil did not get over.'

'They were terrified, absolutely terrified,' says Eamon Ryan, referring to Fianna Fáil at the time. With the backbenchers up in arms, things were about to get worse as Cowen and Lenihan went to Brussels on government business, leaving Mary Coughlan holding the line. She was the ranking minister at a specially convened parliamentary party meeting on Wednesday and was verbally lynched by her colleagues. At this meeting, a truculent Coughlan warned TDs and senators that the taoiseach would be 'summoned back' from Brussels to deal with them.

'There was an EU summit meeting the day after the budget which I had to go to,' says Cowen, 'and there was a parliamentary party meeting, and Mary Coughlan was the senior minister. She chaired and supervised it as tánaiste.' Coughlan, who was already coming under pressure about her performance, is said to have endured a tough time as chair of the meeting. She had to withstand an even rougher ride in the Dáil facing the opposition.

Mayo TD Dara Calleary still fumes that the figures upon which the proposed cuts were based were wrong, and says the whole thing was mishandled. 'It was handled very badly, and part of me thinks it is very hard to take away something from someone who has it,' he admits. 'Mary Harney was the minister, and she was not at the PP [parliamentary party] meeting. There was a meeting after the budget, where the junior health minister, Máire Hoctor, briefed the parliamentary party on the impact of the figures. The terms of eligibility were wrong. They were wrong.'

Coughlan faced a pitiless Dáil on Thursday morning. At leaders' questions she said that the government had taken the medical cards away from 'high court judges, senior civil servants and property tycoons'. Her performance, which sought to give the impression that only the very rich were impacted by the cut, was poor and was seized upon by the opposition parties. The debate descended into chaos. Under such pressure, the tánaiste sought to stick to her message, but she endured a torrid time. Her standing was weakened by this performance.

To try to quell the raging backbenchers, and in the first sign of a climbdown, Mary Harney later that day adjusted income threshold limits. But this had no impact and by the Friday an all-out backbench revolt threatened the stability of the government. Not only were recalcitrant TDs such as Mattie McGrath, Jim McDaid, Tom Kitt and Noel O'Flynn vocal in their opposition, but many party moderates were also furious, knowing they, too, would feel the wrath of constituents that weekend.

On Friday morning Coughlan met with five backbench TDs – Michael McGrath, Michael Moynihan, Christy O'Sullivan, Thomas Byrne and Michael Kennedy – to hear their grievances. 'A large number were concerned about what the proposals were,' says Cowen, who sought to regain control of the situation on his return from Europe that day. On landing in Dublin he was greeted by the news that Wicklow TD Joe Behan was about to announce a shock resignation from the Fianna Fáil party in protest at the cuts. 'So when I got back on Friday evening, apparently Joe Behan was having a problem. So I said get him up here and bring him in ... [but] Joe had made his mind up and had made his move anyway.'

The Green Party then called for a redraft of the measure. The pressure was mounting on Cowen to do something. He made his way out to RTÉ to appear on the *Six One News* where he explained that the government would 'look into it'.

Cowen's closest advisors thought he should not have so closely associated himself with the error, saying it should have been Lenihan accepting the blame. 'I remember having the row in the car with him saying, "Boss, you shouldn't be doing this, you shouldn't be the messenger for it",' says a source close to Cowen. Discounting the advice, Cowen rolled his sleeves up. 'I sat down on the Saturday with the Irish Medical Organisation people and Mary Harney.'

Two more loyalists – Darragh O'Brien and Michael Finneran

– came out against the move in the Sunday papers and this, as much as any of the clamour, played on Cowen's mind. Given the outcry, Finian McGrath became unnerved and made his displeasure known by threatening to withdraw his support for the government. That Sunday, Cowen decided to delay a trip to China and kept working on a solution to the crisis. After a long weekend, a solution was reached by the Monday. Revised proposals would now see just the wealthiest 5% of over-seventies losing their right to free medical care. Only couples with incomes of more than €73,000 and single pensioners with incomes of over €36,500 would have to pay for their health treatment. 'So by the time the Dáil came back on the Tuesday we were able to say we [would keep in] pretty much everyone,' says Cowen.

Finally, on Tuesday, Cowen reappeared on *RTÉ News* and announced a complete climbdown from the intended withdrawal of the medical card eligibility. 'The problem was that a decision had been taken by a prior government to allow a medical card for all over seventy regardless of your means. How to retrieve that decision if you have to? Once you make that move it is very hard to retrieve it,' Cowen concedes. 'When you hit harder times, those sorts of decisions come under scrutiny because you have to find a proportionate [payment], it is about who pays. When you introduce universal payments, you face those problems.'

Cowen, as he did many times in discussions for this book, reflects on his mistakes and admits he was wrong. He does so in regard to this most damaging of mistakes. 'But that being said, we should have had more detail on it. We were all collectively responsible for it,' he concedes.

When it is put to him that his advisors don't believe he should have taken responsibility, he says, 'Ah no, it was a government decision, it was a government decision, no question about that.'

The timing of the budget was a problem, in Mary Harney's opinion. 'The budget was October so it was ready-made for a protest time, if you understand me. If it had have been September, or Christmas when the weather was bad, then I think people were less likely to come out and protest.' Ministers thought that in September large numbers of people would still have been on holiday. Later in the year people are distracted by Christmas shopping and festive celebrations. It is a stark judgement by Harney, but an honest appraisal of how politicians think in a crisis.

Fianna Fáil ministers, speaking to us, were pretty much in agreement that the greater proportion of blame for the debacle should be laid at Harney's door, as she was the minister for health. Pat Carey says that there were heated conversations; he claims that Cowen 'put it very bluntly to Mary Harney' in a question: 'Does that mean that the Bord na Móna pensioners are going to be affected by this as well?' 'Bord na Móna pensioners', who had worked for the peat processors, proliferated in Offaly, but there may well have been a bit of gallows humour in this statement. 'It was at that stage people were scratching their heads, saying "we are not sure, we better go back and take a look". I suppose he [Cowen] had himself the experience of being in the Departments of Health and Finance. He was annoyed that he had been bounced into this,' says Carey. Conor Lenihan also maintains that the Department of Health 'generated the cut'.

Harney accepts that it was a major mistake but is anxious to contextualise it in the times. 'The income threshold was too low, I accept that, we just had to do awful things. Because health was such a big spending department, something like 25% to 28% of the cuts had to come from health. And pay is over 70% of the budget, and we were touching that as well, so from the remaining 30% we had to find a lot of money. That was the challenge.'

She says that they 'did foresee' the furore but adds, 'If you think this was easy, it wasn't. Any time you are taking something off somebody and not giving them a benefit, then, of course, we were into an emergency situation quite frankly.'

Nevertheless, the cut was not worth the protests.

There were claims by a number of Fianna Fáil ministers in off-the-record interviews we conducted that this was a 'Progressive Democrats' cut, that it was motivated by right-wing ideology. Harney rejects this totally. 'The PD ideology would be people at the bottom should be given the support of the state. Those who are well off, people like me, if I was seventy, shouldn't have a free medical card. Why should I?' Harney insists. 'I always remember Barry Andrews joking with me, "My father's furious with you, because he has to hand back his medical card."' He was referring to David Andrews, a barrister, former Fianna Fáil minister and party grandee.

The error, as so often during this administration, was that the weak, in this case the old folks, felt targeted. And their perception was that they had been indiscriminately chosen, while the fat cats and politicians who had caused the crisis through their recklessness were relatively unscathed.

'I mean it blew up,' says Eamon Ryan. 'People were nervous because it was a scary time, older people particularly because they're not in control. If you look in truth as to where the adjustment was made over the years, younger people got a far worse hit than older people, but younger people have got flexibility, they know how to adapt. But they're the ones who got really hardest hit. But with older people it comes to fear and the inability to move; it just touched a nerve.' He recalls the panic among politicians, particularly Fianna Fáil backbenchers and the eternally jumpy Finian McGrath, who were assailed by pensioners at their clinics.

Ryan's words, better than any, recall the moment when the Fianna Fáil/Green Party coalition lost its nerve. 'You could almost literally [feel it], it's almost funny how some of these things happen. It almost felt like a battlefront. You know, when someone calls "retreat" and suddenly everyone retreats.'

On foot of the medical card fiasco, Fianna Fáil fell to 22% in the polls, and such was the trauma inflicted on the party that the government changed the way it did business. 'We were on about 30% or 32%, but in following budgetary discussions we had far more Cabinet meetings to make sure everything we were doing was politically proofed,' adds Cowen. But the damage was done and discussions about a change of leadership began at this time.

Truly something died in Fianna Fáil that October. Its ability to empathise with its key supporters had been lost, according to John McGuinness. '[To] our core voter, the elderly, it was clear that the government was willing to sacrifice anything,' he decries.

The leadership and the parliamentary party, complacent after years of prosperity, were being dragged into these cuts unwillingly. Conor Lenihan says, 'It was very difficult focusing on cuts because all of these ministers had been, if you like, ministers in the good times. We won elections in the good times, which no other government had done before, by cutting taxes and increasing spending. There was no government before or I suspect since that will ever be able to do that again.'

Conor believes the fiasco was the beginning of the end of the government. 'So it was hugely damaging, yes, politically. I would say it was the first major body blow to the government, in terms of political popularity.'

The large protest at St Andrew's church on Westland Row and the massive protests by the elderly and their families outside the Dáil are seared on the minds of those politicians who witnessed them. 'It was the only occasion at which austerity, in this period, has caused a spontaneous outburst of public anger,' says Conor. 'I think there has been a lot of anger directed at many governments, two governments at least, at the austerity measures that have been taken. But none was really comparable to that particular one.'

The protests, the U-turns and the savage cuts had one positive effect for the government – it brought home to the public the depth of trouble the national finances were in. 'That first budget was the first indication to the public that things had changed here,' Cowen wearily recalls. 'What was unfortunate was that the government was having to consider things that it never thought it would have to consider for the previous decades … Unfortunately, harm was done. We lost a lot of political credit with a section of the population we had been very concentrated on. If you look at the tax changes in the good times, looking after the elderly was very much part of our sort of policy.'

The debacle had sparked mutterings of discontent about Cowen's leadership. Five months into his term as taoiseach, those who had been trying to decipher his mystifying character tics were beginning to wonder whether he was up to the job. His most noble failing in leadership, which clearly manifested itself here, was his willingness to accept responsibility for the mistakes of others – it cost him dearly. There are those who were close to Cowen who felt Lenihan or Harney should have taken the hit.

Pat Carey says Cowen did it because honour compelled him. 'Yes, he had that sense of obligation to do it, he realised it was a huge issue – he was, at the end of the day, prepared to take the rap. He was more than happy to do stuff like that.'

Fianna Fáil TDs were perplexed. They wondered how such an obviously damaging cut should be written into a budget by a group of highly experienced Cabinet ministers in the first place.

And then, if it was indeed deemed necessary, why was it so quickly reversed?

The medical card botch-up meant that Cowen's failings were now being discussed in Fianna Fáil and around the country with intensity. In politics, when a party begins to fall in the polls, the last refuge of the scoundrels is to blame the all-encompassing but elusive phenomenon of 'communications'. Rather than pinpoint the leader's personal failings, their own failings or the archaic structure of the party, the TDs often blame communications and those advising on communications. Somewhat like a medieval court where the king's advisors are targeted, periodically a communications director or a PR consultant is jettisoned *pour encourager les autres.*

Cowen's public performances were uneven at best and his good days now became fewer and fewer. Some said an intangible malaise seemed to periodically overcome him as the macabre Irish vaudeville descended into outright political Armageddon. Cowen suffers from the condition sleep apnoea, which causes the sufferer to stop breathing during sleep. Its symptoms can include daytime fatigue and mood swings. He was often, particularly at the beginning of his term, open, articulate, confident and fluent. But increasingly he appeared apathetic as he spoke to the Dáil, his parliamentary party, party grass roots and the media. His voice would become low, he lacked energy and he would repeat platitudes and civil service dogma until his audience completely lost interest.

Towards the end, the only person who could seem to rouse him in the Dáil was the leader of the opposition, Enda Kenny, whom he derided because of tribal animosities. Many felt Kenny was some way removed from being Cowen's intellectual equal. 'And it was very obvious at that point, whether it was an issue of stage fright or whatever, Brian Cowen was not communicating directly with the public,' says Conor Lenihan. 'And to my mind that ultimately undermined his leadership in a very catastrophic way, and it also undermined the public confidence in the government. You reap what you sow, and unfortunately Brian Cowen was communicating very badly. I don't say this with any degree of relish, because I was one of the few people who was a very early advocate of him becoming leader of the party and government.'

Conor, who had a unique opportunity to observe Fianna Fáil leaders in his family home – Charles Haughey was a close friend of the Lenihans – believes that Cowen's reluctance to engage came about because of the unique economic circumstances. 'He was overwhelmed to a certain extent by the enormity and rapidity with which this downturn both domestically and internationally occurred … He was effectively swamped on a personal level by the crisis as it unfolded.'

As public perception of Cowen's premiership began to morph from over-relaxed, to careless to outright disastrous, the theories began to flow. Among those were that he suffered from stage fright and that he was shy. Either way, many began to mutter that Cowen was a reluctant taoiseach and that he would have preferred to have stayed in a lower profile ministerial role. None of the theories were fully accurate, especially the one that proposes that a man would somehow be forced by peer pressure to unwillingly take the top job.

Pat Carey, as always, offers a more deeply thought out interpretation of Cowen's leadership skills, or lack of them. 'I don't think Cowen was a reluctant taoiseach,' he says. 'Punctilious is the word I would use. He understood procedure, he respected the process of government. Maybe he didn't have the killer instinct, the ability just to cut people off, and in some ways he was too collegiate.'

Carey, an extremely astute and fair observer, says there were other features of his leadership style that perhaps weren't suited to the extraordinary times. 'He could never be accused of rushing things. He tried to bring the slowest learner along with him. He very quickly would have gotten to grips with the most complex of matters ... I remember clearly. He would be chairing Cabinet sub-committees. It baffled me. We decided we would publish the twenty-year strategy on the Irish language. It had sign-off from the Cabinet sub-committee and it went to Cabinet, but by Jesus, did he put me through it in both languages.'

Cowen's insistence on concentrating on the mundane minutiae of government in the midst of an unprecedented crisis was another feature that those in the Lenihan camp were to latch onto as a criticism. Carey says, 'You wouldn't want to go in half-baked to him, oh yeah. Even the most complex financial stuff, he was always seriously on top of it ... He is seriously underestimated, probably because of the way he allowed himself to be portrayed.'

Mary O'Rourke echoes some of Carey's observations. But she, too, had the opportunity to observe most of Fianna Fáil's modern leaders at close range. She feels that he stayed too close to his long-time social friends. 'The funny thing about Brian Cowen, he was a very approachable guy, but he didn't see that he had to change at all when he became taoiseach. "Why should I change?" But when a politician reaches the position of taoiseach, there is a requirement to understand that he must separate himself from his subordinates.' Cowen understood this, as he has said in his interviews with us, but he did not put that concept into practice.

O'Rourke succinctly summarises the criticisms that were heard most often during Cowen's years as taoiseach: 'He didn't want to do it [communicate]. You just can't be the same chap at the bar when you are taoiseach … He would come to the IT Athlone a lot and would launch something and read a script. He would no more need a script all full of guff.' O'Rourke felt, as she looked at him during those wooden visits: 'If only he could be like he used to be, normal.'

O'Rourke, McGuinness, Conor Lenihan and others all say that Cowen seemed 'reluctant' to be taoiseach, that there was a huge part of him that wished he was still able to meet his mates at the bar and not have to worry about public perception. We asked Cowen how he felt about getting the job he always coveted, at a time of crisis. His answer is intriguing. 'It is not that I coveted the job actually, I genuinely didn't set out to be taoiseach. Most people who set out to do those things, it never happens for them because they seem to have an ulterior motive beyond doing the job. I am always of the view "do the job you have and whatever may come will come".'

Cowen, unlike many of those in high political office, genuinely understands the working man. He defends his time as finance minister, when revenues boomed, particularly in social welfare and job creation. In his interviews with us he articulated his empathy for the ordinary person in a way that he didn't when taoiseach.

'People often forget [about the individual] and people quote statistics. Why wouldn't a lad be looking for a few more bob? But if you are not going to give the pensioners a few bob, when were you going to do it? If you listen to enough people around the place, you'd never do anything. I just felt, people are getting more money, what's wrong with that? But people were saying you are losing a bit of your competitiveness. Okay, but people were coming here to work, so ordinary people are as entitled to get a piece of the action as everyone else.'

This theme, an expansion of his predecessor in Finance Charlie McCreevy's 'if I have it I'll spend it' motto, is controversial to say the least. Cowen acknowledges that, but he feels there is an element of classism in the debate. 'But don't be cribbing about working people looking for an extra bob,' he said. 'If I am a plasterer working or a carpenter or a tradesman that's the way ... that's natural and how things worked. I hear all these people all talking at the Inquiry – we should have kept down this and kept down that ... everyone is entitled to a piece of the action.'

That the taoiseach didn't display all his intelligence, talent and humanity to a requisite extent was a continuing disappointment to his friends, advisors and political colleagues. His own assessment of his public relations is blunt. 'Looking back on it now, you can say I didn't communicate as well as I could have.' In contrast to Bertie Ahern, Cowen severely limited his media outings, with media engagements and TV interviews being much shorter. The taoiseach then was pursued daily by a pack of journalists, who periodically cornered him for 'doorsteps'. He complied, and fulfilled his expanding media duties in a far more humble fashion than his successor, Enda Kenny, who is the least media-friendly taoiseach of modern times.

Cowen, as the man in charge at the time of economic failure, and as the man most publicly associated with it, has continued to be judged more harshly than other taoisigh. Lenihan, conversely, lived a charmed life, partly because he embraced the media and communicated more obligingly. He and his 'Kitchen Cabinet' had recognised a vacuum when he was promoted. 'I sat down with Brian over the summer after he became minister for finance and told him that from listening to my own constituents in Tallaght that the public didn't understand the context of why these decisions had to be made,' says Conor Lenihan. 'So I suggested that he do work on the communications side and that he do more live interviews so that his interviews couldn't be recorded and misrepresented afterwards.'

Conor, who had been a political correspondent for the Denis O'Brien-owned radio station 98FM, believed that speaking directly to the public through live television and radio interviews was preferable in the main to print interviews. Print could, of course, be manipulated, but the politician must be an adequate broadcast performer. This is not always the case, but Brian Lenihan was a consummate and smooth interviewee. 'So from the autumn onwards, you would have seen Brian doing a lot more live interviews, phoning into programmes like *Morning Ireland*, Seán O'Rourke's *News at One* and appearing live on TV as opposed to in recorded reports ... and that is because things were very volatile internationally and my feeling was that we needed someone to champion and explain what the government was doing.' Given Cowen's stubborn refusal to engage with the media, Lenihan felt the need to articulate the government's actions.

Government TDs, coming up to Christmas, a traditional respite for the Dáil, had bad forebodings for 2009. 'Shit, we are in for a rocky road. We are coming into nightmare local elections: we were in the middle of our selection process at that stage,' says Dara Calleary. 'I think everybody was taking a breath, looking forward to taking a breath after that madness. Getting ready for the year ahead, you are always reading the end-of-the-year reviews, previews, how things were going to be ... Obviously he [Cowen] could see it coming from all sides in the party. He was getting it from councillors who were going into the fray [in forthcoming local elections], and so he had to deal with it.'

January 2009 would mark the ninetieth anniversary of Dáil Éireann, but Calleary, for one, wasn't feeling enthusiastic about

Ireland's floundering institution and damaged taoiseach, especially when he considered the emerging political force that was Barack Obama in the United States. Calleary, who was younger than most of his colleagues, felt the pervading mood: 'This really cool guy [Obama], isn't he brilliant? And all you are is useless. How come Irish politicians can't excite people the same way?'

Alongside all the government's political problems, the banks continued to dominate the minds of Cowen and Lenihan.

5

CHAOS AND DISORDER

Anglo Irish Bank's parasitic damage to the state intensified in the early days of 2009 as it was taken into state ownership. 'Again you were wondering why can you not just drop them? Why would you do this, why not shut them down? I remember Seán FitzPatrick on *Marian Finucane*, and I just remember thinking what a little prick, what an arrogant bollix. That worried me, when we were getting ready to nationalise them,' says Dara Calleary. 'Ultimately that worried me, that arrogance, and that concept of no idea of what had happened. No concept of responsibility. That really worried me about what information had been provided, whether to nationalise them, and you getting a sense that this was going to be a tsunami of a storm.'

In late 2008, in the weeks after the introduction of the bank guarantee, the board of Anglo told the government that it needed help in raising capital. Financial consultants Merrill Lynch and Pricewaterhouse Coopers (PwC) were sent in to advise the government on what the next steps should be. The government announced plans to inject €1.5 billion of capital for a 75% stake in the bank, effectively nationalising it, and immediately the Dublin and London stock exchanges suspended trading in Anglo shares. The final closing share price of €0.22 represented a fall of over 98% from its peak.

The mounting crisis led to casualties at the bank. David Drumm and Seán FitzPatrick resigned in mid-December. They left over a scandal connected to illicit loans to directors and a dubious back-to-back loan arrangement with Irish Life & Permanent – a scandal which itself had been used to distract from the true, dire, state of the bank's balance sheet. But their departures would have been necessary anyway. 'Liquidity concerns mounted over the course of December and January: approximately €3 billion in corporate deposits were lost and the liquidity position in the days leading up to nationalisation was extremely fragile,' Brian Cowen says of the situation. Further credit downgrades were imminent and were expected to drive a further €6 billion of outflows in the near future.

It was not felt that the use of Central Bank or National Treasury Management Agency (NTMA) options to replace this liquidity would be appropriate. It was decided, following consultation with the Central Bank and the Financial Regulator, that greater certainty could be provided by taking the bank into state ownership – nationalisation. The NTMA and Merrill Lynch were in agreement. The nationalisation of Anglo, which had been at the core of the arguments on the night of the guarantee, was now actually happening.

Four months on, Brian Lenihan was getting his way and his aims were probably helped by the fact that Cowen was on the other side of the world and could not have argued much even if he wanted to. 'At the time the decision was made, I was in Japan leading a trade mission. I received a phone call from the minister for finance stating that it was necessary to proceed with the nationalisation decision immediately,' Cowen recalls. While the bank at the core of the nation's financial troubles was being taken over by the state, Cowen was meeting the Japanese emperor and visiting Toyota. However, he remained in constant contact. According to one source, a civil servant on the trip, press secretary Eoghan Ó Neachtain saw his hotel room become the base of operations. 'We usually had a delegation room that was like an office,' says the aide, 'but because of cutbacks the press secretary's room became the delegation room and so therefore I don't think anybody slept in that bed all that week.'

Cowen was alerted to the need for further action on Anglo by Lenihan. 'Brian rang me about that [Anglo nationalisation]. He said this stuff had emerged as a result of the due diligence in the context of recapitalising the bank … this stuff had arisen and confidence had leaked out completely. The bank itself and the management, there would have to be a total change and we were going to have to step in as a country.

'I said "Who is saying this to you?" We went through the whole thing. The NTMA, the Central Bank were all saying it and it was pretty unanimous … he had no other option at that point.'

Lenihan's advisors, Kevin Cardiff and David Doyle, and the Central Bank agreed that taking the bank into state ownership was necessary to protect the wider banking sector. Cowen recalls asking Lenihan during the phone call: 'When do you have to do this?' and Lenihan replied, 'I have to do this pretty immediately.'

Cowen was not convinced that nationalisation was the best answer and felt it could further weaken confidence in the fragile Irish banking sector. He said to Lenihan: 'Okay, well get the tánaiste to call a Cabinet meeting. I agreed to that. So it was pretty clear there were no other options.'

Anglo was nationalised on the evening of 15 January 2009, the night before it was due to hold its emergency general meeting in Dublin's Mansion House. This move brought the bank into state ownership, the state becoming the sole shareholder, liable for all the debts of the bank. The world's most toxic bank was now the burden of the people of Ireland. Shareholders who were wiped out were livid; many of them broke down in front of the television cameras.

The nationalisation of Anglo was yet another blow to Cowen's authority. He had vehemently opposed the move back in September and his opponents in the parliamentary party knew it. And if they didn't know it, Lenihan made sure they did.

John McGuinness, then a junior minister, was with Cowen on the trip to Japan. He was emerging as a formidable opponent of the taoiseach and he felt that the treatment of Anglo was symbolic of their increasingly differing strategies. 'Brian Lenihan wanted to do things differently and I believe he would have been more difficult with the bankers were it not for the others within that Cabinet, and the taoiseach who wanted to be a little bit less difficult with them.'

However, following the shock announcement to the public that the bank was being nationalised, many opposition TDs and commentators were alleging that Lenihan was too soft on the bankers of Anglo, AIB, Bank of Ireland and the others. Cowen disagrees. 'No, I don't think that is fair … Were people being fully transparent with him or were they in denial or did they know what was going on at all?

'So he had to, from his own experience, work that out from meeting them … but certainly he became very concerned about the quality of the information coming. There was more and more negative data coming back about the banks and the state of their loan books, and the nature of how it was being discovered was adding to the slow emergence of the horrific truth. And the problem was that it takes time,' says Cowen, 'even when you have sent in people like PwC to do this exercise of profiling the thing and getting a sample, a representative sample as to what sort of activity was going on, and from then trying to figure out what is the level of impairment, or what's the problem, or what is the story.'

Cowen remains scathing about the banks, for he was also accused of being too close to them. 'It was appalling where it [banking] had gotten to. Looking back now, people say "Was he soft on them?" ... No, he wasn't soft, he was just trying to manage the situation in the time period. He had to get as good a read as he could. He realised the regulatory system wasn't as hands-on as it should have been. Here you were depending on people who were already getting very defensive when the information was needed.'

Aside from the Anglo crisis, the government that Cowen led into 2009 was riven with anxiety. John Gormley of the Greens appeared increasingly jittery and members of Cowen's own party were becoming ever more sceptical about the taoiseach's abilities.

All the while, the public was in shock. Willie O'Dea recalls, 'Through the Christmas period there was extreme apprehension as to whether the country was going to go over the cliff altogether or what was going to happen to the party ... the reaction of the public was you've let it slip, you don't know what you're doing, the whole thing's out of control, it's a disaster, we'll absolutely never vote for ye again, and so we came back apprehensive.'

Gormley told Green Party members in his New Year message: 'We are not in government for the sake of being there. If we are not advancing our aims, then we must – and we will – think again.' This fuelled fears in Fianna Fáil that their coalition partners were uncomfortable about backing tough budgetary decisions. The financial problems that were engulfing the government were causing significant instability and already both parties feared heavy defeats in the looming local and European elections.

Economic clouds were growing darker, and the pressing concern for ministers, when the Dáil returned in January, was a recovery programme for the Irish economy aimed at restoring the national debt to normal levels over five years. The plan, which was to be finalised in a matter of weeks following talks with employers and trade unions, included at least €3 billion in further cuts to public sector pay and spending programmes for that year. It was becoming clear to all that Ireland was in deep economic trouble. Final exchequer figures for 2008 show tax revenues fell below €41 billion – more than 20% below the government forecast of €49 billion for the year.

At the first Cabinet meeting of the New Year, Lenihan briefed ministers on his department's latest assessment of likely tax revenues and borrowing requirements for 2009.

'I just came back apprehensive and thought this is going to be a very, very rough session and so it turned out,' O'Dea says. Given the scale and pace of the crash, Professor Alan Ahearne, then an economics lecturer in NUI Galway, predicted the country would need to borrow a staggering €20 billion that year just to keep going. He said the government's revised revenue forecasts had to be brutally honest because 'nobody believed the growth and debt numbers in the last budget … they were far too optimistic'.

Coming clean to the public, an increasingly embattled Cowen extended the timeframe by which he said his government would get the public finances back under control. 'I think we have to, over a period of time, more likely five years than three in my opinion, bring equilibrium back between the current spend and the tax revenue,' the taoiseach told the Irish people. 'You can then continue to borrow for capital investment purposes. There is a return on that.'

Even with falling inflation, workers – and particularly commuters – were hit by a series of increased charges. Bus and rail fares rose by an average of 10% from 1 January. Motorway toll charges were increased by 10 cents per car and 30 cents for larger vehicles on the M4 at Enfield, the M1 at Drogheda and the M8 at Fermoy. Toll charges on Dublin's East Link bridge increased by 5 cents per car and 20 cents for larger vehicles. The charge for visiting a hospital A&E unit without a letter of referral from a GP went up from €66 to €100. Also, for the first time, the government had begun to introduce cuts to public sector pay.

In addition to the mounting concerns for the domestic economy, international condemnation of Ireland's banks was cranking up. In Germany, the guarantee and the increasing fear about Anglo Irish Bank and Irish Nationwide had led to the public charge that Ireland was the 'Wild West' of the eurozone, a comment that stung Lenihan. The label 'Wild West' had first been used by *The New York Times* in 2005 to describe Ireland's light-touch regulatory system, but its re-emergence in January 2009 was damaging. A joke soon spread across the boardrooms of Europe: 'What is the only difference between Ireland and Iceland? One letter and six months.' In Iceland, the state had refused to intervene and save the banks, causing a massive crash. As a result they were mocked by top European bankers and politicians. Lenihan had a monumental task to try to restore Ireland's finances, but becoming an international object of ridicule was extremely damaging to his mission.

Fianna Fáil members' tendency to follow their leaders in an unquestioning and sometimes overly loyal manner was the fundamental reason for the party's success as a political movement. But, under the pressure of the most monumental financial crisis the country had ever faced, Cowen's authority was crumbling, just eight months into his reign. Even some of Cowen's greatest loyalists were expressing doubts about their leader.

Junior Health Minister John Moloney, Cowen's constituency colleague and long-standing friend, caused controversy at a private event when he savaged his own leader's apparent disappearing act. The *Sunday Independent* published a front-page story written by John Whelan, who went on to become a Labour senator, based on comments made by Moloney at the Laois Chamber of Commerce annual black-tie ball. Whelan, who had recently been laid off from his job as a newspaper editor and had written a dole diary in the paper, was asked would he MC the event, which took place at the Killeshin Hotel on 9 January. He took notes of Moloney's keynote address and among those reported comments were strong criticisms of Cowen. 'No one knows what's gone wrong with him' and 'he's not the man we know' were among the phrases reportedly uttered by the Fianna Fáil junior minister.

There was uproar when the story appeared, with Whelan and Moloney taking part in a rather unseemly war of words over the airwaves. Moloney accused Whelan of engaging in a vendetta against him and insisted he had full confidence in his leader. Moloney had not believed that his remarks were for quotation. 'If I had something to say against my best political friend for many years, would I go into a room where there are three people that I have never met before and discuss Brian Cowen in a negative fashion?' he asked.

Whelan insisted he had quoted the minister accurately. 'In this instance, John Moloney got caught shooting his mouth off. He was pandering to the constituency concerns in Portlaoise while swearing his undivided loyalty in Dublin,' Whelan wrote of the event. Moloney, a respected TD, and an intimate friend of Cowen, was chagrined and, whatever the contention between the two men, many believed that the reported comments had the ring of truth about them.

With events moving so fast, the relationship between Cowen and Lenihan was also beginning to deteriorate. The finance minister had begun to vent his frustrations at his leader. 'I think he was very keen to become leader of the party; he was very frustrated at times by both Brian Cowen and the tánaiste, Mary Coughlan,' says Conor Lenihan.

Others have accused Lenihan of briefing against Cowen, even at this early stage. One civil servant, who was close to the taoiseach, offers, 'I would say Brian Lenihan constantly tried to undermine Brian Cowen. Brian Lenihan would give a briefing, then he started developing his own crew in the parliamentary party. He started giving them extra briefing. John McGuinness was part of it, Michael McGrath, Thomas Byrne and Seán Connick. Quite a few of the 2007 intake. He kind of started building,' says the source.

For Pat Carey, the pace of events caught many off guard. 'There were so many things happening all at once. Lenihan would be trying to be in three, four and five places at the same time. He and Martin Mansergh [were] putting through legislation, but as he was often doing other stuff, he often missed briefings or parliamentary party meetings.'

In early February social partnership talks broke down, forcing the government to introduce a new levy on public sector pensions. Cowen outlined measures the government had agreed that would cut €2 billion in public spending. However, the taoiseach told the Dáil that the government had decided on a recovery strategy in the absence of agreement with the social partners. In the news conference that followed, Cowen said he recognised that the government's decision was unpalatable and not immediately welcome. 'We can do it if we pull together, and I am confident we will pull together to overcome this challenge.'

Both Cowen and Lenihan spoke at a lengthy private meeting of the Fianna Fáil parliamentary party on the night of the announcement. While there was no significant dissent expressed at the meeting, Lenihan was asked detailed questions about the implications of the new pension levy for public servants, especially teachers, gardaí and nurses. Most questions centred on the implications for the take-home pay of those in the lower and middle income ranges.

Several Fianna Fáil TDs have recalled their deep anger at the lack of consultation on this measure, which they felt was a further attack on their core voter base. Former Fianna Fáil minister Dr Jim McDaid questioned the government's mandate and called for an election. 'We do not have a mandate for what we are doing,' he told Newstalk radio. 'Perhaps it is time we should call a general election.' McDaid was given to rash declarations and he was getting well ahead of himself calling for a general election, but it does give an indication of how unstable the government already was, less than a year after Cowen had become taoiseach.

By then, Lenihan knew that an emergency budget would be needed as early as April. 'Immediately Brian began planning the next budget, which was a whopper,' says Mary O'Rourke.

Lenihan, always distrustful of officials in his department, was anxious to have someone he could call his own man in Finance with him, and had been on the hunt for a special advisor for a few months. Having courted the likes of economist David McWilliams, the name of Alan Ahearne was the one that lingered in Lenihan's thinking. O'Rourke says of her nephew: 'If you are in a ministry, having been in one before, you can never trust the civil service.' She corrects herself, however: 'Sorry, you can with your money and with policy. But in the end they don't ever see the political side of things. You have to knock about and talk and talk and talk.'

After meeting Ahearne a number of times, in March 2009 Lenihan asked him to be his special advisor. Leaving his wife and young family behind in Galway, Ahearne moved in with an uncle in Castleknock in Dublin four days a week. While that was hard, nothing could prepare him for what he encountered in Merrion Street. 'From the first day I went in, it was incredibly stressful,' Ahearne recalls. 'A constant battle. I remember meeting someone two weeks after I started and he said, "Jesus, you don't look good, you look pale and your eyes look terrible." It was awful.

'But when you are part of a team in a battle, you do become quite close. The team was also the Central Bank governor John Hurley and later Patrick Honohan, [and] John Corrigan from the NTMA. Senior guys from the department, guys like David Doyle, Kevin Cardiff and Jim O'Brien. Then there was Cathy Herbert [Lenihan's political advisor] and me. We met a lot – many, many times. We nicknamed the room we met in the "war room". It was war, every day a new battle. We were a virtual war cabinet, with Lenihan as the Churchillian leader.'

The former US federal official continues: 'It was always very stressful, I remember going in on the train every morning thinking, what missile is going to be launched at us today? A constant feeling of being in the trenches, a new battle every day.

'Lenihan was a fantastic general in meetings. He was a natural leader,' adds Ahearne.

At that most traumatic time, in the run up to the April budget, the arrival of Ahearne was greeted with approval by many Fianna Fáil backbenchers. Lenihan quickly realised that his new advisor would be better able to explain to the TDs and senators what was going on than he would. He became a valued conduit. 'He then started the process of Alan Ahearne coming in and people said, "Well thanks be to Jesus somebody knows what they are doing and what is going on",' says Pat Carey.

Many of the senior politicians in Fianna Fáil had been around during the Haughey years, so they were more battle-hardened when it came to facing a political crisis. The Greens, however, were political ingénues compared with crisis veterans like Cowen, Martin and Harney.

Eamon Ryan had become the Green Party point man on the crisis and had developed a habit of taking assiduous notes at Cabinet, much to the annoyance of Cowen. But Ryan was about to get a big wake-up call. About this time, he had lunch with Michael Somers, Brendan McDonagh and John Corrigan of the NTMA, economist Peter Bacon and David Byrne, a former EU commissioner. 'It was a scary lunch because we realised what had been a banking problem was now a sovereign problem,' he says.

Ryan says they looked at a number of remedial options. The men at this lunch also discussed 'nationalising, the state to do it itself and go in and take over all the banks'. This would have been an enormous, probably impossible, undertaking and indicates the gravity of the problems that the men – almost exclusively men – at the centre of this calamity were confronting. Lenihan was worried about a 'sovereign debt' problem before January – a situation whereby a country can no longer meet the demands of its public debt. Ireland was now coming close to this cliff.

In late March, Ryan and his wife, journalist Victoria White, found themselves at the heart of an embarrassing episode, when the *Sunday Express* in Britain reported that Ireland was on the verge of bankruptcy. They believed that White had voiced such concerns at a dinner party with friends. The story ran the same weekend as the Green Party think-in in Wexford.

'Ryan is "deeply worried" about the economy and "totally disgusted" that Ireland's leader, taoiseach Brian Cowen, gets paid more than US President Barack Obama. The comments came to light in conversations between Ryan's wife Victoria White and friends, which have been revealed to this newspaper,' read the

Express story. 'White, a former journalist, said that her husband was "sick with worry about the condition of the Irish economy". She said her husband believed the government would soon "not be able to pay for social welfare or pensions because the country was on the brink of bankruptcy".' Green Party advisors said they wouldn't comment on third-hand alleged conversations – apparently at the last minute, a denial had come, but the *Express* printed the story nonetheless.

Cowen was unlucky at the timing of his accession to the office of taoiseach and he was deeply unfortunate with the economy. But often during his premiership he, or the people around him, did his cause no good by allowing petty issues to become more damaging than they should have. Journalist Ken Foxe broke a story in the *Sunday Tribune* in March that two unflattering nude portraits of Cowen had been hung illicitly in two leading art galleries in Dublin. Visitors to the National Gallery and the Royal Hibernian Academy (RHA) Gallagher Gallery got a laugh from the displeasing, clearly satirical paintings of the taoiseach, but the reaction of Cowen's supporters distinctly lacked a sense of humour.

The first painting, displayed in the National Gallery by an anonymous prankster, featured an undressed Mr Cowen perched on the loo holding a roll of toilet paper. A guerrilla artist, thirty-five-year-old teacher Conor Casby, had entered the gallery carrying a shoulder bag and wandered around a number of rooms before making his way to the National Portrait Collection, an area which holds paintings of Irish historical figures. A caption for the artwork gave a brief description of Mr Cowen's background. It read: 'Brian Cowen, Politician 1960–2008. This portrait, acquired by the National Gallery, celebrates one of the finest politicians produced by Ireland since the foundation of the state. Following a spell at the helm of the Department of Finance during a period of unprecedented prosperity, Brian Cowen inherited the office [of] Taoiseach in 2008. Balancing a public image that ranges from fantastically intelligent analytical thinker to big ignorant fucker from Offaly, the taoiseach proves to be a challenging subject to represent.'

The unsavoury picture was viewed by bemused patrons until security staff spotted it more than an hour after it had been hung. Since the National Gallery holds and displays priceless artworks, it was a rather embarrassing security lapse. Gallery management alerted gardaí at Pearse Street station, who were called in to examine the portrait and CCTV footage. A second nude image of the taoiseach was displayed in the RHA Gallagher Gallery a few days later. In this, Cowen was pictured dangling a pair of Y-fronts from his fingertips.

The story of a garda manhunt for the artist was picked up not just nationally but globally, to much hilarity. Some of the Cowen family, however, are believed to have been furious when RTÉ followed up the story on the main evening news. The report was light-hearted in tone, putting the value of the art at virtually nothing, with newscaster Eileen Dunne referring to the fact that the taoiseach was 'not thought to have posed for the artist' in the introduction.

Twenty-four hours later, Dunne was forced to read out the following grovelling apology: 'On last night's programme, we carried a report on the illicit hanging of caricatures of An Taoiseach in two Dublin galleries. *RTÉ News* would like to apologise for any personal offence caused to Mr Cowen or his family for any disrespect shown to the office of the taoiseach by our broadcast.'

Eoghan Ó Neachtain made a complaint about the story, which he said 'went beyond the news values of RTÉ'. In one of the dafter statements in the imbroglio, Fianna Fáil Dublin-North TD Michael Kennedy called on RTÉ director-general Cathal Goan to 'consider his position' over the report. Members of the Cowen back-room team told us that Brian's wife, Mary, who had a strong distrust of the media anyway, was most put out by the tone and tenor of the RTÉ report. RTÉ then came in for severe criticism for bowing to the pressure to apologise.

The national broadcaster had deemed the report to be inappropriate before complaints were received, a spokeswoman later said. Consequently the report did not run on subsequent bulletins and was taken down from the RTÉ website. The matter then took a twist when Cowen insisted that Ó Neachtain, the trusted government press secretary, had called RTÉ without referring the matter to him.

Then Ray D'Arcy's show on Today FM received emails relating to the hanging of the art and gardaí paid a visit to the station seeking access to them. Fine Gael's Justice spokesman, Charlie Flanagan, said it was a 'shocking overreaction' for officers to demand that the commercial station surrender emails relating to the prank, and was a menace to freedom of expression. The opposition claimed the government's 'heavy-handed' response had escalated the caricatures into a global talking-point and was a negative reflection on Ireland.

Prankster Casby was questioned by gardaí over the unauthorised hanging of the two portraits in the National and RHA Gallagher Galleries, but he ultimately was not charged. He handed over five paintings of other senior politicians to gardaí. Cowen's administration was rapidly finding itself adept at bungling from the tragic to the comic.

This mini crisis passed as attention fixed back onto the economic crisis. Lenihan was becoming increasingly frustrated at the lack of understanding among his Cabinet colleagues about the scale of the crisis facing the country. Ahearne says Lenihan's attempts to grasp the nettle in 2009 were continually interfered with by Cowen, other ministers and backbenchers. 'Yes, he was dragging a whole lot of people with him. There was opposition to the cuts from the backbenchers and from within the Cabinet. They were totally unrealistic.'

Life for Pat Carey became difficult – it was his duty to look after the Independents who supported the government. A government needs a majority to pass legislation and by this stage, the majority was wafer thin. With numbers tight in the Dáil, chief whip Carey had a Herculean task in managing numbers for Dáil votes. This involved keeping the government-supporting Independents Michael Lowry, Jackie Healy-Rae and Noel Grealish happy. 'Every day was an emergency day and we were constantly looking out that Jackie Healy-Rae was going to be all right, and Michael Lowry. Our own crowd were becoming unduly stroppy,' explains Carey. 'Lowry was and still is a pragmatist. Even when I was moved into Cabinet, if he wanted something for his own constituency, he would simply wander the ministerial corridor and talk to the minister. He would sit in the office. For Lowry and Healy-Rae, as long as you were able to deliver something for them, they were pragmatic and they were loyal.'

So delicate was the balance in the Dáil, Carey had to schedule Dáil votes earlier than usual to humour Healy-Rae, who preferred to head home to Kerry at a time that suited him. 'To be fair they were okay. The only thing with Jackie was he liked to get away early on a Thursday so we used to have easy votes on the Thursday so he could get away.'

For months, Lenihan had also been working very long hours while preparing to announce his solution to fix the banks – the

National Asset Management Agency or NAMA. 'He was in early in the morning always. Now that is a family thing, we are all bloody early risers. He'd be in before 8 a.m. mostly and he would work on,' says Mary O'Rourke. 'I remember him saying, "I am working on this NAMA legislation, it is going to be very big."' She noticed the effects of the financial crisis on her nephew. 'I knew Brian was working very hard ... my husband died on the 30th of January, and we always have an anniversary mass and it is always a real family occasion. Brian always came to the mass. I remember him coming down, and he had a dark heavy coat, I can see him vividly ... and I thought Brian looked very tired, even from away across the church,' O'Rourke recalls. 'He came down to the house, he loved the social occasion, in a kind of an innocent kind of way. He was a moderate drinker and he loved the chat. If you talk a lot, you don't drink a lot, simply because you are talking all the time.'

The burden of trying to save not only the Irish banks, but also the Irish economy, which was in freefall, took its toll on Lenihan in those dark months in early 2009.

With Anglo nationalised, and others likely to follow, Lenihan knew something further had to be done to stabilise the banking sector. The bank guarantee had failed to prevent a flight of deposits out of Irish banks to other more stable banks, and those Irish banks weren't lending to anything like the extent required to keep the economy running. He realised something had to be done with the billions of euro worth of toxic loans that remained on the books of banks, loans that had been taken out by developers and other entrepreneurs no longer in a position to pay them back.

The finance minister believed he needed to perform another bold and innovative manoeuvre to get the banks lending again. Despite significant resistance from his officials, Lenihan quietly commissioned the economist Peter Bacon to develop an idea that would allow the state to deal with those toxic loans and put the banking sector back to work. 'Against that backdrop, it is imperative that initiatives should be undertaken that will lead to stability in bank deposits and term debt liabilities and eliminate the need for a renewal of the guarantee,' Bacon informed Lenihan.

Bacon recommended the government establish what became NAMA. This agency would take control of the toxic non-performing loans, buying them at a massive discount. Its job would be to try to sell those loans over a ten-year period. The banks in tandem would also be recapitalised by the government, to allow them to lend again. Lenihan approved of Bacon's vision and agreed that NAMA should be under the control of the NTMA. Bacon had proposed the establishment of the largest property portfolio management company in the world.

Lenihan declared that NAMA's purpose was two-fold. First, to rid the busted banks of their toxic development loans and re-capitalise them so they could lend again. Second, to restore a functioning property market. 'NAMA will ensure that credit flows again to viable businesses and households by cleansing the balance sheets of Irish banks. This is essential for economic recovery and the generation of employment. It will ensure that we avoid the Japanese outcome of zombie banks that are just ticking over and not making a vibrant contribution to economic growth,' he said.

On Wednesday 15 April Lenihan, for the second time in six months, delivered an emergency budget. This one was to cut spending and increase taxes by €3.25 billion. When he delivered the bad news to the Dáil, there was astonishment at its severity. The rates of the income levy were doubled and the entry points for each rate were reduced: mortgage interest relief was reduced to the first seven years on principal private residences. Health levy rates were doubled to 4% and 5%, excise duty on cigarettes went up by 25c per pack of twenty and excise on auto-diesel went up by 5c per litre. The existing early childcare supplement was halved initially and totally abolished by the end of 2009. The child benefit payment was to be means tested, or taxed in the budget for the following year (this plan was later abandoned). Jobseekers' allowance for the under-twenties was halved to €100 per week so as to incentivise the young unemployed to participate in training programmes.

Lenihan also announced several changes to the remuneration of TDs and senators following the decision to cut the number of junior ministers by a quarter. Here was a perfect example of how the crisis motivated Lenihan to move on a system of payments which was totally out of step with where the country found itself. No longer would deputies receive long-service payments or increments, and there was a 10% reduction in all expenses. The outrageous arrangement whereby former ministers were paid ministerial pensions while they were still members of the Oireachtas was ended. The allowance paid to the Oireachtas committee chairs was halved and the payments to whips and vice-chairs were axed.

Billy Kelleher says, 'The budget was very harsh. It was exceptionally harsh. At that stage you could sense that the government were really struggling on a daily basis, even to get to explain itself, to get ahead of just being perceived as crisis managing.'

Dara Calleary believes the Irish people were already becoming acclimatised to the cuts: 'The April budget 2009 was very, very tough but people were ready for it. See, the problem with 2008, people were not ready.'

The decision to purge the junior ministerial ranks caused outrage within Fianna Fáil. Cowen decided to sack seven ministers and promote two to cull the numbers down from twenty to fifteen. He said that the purge reflected the fact that the government was giving a lead in making sacrifices and reducing costs. The ministers who were not reappointed were: Noel Ahern (Dublin North-West), Seán Power (Kildare South), Máire Hoctor (Tipperary North), Mary Wallace (Meath East), Michael Kitt (Galway East), Jimmy Devins (Sligo–North Leitrim) and John McGuinness (Carlow–Kilkenny). The seven axed ministers, who returned to the backbenches with varying degrees of anger and disappointment, were consoled by severance payments worth up to €53,000. The two backbench TDs promoted to fill the two vacancies were Áine Brady (Kildare North) and Dara Calleary (Mayo).

The sackings of John McGuinness and Noel Ahern, the brother of Bertie Ahern, caused most surprise. McGuinness claimed he was given the boot because of his toxic relationship with Mary Coughlan. McGuinness and Coughlan clashed over what needed to be done to address the needs of the country. McGuinness was eager to see reform of the system and felt he was being undermined by his senior minister; he felt she lacked competence in a senior economic ministry. McGuinness did not go quietly and was to become the leadership's most vocal critic. He took to *The Late Late Show* and later the *Sunday Independent* to vent his anger over his dismissal, and he savaged Coughlan for being out of her depth in her job. He revealed the deep tensions between the two. 'Mary has her views on things and I had mine. I was willing to press them and ask for change.' McGuinness was also scathing about the lack of leadership being given to the country by Cowen and Coughlan. He blamed Coughlan for his demotion and claimed she had threatened to resign if he remained in office.

On *The Late Late Show* he said there was paralysis in government: 'there is a lot of discontent in the party at the moment'. He added that elected representatives were not being listened to and there was a disconnect between the parliamentary party and the leadership. 'I have confidence that Brian has the ability; he is a decent family man who understands the normal troubles of people's lives but he needs to shift his mindset from being the leader of Fianna Fáil to having a clear understanding that he is now the leader of the country. We need to put the country first.'

He did not spare Coughlan. 'She made it quite clear that she would consider her position if I was brought back to that or some other ministerial capacity,' McGuinness told us for this book. He also questioned her capabilities, insisting that she did not have the skills to run the Department of Enterprise, Trade and Employment. McGuinness said that while he had a reasonable personal relationship with Coughlan, her style of management was very different from his. 'She's not equipped to deal with the complex issues of dealing with enterprise and business within the department. And neither is the department,' he told *The Late Late Show*'s host, Pat Kenny.

In response, the tánaiste's departmental spokesman strongly denied the claim that she had insisted on McGuinness' demotion and described as ludicrous the criticisms being made by McGuinness regarding her competence. 'We have no axe to grind with the man. There was no ultimatum. I wonder where all this is coming from.'

Cowen rejects the criticisms levelled by McGuinness at the government's handling of the economic crisis. 'I don't agree with John on that. I spoke to him when I had to make the decisions I had to make.'

McGuinness, behind a sometimes stern and unyielding exterior, is an extremely likeable man, with a wry sense of humour. But he has gained a reputation for opposing Fianna Fáil leaders.

He had rowed with Bertie Ahern, was emerging as Cowen's chief internal critic and went on to be an opponent of Cowen's successor, Micheál Martin. Articulate and cutting, the timing of his attacks on Cowen and Coughlan, coming after he had been sacked, allowed colleagues to say that he was motivated by personal bitterness. Cavan–Monaghan TD Margaret Conlon said in the wake of the outburst: 'If John McGuinness had all these wonderful ideas, he was a junior minister in the department for two years, what innovative reforms has he introduced?' She added, 'I think if you have grievances to air, air them in the appropriate forum, which is at the parliamentary party meeting.'

Pat Carey, an often cutting commentator himself, believes that McGuinness, who surely had ambitions set on Cabinet, was personally hurt by the cessation of his ministerial career. Carey says there was 'crankiness' and that many of the demoted junior ministers were 'not happy campers. People like John McGuinness – they were sore.' He adds that McGuinness had fallen out with a few people in the department. 'What I heard from officials in the department was that McGuinness was very difficult to work with, extremely difficult. He was a difficult man to take a brief. That department would be as enterprising as the private sector, and you would think he would be fully at home there … but John, since he joined the parliamentary party in 1997, a few of us would have dinner inside in the members' restaurant on a Wednesday night before the vote. There was myself, Michael Collins, Noel O'Flynn and John. We would chatter, but even then John would pick a row over anything, and did.'

Another factor in the criticism of Cowen was the growing confidence of Brian Lenihan, who had begun to agitate within the party against the leader. 'People [in the party] grew in their confidence of Brian Lenihan, and the public generally, and that seemed to embolden him,' one source, a senior civil servant who worked with Cowen and Lenihan, told us. 'I'd say after a year in office or so, from that time on he was constantly trying to undermine Cowen … all those kind of little manoeuvres like not bringing things until the very last minute. Turning up for meetings late and all that kind of stuff.'

McGuinness confirms that Lenihan started agitating around the time that he and others were sacked. It is a time-honoured ploy in politics to recruit supporters for your campaign against a leader from the ranks of the disaffected. 'When Brian Cowen did the reshuffle and he had to reduce the number of junior ministers, from then on Brian Lenihan began to openly articulate the view that this man had lost his way,' says McGuinness. Lenihan told McGuinness that the cuts and reforms he wanted to introduce were being resisted from the top. 'He said that the changes that were absolutely necessary to be made to save the country were not going to be made because of the tribal nature and personality of Brian Cowen.'

Fianna Fáil's long periods of success were driven by a collective thirst for power, to stay in power and to hold power for as long as possible. That gave the impression at times of togetherness, which hid deep internal divisions. To this day the sense of family and camaraderie at party gatherings is tangible. And loyalty to the leader is usually maintained until the bitter end. That loyalty is often maintained with the coin of advancement. Whereas Ahern had few friends in the parliamentary party, Cowen had scores of them, and he sought to promote them. This alienated those who had advanced under Ahern. 'The people that he was promoting were the people that were closest to him,' says McGuinness.

Cowen replies to this criticism: 'The comments by John McGuinness are predictable really. John has been consistent in his criticisms of every party leader he has worked under. The facts are that I appointed people to positions on the basis that they were up to doing the job. It is not true to say that every appointee was a friend of mine. Many, however, became friends on the basis of mutual respect that grew up between us working closely as colleagues in difficult times.

'There were even some friends who held positions that I asked to step aside. These were experienced, competent people, who had to step back in order to give others the opportunity to serve at minister and minister of state level.

'It [choosing minsters] is one of the more difficult aspects of a taoiseach's job, that never meets with unanimous approval from the parliamentary party. That is why it is left to the party leader's discretion to make these decisions. There are always those who are disappointed if they are not included. In the interests of facilitating new blood into the government, I had to identify team players who were prepared to promote positively what the government was trying to achieve in politically difficult circumstances. No party leader can meet the aspirations of all who would be happy to serve. If there was any criticism in that regard that came to my attention, it would have been that I was overly conservative.'

In May the coalition faced the voters at the local and European elections. It was not a pleasant experience. When there is a stable electoral cycle these elections usually fall at the mid-term. The seats for local councils are filled at the same time as the elections for the European Parliament. They are not always a guide for the subsequent general election – Fianna Fáil returned to power in 2007 after bad 2004 local and European election results – but these polls are a very good guide to the national attitude to the ruling parties.

The campaign got off to a poor start. Cowen looked jaded at the party's election launch at the Radisson Hotel on Golden Lane in Dublin. Senior members of the party sensed problems. Carey articulates a view held by many within the party. The stature, success and charisma of Bertie Ahern meant Fianna Fáil had become over-reliant on his presence. 'In Bertie's time everything revolved around Bertie. So when he went there was a whole apparatus that went with him. A lot of things just fell by the wayside.' Ahern had a legendary capacity for work and was in contact with every local organisation, but he was also a bit of a control freak. Cowen was not and some felt he took his eye off the ball and allowed party structures to fall into disrepair. 'The organisation had become very flabby at that stage,' says Carey.

Come election day, Fianna Fáil and the Green Party were hammered by the electorate. In the local elections, Fianna Fáil secured only 25% of the vote, down from 41.65% in the 2007 general election. Cowen's party lost 135 local seats. Their heavyweight opponents, Fine Gael, gained eighty-eight councillors. The Green Party, who had a far lower number of councillors in the first place, thirty-two, still lost fourteen seats.

Face was somewhat saved for Cowen when his party lost only one European seat, the one held by Eoin Ryan in Dublin. Nevertheless, they returned with three seats, profiting from an extraordinary campaign run by Pat 'the Cope' Gallagher in the North-West constituency. The losses may have been even worse, only for the ill-judged intervention of Fine Gael advisor Frank Flannery, when he suggested in an interview with John Lee in the *Mail on Sunday* that Fine Gael and Sinn Féin, ideological enemies, could enter coalition one day. Fine Gael felt this controversy cost them votes and Flannery was benched by a bemused Enda Kenny.

Opposition TDs also took seats in two constituency by-elections that were held concurrently with the local and European polls. Fianna Fáil's Séamus Brennan had passed away in 2008 and Independent Tony Gregory died in January 2009. In a curve-ball contribution from the media, RTÉ's and perhaps the country's foremost economics editor George Lee became Fine Gael's newest recruit and filled Séamus Brennan's seat. (Lee's life as a TD was to be short-lived, and after nine months he was gone, claiming to have been frozen out of the action by Enda Kenny and the Fine Gael hierarchy.) Tony Gregory's team supported his election agent Maureen O'Sullivan, who won the seat. Both newcomers were to vote against the government, further diminishing its majority.

But considering the Cabinet had less time to canvass and given the austere measures they had introduced over the preceding year, the overall result was not a catastrophe.

The Greens mistimed some of their announcements, concedes Eamon Ryan. 'At those local elections in May 2009 we announced, not very cleverly, the need for a revised Programme for Government.' Ryan maintains that the parties needed to redraw the Programme for Government, which had been agreed with Bertie Ahern in the summer of 2007. It was a contract formed from a blend of the Fianna Fáil and Green Party 2007 general election manifestos with all the compromised policy objectives they could fit in. 'We needed a new Programme for Government … the world had completely changed, what were we doing working to a programme that existed in a completely different world?'

The Greens were also worried that their supporters would not get behind NAMA unless they got policy concessions elsewhere. The Greens' negotiating team of Ryan, Junior Minister Mary White and Senator Dan Boyle faced off against Noel Dempsey,

Mary Hanafin and Dermot Ahern. Various members of both parties had an input as the negotiations stretched through the year. The Greens faced a different animal in Fianna Fáil than it had faced in 2007. Fianna Fáil was now a wounded beast. 'The truth is we had a very powerful position going into the negotiations and we did use it,' Ryan remembers. The big casualty in the talks from Fianna Fáil's point of view was education. Much to the disgust of Minister for Education and Science Batt O'Keeffe, who had taken the brave step in signalling the return of college fees, the Greens insisted his proposals be dropped. O'Keeffe was a close friend of the taoiseach and the two socialised most evenings in the Dáil bar. Small, personal defeats such as this subtly undermined Cowen's standing – as his political position weakened, he could no longer protect his friends.

'That renewed Programme of Government was much Greener than the one we started with. We went from being in a position where we weren't needed in government to one where we were absolutely essential,' says Ryan. 'The very significant attempt to protect education spending – particularly throughout that process in terms of class sizes, college fees – was key for us.'

The Greens were a disparate party within this coalition, and throughout the crisis the two parties were compelled to parlay to keep the smaller organisation together. The Greens' leadership, having secured a revised Programme for Government, still needed approval from the party membership for NAMA legislation and the budget cuts.

Relations between Lenihan on one side and Cowen and Coughlan on the other were not helped by the publication of a major report detailing potential savings across the public service, compiled by economist Colm McCarthy. It became known as the 'An Bord Snip Nua' report, due to McCarthy's role in a similar process nicknamed An Bord Snip in the 1980s. The McCarthy report proposed cuts in public spending and in public service staff numbers, pay and pensions, and reducing the number of Irish embassies abroad. It also recommended the abolition of a number of government departments and quangos.

Lenihan felt the process was necessary to condition the country to the new reality, but it also gave him political cover. 'Nothing can be immune from examination,' the minister for finance warned.

Cowen, Coughlan and others in government were less enthusiastic about it. Éamon Ó Cuiv, whose Department of Community, Rural and Gaeltacht Affairs was targeted for the chop, claimed the McCarthy report showed what would happen if an 'economist from Dublin 4' was running the country. In government circles, the special group's report was being described as a Department of Finance wish list. It signalled the shift of power to Finance after a decade of policies favouring social partnership under the auspices of the Department of the Taoiseach.

Since before the April budget, there had been increasing friction between the two government departments, of Finance and of the Taoiseach, over when to publish the report. Lenihan again appeared to have a different view from Cowen's on the matter. Tánaiste Mary Coughlan, in the Dáil, under pressure from Labour leader Eamon Gilmore, gave the clearest indication of government hostility to the McCarthy report, though it had been commissioned by her own finance minister. 'There are many recommendations within McCarthy that don't make sense; many,' she said. 'But it will be a matter for the government to make the appropriate decisions.'

Lenihan was furious at Coughlan but bit his lip, publicly at least. Conor Lenihan says, 'Members of the government outside

Finance looked at the McCarthy report as a showpiece event, but it was anything but … It was a serious effort on the part of my brother to instil not just a culture of cutbacks but actually a culture of restricting the whole structure of the way the state was operated.'

Further fissures appeared between his brother and Cowen over An Bord Snip Nua. 'Of course there was no support for Snip, but that's what was required. We needed to rapidly restructure the state, how it worked, restructure the size of the government, the size of the Dáil, the number of local authorities, the hospital provision.' Conor views the resistance to An Bord Snip Nua as an effort to undermine his brother, but Cowen maintains he supported Lenihan at this time. And having been minister for finance, he knew that the Department of Finance was often 'gung ho' when it came to cuts.

Lenihan, ever the patrician, felt that cutting that symbol of Irish prestige abroad, embassies, was just not on. Micheál Martin, who as minister for foreign affairs oversaw embassies, recalls: 'He'd no stomach for cutting embassies, which made life a bit easier for me. An Bord Snip said get rid of I don't know how many embassies.' Martin claims Lenihan came to his office and said, '"We can't do that can we?" Lenihan got that in fairness to him, he had a soft spot for Foreign Affairs; one thing Brian Lenihan had is he had a broader understanding of government and how it works.'

This emerging crisis was virgin territory for Cowen and his ministers. 'We needed to address these things as a matter of urgency,' says Conor. 'There was a huge slowness on the part of some people in the government, particularly the taoiseach and the tánaiste, to entertain that very idea.'

And, as always, an element of farce was never far away from

this administration. It emerged that McCarthy had been paid €800-a-day, or €35,000 for forty-five days' work, to impose crippling cutbacks.

6

THE STATE OF THE NATION

The contrast in personalities between Brian Cowen and Brian Lenihan became more and more acute as the crisis escalated. Colleagues felt that Cowen was shrinking into himself. Gone was the ebullient, forceful politician of the recent past. He seemed stunned by the gravity of the political and financial tribulations facing him. Fighting on many fronts, he neglected the vital requirement to bring the public with him. Meanwhile Lenihan seemed emboldened by the crisis; he was becoming the friendly face of the government and he revelled in it. He loved speaking to the media, both on and off the record, and took to heart his brother Conor's advice to do many television interviews.

In July Brian Lenihan was invited to attend the MacGill Summer School. The summer school was set up in 1981 to cele-brate the memory of local writer Patrick MacGill and features debates between public figures in a relaxed, convivial atmosphere. Lenihan was up against George Lee, the recently elected Fine Gael TD, and Labour leader Eamon Gilmore. In 2009 the school took place a week after the publication of the McCarthy report and its agenda focused on the economy. On the night of Leni-han's appearance, 900 people squeezed into the main dance hall of the Highlands Hotel, a room that normally holds 500.

When he took to the stage, Lee said that he was tired of being told by the 'people who wrecked this economy' how to get out of it. He rambled on a bit. He was followed by Gilmore, who was introduced as the most popular man in Ireland. Gilmore said that cuts alone wouldn't be enough to save the country.

Lenihan seemed far more self-assured than he had in the preceding months, which was quite a triumph of self-confidence considering the calamities that had befallen his government. He accepted that the previous Fianna Fáil government had allowed a property bubble to emerge. He passionately evoked the contributions of Seán T. Lemass and T. K. Whitaker, and said Ireland needed that sort of courage once again. However, Lenihan's statement to the press before his address, that parts of the McCarthy report would be implemented before the budget, did not go down well with his Cabinet colleagues. Cowen had said that nothing would happen on the matter before the budget, and the next day the papers reported this as a clear sign of a schism between Cowen and Lenihan.

By the time the debate was over, it was close to midnight. As the dance hall emptied, Lenihan sipped white wine and seemed content. There were prominent political figures everywhere. In one corner you would see Fine Gael leader Enda Kenny and his advisor Frank Flannery; in the other was tánaiste Mary Coughlan, who bought reporters a round of drinks.

Speaking to one of the authors of this book, Danny McConnell, after his address, a visibly charged Lenihan aired his frustration at the lack of understanding among some of his Cabinet colleagues of what needed to be done to fix the country. 'They just don't get it,' he said. He claimed he was not getting the support in Cabinet for the actions he proposed.

But the response to his impassioned speech gave the finance minister further confidence to speak to the people when offered an opportunity. He intimated to those close to him the impact of that night, saying 'I really felt I touched the people' and that it gave him confidence to continue on that path of reaching out. The event emboldened Lenihan to communicate more directly, says Mary O'Rourke. 'From then on Brian resolved to keep on the path of talking, to tell people what things were like, how bad things were.' Sections of the public and the media, particularly those who benefited from Department of Finance briefings, were grateful for this commitment to the 'path of talking'.

Cowen and his supporters thought he should take a different path. As the crisis deepened, panic gripped Ireland. Many younger citizens had known only economic growth and years of plenty. Now the banks were in a state of collapse and they had virtually stopped lending into the economy. Mortgage lending halted; car loans stopped; businesses, big and small, saw their credit, so vital to commerce, cut off and those businesses began to close. And the job losses, probably the most demoralising blow to national morale, started apace. The PC giant Dell closed its centre in Limerick, announcing 1,900 redundancies. Waterford Crystal, one of Ireland's most iconic brands, closed its last major glass-making plant in the south-east and laid off 480 workers. The Ulster Bank Group revealed plans for 750 voluntary redundancies. Supermarket chain Superquinn shed 400 jobs and closed its Dundalk store. The SR Technics plant in Dublin Airport closed and let go 1,135 well-paid aircraft staff. Multinational microchip firm Intel reduced its Leixlip workforce by 294 through compulsory redundancies. It seemed that every government announcement referred to budgetary cuts.

Cowen, a privately compassionate and decent person, failed miserably in projecting that side of his personality, and he seemed strangely unable to explain to people in simple language what was happening. He was not performing the relatively simple task of empathising with Irish citizens. The media and their backbench co-conspirators now hit upon a new way of criticising the taoiseach's communication skills – they demanded he must do a 'state of the nation' address.

As the job losses mounted throughout 2009, Cowen was urged to speak to the nation in the style of a US president and tell the people what exactly was going on in the country. Speculation on his giving such a speech was to continue until the end of his term in office. Given the increasingly desperate state of the economy, Cowen's supporters were also calling on their taoiseach to go on TV and address the nation. These calls were repeatedly met with a steadfast refusal.

'We began in the parliamentary party meetings to wish Brian Cowen would make some statement to the nation,' says Mary O'Rourke. She speculates that 'the terrible thing which stopped Brian Cowen I think is it would all go back to Charlie Haughey: "We all have to tighten our belts, we are living way beyond our means." That was the prototype of the state of the nation.' In January 1980, in a previous financial crisis, shortly after becoming taoiseach, Haughey appeared on television. Staring at viewers through his hooded eyes, he said he was there to talk about 'the state of the nation's affairs'. He added the infamous line 'as a community we are living away beyond our means'. Since Haughey lived in a mansion in Kinsealy, Co. Dublin, paid for through unexplained means, many of those in the know at the time found the speech laughable. When it was revealed at the Moriarty Tribunal years later that Haughey had taken at least €8 million from rich benefactors to help him clear his loans, the true scale of the black joke was apparent to all. It was hardly an auspicious precedent for a Fianna Fáil taoiseach.

Cowen's personal finances were not a concern in this sense, but his supporters understood there were dangers of a negative reaction to a state of the nation address from a public wary of politicians in a less innocent age. Still they thought the pluses outweighed the minuses. Fianna Fáil Tipperary South TD Mattie McGrath was one of those: 'Colleagues and I begged him on several occasions to address the nation. If he levelled with the people as to how bad things were he would have gained a lot of respect.'

His inner circle, too, wanted him to participate in a state of the nation address. One of Cowen's senior advisors said, 'We wanted him to do more media, he was a good media performer when minded to do so. We wanted him to do the state of the nation thing and told him so.'

The inner Cowen team was also concerned about his appearance and believed that his personal image was having a negative impact on the perception of the government and of him as leader. 'He always looked unwell, always looked tired and unfit. Constantly, again, there were efforts inside made to try and get him to lose a bit of weight and all that kind of stuff,' says one source, a senior civil servant. If carrying a bit of weight was a sin, then many in the Dáil and on the press benches were also sinners, but Cowen had a natural tendency to look slightly dishevelled.

Pat Carey, too, wanted Cowen to do a national address but said, 'He always resisted it and it got to the stage it went on too long and then it was too late.'

P. J. Mara, Haughey's press secretary and a mythic figure in Irish public relations, stated in 2012 of Cowen's failure to speak: 'If a government isn't engaging with the electorate, they are doomed. He was told this by me at least four times, five times over a period of nine months. It is one of the great mysteries of modern Irish politics.'

During the 2007 general election, with Bertie Ahern paralysed by the allegations emerging about his personal finances, Cowen had taken over and almost single-handedly, through accomplished and bullish media performances, pulled victory from the jaws of defeat. The contrast with his current demeanour was disquieting. Yet Mary Harney, familiar with that bullish 2007 Cowen, said she watched him shrink before her eyes. 'It's a pity. I think Brian Cowen became so overwhelmed by the problems that confronted him. Talk about being the unlucky general! It was sad. He became very media-shy. Very media-shy.

'He was certainly capable of making decisions and unpopular ones at that,' she says, pointing out that he backed her on the difficult choices she made in Health. 'He had character and guts. And that would be my summary of him. But he became extraordinarily media-shy about going out there and explaining what was happening and building up a relationship with the public – whereas Brian Lenihan did … And that was an error and I'm sure he will say that himself, he will acknowledge that.'

Cowen does acknowledge that his failure to bow to all this pressure to do a state of the nation was a major error. Our interviews with Cowen were full of surprises, and this admission shows that he is not as aloof and stubborn as he is often portrayed. We expected him to brush it off as an inconsequence, as PR frippery, but he says, 'Looking back now it would have been better had I done one [a state of the nation]. No point in saying otherwise.'

While trying to explain this failure, Cowen proceeds to damningly assess his ability to deal with the crisis: 'I suppose crisis management is being out ahead of the issue and trying to put a context on it for people so they can understand what is actually happening … I didn't succeed in that. That much is obvious. I mean I didn't succeed. Sometimes you can be hard on yourself but I didn't succeed on that front.' Cowen believes he failed in this vital area. A member of Cowen's family told us that in the years after he resigned as taoiseach 'he blamed himself for mistakes, and replayed those mistakes over in his head'.

He has many regrets to express. 'It is like everything – if you could have your time back again what would you do differently?' Cowen asks rhetorically and continues: 'Only a fool would say you wouldn't change anything. So, you would do things differently; obviously one of the things is something like that [state of the nation].'

Some in his back-room team told us that they discouraged doing a state of the nation speech because the situation was changing so rapidly. Cowen doesn't agree. 'It wasn't just an incremental change, there was a serious reversal in the fortunes of the country and there was a need probably to get out there to the country and put it to the people, "this is our plan".'

What frustrates Cowen and those close to him most is that he understood the plight of ordinary people in a way that many of his political contemporaries didn't. 'Now we did have our plans, and we took decisions, but it wasn't seen as a plan where people could have a bit of hope,' he says, in oblique terms admitting they were not in touch with the people. 'They were like "Janey Mack, will this ever pick up or is it going to continue into a downward spiral?"'

But during those years of crisis, according to Micheál Martin, 'there was a degree of caution there that was probably warranted. I remember Brian Cowen saying to me, the drop in revenue was catastrophic in the one year. No one had predicted it.'

Those of us who have observed Cowen up close for many years see an essentially shy and sensitive man. The fist-pumping, finger-pointing firebrand of the Dáil Chamber was often a show and, allied with formidable articulacy, a rather effective show. Though he has been revelatory with us, observation leaves the suspicion that his shyness and caution prevented him from making a lachrymose address to a TV camera that might merely have invited ridicule. It was the tragedy of this abundantly gifted man that he was encumbered with self-doubt when it came to essential facets of leadership.

The contrast between the two Brians was manifest. Cowen's refusal to engage in a coherent media strategy meant Lenihan filled the vacuum and was becoming the face and voice of reassurance in government. Lenihan pulled off the skilful manoeuvre of becoming an object of public affection while carrying out grim work. This ratcheted up tensions between the two men.

As Willie O'Dea says, 'What I was fascinated by was the sort of deterioration of the relationship between the two of them … Lenihan came in as his proposed right-hand man, minister for finance and all that. As things got worse and the media continued to speculate about a change of leadership and focus on Lenihan, that caused tensions, tensions that were fairly evident.'

Cowen, as he expanded on why he believes his communications strategy failed, cited the figures to illustrate the gravity of the collapse he was facing as taoiseach. He says the public was shocked at the pace of decline. He does not say that he was shocked by the country's rapidly collapsing fortunes but that is the implication: 'There was a contraction of 3% in 2008, then it was 8% in 2009; it was unprecedented.'

Partly in an attempt to address Lenihan's new-found popularity and to accede to the calls from Fianna Fáil backbenchers to 'do more media', Cowen committed to do a number of key interviews. He gave an interview to the *Sunday Independent* in August and two weeks later he went on *The Late Late Show*, where he was new host Ryan Tubridy's first guest. Upbeat and expansive, Cowen was asked for the first time about his lifestyle and some press claims about his drinking. He denied that he drank too much and won applause when he stated he simply enjoyed a drink or two at weekends, relaxing with friends, once his work was done.

He also said that the following 100 days would be 'crucial' for the country, with the re-run of the Lisbon Treaty, the passage of NAMA legislation and a belt-tightening budget to pass.

Generally the interviews were well received. The problem, according to his critics in Fianna Fáil, was that he then disappeared from public view again. At this time a poll was done which showed that only 15% of the public supported him as taoiseach. What many in the party expected to be a blitz of public relations just fizzled out. The unevenness of his approach to public relations, the lack of energy that went into that vital aspect of modern politics, dogged Cowen to the end of his tenure as taoiseach.

Micheál Martin says that Cowen 'didn't do optics, or presentation, he wanted to get the decisions right'. However forensically Cowen did his work behind the scenes, it was not going to tackle his plummeting popularity. Cowen was something of a throwback, according to Martin. 'I think Brian's strategy was to have everybody on board. He believes in the constitutional framework that we operate within ... He believes in the idea of Cabinet decision making. He was very clear on those kinds of basic principles. That's how he operated, he was almost old-style in some respects.'

If Cowen's feelings on the course his government and country were taking at this time were anything like those of his colleague, Willie O'Dea, it was probably best he didn't do too much media. O'Dea recalls: 'It was quite grim; Jesus, very, very grim. You couldn't possibly imagine a worse position to be holding than [that of] a Cabinet minister when the government was disintegrating. The economy, our support was disintegrating … People became openly hostile, it's an awful position to be in.'

Just as Cowen was kicking off his media assault, Mary Harney announced she was withdrawing cancer services from Sligo General Hospital. Two Fianna Fáil TDs, Jimmy Devins and Eamon Scanlon, resigned the party whip. Cowen supported his health minister rather than his party colleagues. 'That again displayed to me his character and his guts,' says Harney.

Cowen, already fighting on so many fronts, was by now beleaguered on the battleground where his government's existence could be snuffed out in a day – the Dáil. When the government was formed after the 2007 general election, it had enjoyed a majority of thirteen. Independent Finian McGrath removed his support, Séamus Brennan's seat was lost, Joe Behan had relinquished the Fianna Fáil whip and resigned completely from the party and Dr Jim McDaid had also lost the whip for voting against the party. The election of Pat 'the Cope' Gallagher to the European Parliament had temporarily reduced the number of TDs in the Dáil to 165. The resignations of Scanlon and Devins left the government majority on a knife-edge. With the support of PD Mary Harney and two Independent TDs, Michael Lowry and Jackie Healy-Rae, the government commanded the support of just eighty-two TDs, with seventy-nine opposition votes.

Facing into the '100 days' Cowen had referred to in his *Late Late* interview as vitally important, the government had to try to pass yet another draconian budget which sought to reduce spending and increase taxes by €4 billion. The administration passed its NAMA legislation and with an ever more sceptical Europe looking on, it had to force through the Lisbon Treaty referendum at the second attempt in October.

Micheál Martin had managed the campaign, adamant that it should go to a second vote. Not all his colleagues agreed. Some believed that large sections of the treaty could just be passed through the Dáil without putting it to a referendum. 'Now even Brian Lenihan at the time was really annoyed about it [the referendum] because he was dealing with the storm clouds that were gathering,' says Martin. 'He didn't feel that this helped us with Europe. Brian was even putting forward that you can actually do parts of Lisbon by legislation but I was dead set against that and said that you have to respect it ... If you tried that it would be politically disastrous.'

The campaign that had proved so successful on the No side in 2008, which had created so much doubt with the people, was negated. Martin had secured concessions from Europe, including the pivotal guarantee of each country retaining an EU commissioner, which pushed the vote through. 'But I had to deal essentially with the handling of the defeat and that took up my first year as foreign affairs minister, and I must say it was probably the best-run project electorally and politically I was involved in.' The second Lisbon Treaty referendum passed by a sizeable majority – 67% to 33% – in late October.

But the sense of victory was short-lived. That autumn a furore blew up when the dogged reporter Ken Foxe exposed an embarrassing series of stories that damaged the government. In the articles, which ran in the *Sunday Tribune*, Ceann Comhairle John O'Donoghue was revealed to have filed exorbitant expense claims over a number of years. O'Donoghue had served under Bertie Ahern as justice minister and minister for sport and tourism from 1997 to 2007. After that election, the Kerryman was nominated ceann comhairle, against his wishes.

The position of ceann comhairle, or speaker of the Dáil, was supposed to be above parliamentary criticism or general political confrontation. However, O'Donoghue became the wrong man on the wrong spending spree at the wrong time. The newspaper detailed the extravagance that had become acceptable among a small coterie of senior politicians. Figures released in October 2009 showed he had incurred about €90,000 in expenses on foreign travel since becoming ceann comhairle in June 2007. The claims from the ceann comhairle's office were seen as excessive in the light of the country's poor state.

Other papers quickly got in on the action. The *Mail on Sunday* revealed that two of the official trips coincided with the Prix de l'Arc de Triomphe race meeting in Paris. O'Donoghue, who was accompanied by his wife, Kate Ann, splashed out €12,905.14 on two trips in 2007 and 2008. The trips were billed as official business, with the ceann comhairle 'attending functions as a representative of Ireland'.

In 2007 O'Donoghue had spent two days at the races. His meeting with the president of the French national assembly, ostensibly the reason for the trip, only took place en route from his hotel to the VIP suite at Charles de Gaulle Airport. A €700 lunch is described in documents as 'official entertainment – lunch in honour of Tourism Ireland and France Group'. However, the credit card slip reveals the lunch was bought at the Longchamp racetrack.

Given previous excesses highlighted when he was a minister, these revelations were embarrassing. Before becoming ceann comhairle, avid race-goer O'Donoghue had already enjoyed lavish trips to the races in Paris and Cheltenham. These were said to be justified, however, on the grounds that he was supporting Irish interests as minister for sport and tourism.

The media, the public and opposition politicians now questioned the legitimacy of the ceann comhairle taking these tax-payer-funded foreign trips, when he had no such responsibilities. With Ireland in the depths of recession, the ceann comhairle's credibility drained away as the revelations flowed. On one of the trips, the couple flew from Kerry to Dublin at a cost of €227.50. They then caught the early morning Aer Lingus flight to Paris CDG for a precipitous €1,608.54. Transport in executive cars cost €1,543 over three days. They stayed at the Hotel Raphael, where their room cost more than €500 per night. One evening they went to the Michelin-starred Butte Chaillot restaurant, where a party of five people dined at a reported cost of €329.20 to taxpayers, which was called 'official entertainment'.

For five weeks O'Donoghue refused to comment on the revelations, saying that his unique political position meant that he could not. So detailed were the expense revelations that it was inevitable that the parliamentary convention not to attack the ceann comhairle in a partisan way could not prevail. Labour leader Eamon Gilmore became O'Donoghue's chief assailant and issued a statement saying the disclosures 'appear to suggest a pattern of extravagance which is unacceptable to the taxpayers who are paying the bill'. Eventually O'Donoghue resigned, delivering a bombastic oration as he stepped down from office. He was replaced by Fianna Fáil Louth TD Seamus Kirk. O'Donoghue remained as a TD and was expected to vote with the government.

The scandal over O'Donoghue's spending was extremely damaging to the image of the government and served to paint senior Fianna Fáil politicians as aloof and utterly uncomprehending of the plight of working people.

Meanwhile the government, having already hit public sector workers with the loathed pension levy in February, was now looking intently at cutting public sector pay, one of the sacred cows of the boom years. They would have to confront the issue with the December budget approaching.

This major, multi-billion euro pay issue became a deeply acrimonious ideological breach between Cowen and Lenihan. Cowen, as a devotee of social partnership and consensus government, was keen to salvage any possible pay deal with the unions and employers to combat the sense of uncertainty swirling around the government and the country. Given the failure to reach agreement on a new social partnership deal earlier, and in a bid to deliver €1.3 billion worth of savings in the public payroll, Cowen convened a new round of talks.

Social partnership was the name given to the series of national pay agreements that were initiated by Charles Haughey in 1987. The agreements were struck between the government, main employer groups and the trade unions. The partnership agreements were credited by their supporters with bringing an industrial peace to Ireland that was fundamental to inducing an economic boom. But critics felt that they had contributed to wage inflation and a drift into non-competiveness.

The Croke Park Agreement, signed in June 2010, was Cowen's attempt to continue the social partnership model. A deal on pay agreed between unions and the state at a time of great crisis was deeply controversial and became very divisive among the public. Cowen also introduced it against the strong wishes of his finance minister and others in his party.

He spoke to us about his thinking on social partnership: 'We are the authors of it, and we should stick with it, especially now we are in tough times ... It doesn't mean you come out with a deal you can't afford, but you must respect the process, because [if you don't] then who is going to listen to you? You can't act in bad faith.'

Cowen, like many Fianna Fáil traditionalists, believed his party was the true party of labour and he was not giving up social partnership easily. He wanted to bring the unions with him. 'Everyone needs a bit of room to manoeuvre. You want people to be responsible … and they were more likely to be responsible if they knew the details of what was going on.' He doesn't directly blame Lenihan for the campaign against a pay deal, but says that, in his position, he could not afford to be as tough as some commentators wanted him to be. 'There was a popular movement in some elements in the media; it was never my way to take a macho approach, in terms of running the country.'

Lenihan was most certainly not in favour of continuing social partnership in the fashion that Cowen was. He felt the country could ill afford to enter into any agreements and wasn't shy about letting people know this. 'Lenihan didn't want anything at all to do with it,' says Pat Carey. 'He felt it absolutely made no sense to be doing a deal with anybody. He would get quite exercised about that … On the other hand, Brian Cowen felt whatever chance we had of muddling through, we must try and have some level of industrial peace.'

Carey believes Cowen has been unfairly characterised as pandering to union chiefs, and, in fact, was more empathetic with the working man than Lenihan, the remote Cambridge law scholar. Carey remembers that 'when the [public pay] cuts began, the atmosphere in the back-up office, people being paid very low wages already, coming back after the vote and one or two of them crying their hearts out, "How in the hell am I going to pay the mortgage?" … That fed through to Brian Cowen, too. Things were bad enough without making them worse for people. But Lenihan felt you have to do the right thing, to do whatever is necessary no matter the cost.'

While Lenihan was opposed to the social partnership arrangement, Cowen remained wedded to it and had a strong ally in Dermot McCarthy, the secretary-general to the government, in his quest to keep social partnership alive.

Dara Calleary, the junior minister for labour affairs, was central to social partnership policy. 'One of the difficulties at that time is that the Department of An Taoiseach runs civil service and social partnership and the Department of Finance was Department of Finance and public service. So you had two departments responsible for public service, and two different ways of doing things,' he says, in an acknowledgement of the dichotomy amid which the Department of Public Expenditure and Reform now runs all public service and pay affairs. He feels the clash was more between the Departments of Finance and of the Taoiseach. 'There was conflict not necessarily between the two Brians, as there would have been conflict between the permanent governance within the taoiseach's department and the permanent governance in Finance.'

Cowen and Lenihan identified that they needed to save €1.3 billion from the public pay and pensions' bill. Pay cuts would have to form part of the package of reductions on budget day. Unions immediately took to the media to protest. They said that, on top of the pension levy earlier in the year, too much was being asked of their members. For many in the private sector, such militancy was galling given the 250,000 jobs which were lost in companies across the country in eighteen months. The public discourse became worryingly divisive as crunch talks began in November in Government Buildings.

Eamon Ryan offers one explanation of Cowen's motivation in seeking to hammer out a deal. 'We had a big, big budget problem because we still knew the scale of the gap. It's all public pay, in terms of in the big departments in the public sector,' recalls Ryan. 'Brian Cowen was coming in from that context saying "I think there's a way we can do this. We can get a really good deal in terms of productivity, in terms of work arrangements."'

After one national strike on 24 November, the unions signalled their intention to hold another on 3 December and Cowen wanted to salvage a deal at any cost. This was against Lenihan's wishes. Cowen told the unions he was willing to modify Lenihan's draft plans, which proposed swingeing pay cuts. The draft deal that called off the strike carried an overall transformation programme for the public service and brought into play a union proposal to grant a twelve-day unpaid leave scheme to produce savings. The unions reckoned that savings of over €800 million could be made through this agreement on unpaid leave.

A dubious Department of Finance immediately poured cold water on the merit of the deal, saying the savings would be at best half of what the unions estimated, considerably less than the €1.3 billion target sought by Lenihan. Cowen and a reluctant Lenihan met the trade union leaders. Cowen, in his interviews for this book, spoke publicly for the first time about the controversy that was to break. 'My attitude was if you share the problem with people [social partners], you will be able to spread the responsibility to the work force ... at least let them know the problems we were facing.'

Going into a Cabinet meeting on Tuesday 1 December, Cowen thought he and Lenihan were of the same view. 'That was agreed with Brian before the Cabinet meeting,' he says, 'then such and such happened at the Cabinet meeting and some colleagues said, "Should we be having the talks?" I said we have to have them in,' he recalls.

His Cabinet colleagues confirm that his insistence was met

with revolt. Ryan recalls the meeting: 'The fly in the ointment was that there would be a quid pro quo for the pay deal, that there would be twelve days less work. Pretty much immediately in Cabinet there was a sense that that doesn't make sense, that's not a saving, that's just the appearance of a saving.'

Carey agrees that Lenihan and Cowen had 'differing views' on the proposal. 'And I think the union leaders were quite sceptical at the time. That was a very difficult period all right.'

But Cowen didn't give up. He believed that social partnership was at the core of what Fianna Fáil stood for and he lobbied his colleagues. He told us: 'I subsequently made the point to some of my own colleagues, "If you look at the aims and objectives of the party, one of them was we believe in the process of social partnership."' He insisted the idea of the twelve days of leave should at least be explored.

Eventually, the Cabinet ministers gave hesitant approval to officials to tell union leaders they were authorised to negotiate on unpaid leave as an alternative to cuts in pay rates. In return the unions agreed to call off the planned strike. The union leaders announced that a deal had been struck and details of the twelve-day leave proposal began to emerge. There was substantial negative comment from the press and opposition TDs on the Wednesday morning and attitudes to the plan in Cabinet polarised. There was Cowen on one side backing the plan, and everybody else against it. Ryan says that the opposition to the plan was strongly expressed by the Cabinet and that 'we made it clear [to Cowen] that no, this is not a good idea'.

According to Ryan, when the leave plan 'was announced in the Dáil, I think then that was difficult and I remember ringing a couple of people. Ringing Mary Harney, ringing Brian Lenihan, ringing John [Gormley] and then ringing Noel Dempsey.' Ryan

Bertie Ahern, three times elected taoiseach, announces his resignation from office in 2008 at Government Buildings. © *Irish Mail on Sunday*

Brian Cowen, the new leader, outside the gates of Leinster House.
© Steve Humphreys

A triumphant homecoming – Cowen and his family greet crowds on the streets of Tullamore. © *Irish Mail on Sunday*

Justice Minister Brian Lenihan and Minister for Agriculture Mary Coughlan at Leinster House on the day that the taoiseach elect, Brian Cowen, was ratified as leader of Fianna Fáil. © Tom Burke

An Taoiseach Brian Cowen on his holidays enjoying a game of golf.
© *Irish Mail on Sunday*

An Taoiseach Brian Cowen with the Progressive Democrats Minister for Health and Children Mary Harney and Minister for Environment John Gormley, pictured at a press conference at Government Buildings regarding the over-seventies medical card issue. © David Conachy

An Taoiseach Brian Cowen, with Tánaiste Mary Coughlan, Minister for State Pat Carey and Minister for Finance Brian Lenihan, speaking after pay talks with the trade unions collapsed at Government Buildings. © Damien Eagers

Brian Cowen and Brian Lenihan chat with Helen O'Donnell and her daughter while canvassing in the Blanchardstown Shopping Centre for a Yes vote in the Lisbon Treaty.
© Frank McGrath

A new low – an embattled Cowen hits out at the tweet which suggested he was halfway between drunk and hungover during a radio interview.
© Steve Humphreys

Brian Cowen, flanked by Mary Coughlan and Chief Whip John Curran, announces a confidence motion in himself. © Damien Eagers

Cowen and Lenihan during a media briefing at Government Buildings. When this picture was taken Lenihan was already manoeuvring against his leader. © Damien Eagers

The one and only – Lenihan canvassing in Dublin West. He was to be the only Fianna Fáil TD elected in Dublin in 2011. © Gerry Mooney

The isolated leader – Cowen at the Ard-Fheis.
© David Conachy

The new leader and the pretenders. A victorious Micheál Martin stands with
Lenihan, Éamon Ó Cuiv and Mary Hanafin. © David Conachy

The remains of Brian Lenihan being taken from St Mochta's church,
Porterstown, following his funeral mass. © Tom Burke

was rallying support to take on Cowen in his revolt against this plan. He said that the 'Cabinet met again and it was clear: no, we can't do this'. It was made clear to Cowen that his Cabinet would not back him.

'It was a backtrack, it was a loss of confidence,' Ryan adds. 'My personal view is that there was still a case for social partnership but I think on that specific issue he was wrong, it wasn't a real saving and because it was not a real saving, we couldn't do it.'

Cowen also faced the anger of the backbench Fianna Fáil TDs, who now joined the revolt against the leave plan. They lashed out at ministers at a meeting of the Fianna Fáil parliamentary party on Wednesday 2 December. They saw Lenihan as an ally in opposition to the deal.

As for Mary O'Rourke's view: 'Brian [Lenihan] said social partnership simply can't continue and he was right.' Lenihan was on the continent during the parliamentary party meeting when the opposition was expressed – he called his aunt beforehand to give her a briefing. O'Rourke was of the belief that the teaching unions had first proposed the idea to Cowen. She asked her nephew: 'What's this about the unions and the teachers?'

Lenihan told her to go to the meeting and 'speak up'. 'I went and Cowen said he was in a delicate state of talks with the unions and they had come up with this marvellous idea that the teachers had,' says O'Rourke. Cowen pressed the merit of the twelve-day holidays but she was not convinced.

'The thing was the most ridiculous thing. I knew immediately,' says O'Rourke, a former teacher. 'But before I could even get to my feet some other teacher TD said, "That is not on Taoiseach, that won't happen. That's not on." Then about twelve people spoke – I was one of them. I said it was daft.' All of the speakers at the meeting expressed opposition.

Conor Lenihan says, 'Our backbenchers took off like a rocket, including Chris Andrews. Mattie [McGrath] revolted in the parliamentary party. There was a spontaneous combustion in Merrion Street, amongst the public, amongst our backbenchers. This was huge, the media went to town on it, everybody.' Many shared Conor's view that 'this was a completely doolally proposal'.

A lot of the tension exploded around that incident internally. It was felt that Cowen and Mary Coughlan were trying to stitch up a partnership deal and were prepared to give pretty much whatever the trade unions wanted. 'It was completely at odds with what people in Finance wanted. But more importantly the public themselves, private sector workers, felt that public sector workers would escape the kind of austerity that they themselves were now experiencing in their job,' says Conor.

Cowen, the party man, did not get into a shouting match at that meeting. He 'listened to us all, we were never whooshed out of it or anything,' says O'Rourke.

The harsh words were to come later for O'Rourke. She received an irate phone call in her Dáil office from the taoiseach after she criticised the deal that night on *RTÉ News*. Cowen explained to us the context of this phone call.

'It had been decided at a government meeting at the time that we would have discussions with the trade unions to see if we could get agreement on the changes we needed to get through regarding salaries, pensions and reforms in work practices in the public sector.

'It had also been agreed between me and Brian Lenihan in a conversation that we had before the Cabinet meeting that particular week, as we went over to the Cabinet room, that we would try direct talks with the public sector unions as a first option to see if agreement was possible. Even if we couldn't get agreement, which we knew would be difficult in the circumstances, the discussions would have the benefit of spelling out how little room for manoeuvre the government had, given the seriousness of the situation.

'We both agreed and I told the secretary-general, who was with us as we made our way from government buildings to the Cabinet room, to ring the unions before the Cabinet meeting started, and tell them that the government would enter talks with them to see if an agreement could be worked out.

'In the newspapers the following day it was suggested that I had agreed to an idea being floated by the unions that public sector workers would work less hours as a way of reducing the public sector pay bill. Some Fianna Fáil backbenchers, including Mary O'Rourke, were reacting to this publicly, stating that they were opposed to the idea. Talk of "tensions" between me and the minister of finance was being manufactured for some unstated political purpose as far as I was concerned. There was a bit of political mischief going on, I have no doubt, with a view to portraying the minister in a good light at my expense,' he said.

'I was not happy that an experienced former minister such as Mary O'Rourke was being critical in the media when what was being said was a misrepresentation of the government's position. We hadn't conceded on any points beforehand. I felt her contribution was not helpful and told her so. Had the roles been reversed, she would have been within her rights to do the same. I do recall stating that comments on the proposed talks should be left to those directly involved at that stage. As one who guarded her own ministerial turf when in office, I knew she would understand the point exactly. I also recall her minimizing the import of what she had said by admonishing me not to be silly.'

According to O'Rourke Cowen told her to 'keep your nose out of it'. She believes that Cowen's anger was intensified by the fact that she was Lenihan's aunt, and that she was somehow a stalking horse for the minister for finance. 'I was amazed, very amazed, but that is what he said ... he thought I was only doing it for Brian Lenihan's sake but I wasn't, I was doing it because the twelve days was the daftest, stupidest notion.' The concern of backbenchers was reflective of the unease in their constituencies and in the press about what was seen as a cosy deal between the public sector and the government.

Lenihan was making it known that he was deeply sceptical about what was on offer. 'He [Cowen] is insisting this is viable but it simply isn't. There are still some in government, my colleagues, who do not fully understand the gravity of the situation we find ourselves in,' he told Danny McConnell at the time.

Eamon Ryan felt for the taoiseach during the rebellion against the proposal. 'I think that was tough and that was messy – but it was the right decision, it would have been the wrong decision to go ahead with it – and the fact it was in the public domain didn't help.'

Given the uproar from within his own party and the emerging reality that the deal wasn't viable, Cowen relented. The talks in Government Buildings collapsed on Friday 4 December, after it was decided the price being demanded by the unions was too high. It emerged that public sector workers were facing into pay cuts of up to 6% when the budget was formally announced the following Wednesday. At the Cabinet, a weakened Cowen admitted defeat. Was he damaged in the eyes of his colleagues?

'Yeah, of course,' says Ryan.

According to Pat Carey, 'the whole government was damaged. Certainly, there was a divide on the issue. There was the side which felt we can't give in to the unions. Then there was the other side. Mary Coughlan, Brendan Smith would have been in the conciliatory group. There were others in between.'

Conor Lenihan says that his brother was vehemently opposed not only to the twelve-day plan but to social partnership as it existed at that time. Here there was a significant ideological clash with the taoiseach. 'Yes it was a flash point. There was a strong degree of tension around the whole impulse in the government to have a full agreement with the social partners.

'We felt that these partnership agreements were worthwhile when there was money, but given the scale and nature of the crisis there was really not much room for an agreement like the Croke Park Agreement ... It should have been suspended pending the recovery of the economy,' says Conor.

Cowen was extremely cautious about revealing any cross-purposes with Brian Lenihan throughout our discussions. However, he said that he believed Lenihan and the secretary-general of the government agreed 'before a government meeting' to bring in the unions 'and have discussions and see if we can do a deal'. They also agreed that 'if we can't do a deal, it is going to involve some pretty tough stuff'.

Cowen, as taoiseach, believed he did not have the luxury to just cast away social partnership. He felt it was the only structure that would prevent yet another front opening in the crisis. 'My attitude was we have this arrangement in place, you must discuss it with them [the unions], you must discuss and engage and if you can do a deal you do it. If you can't, you can't ... but you can't say we will throw away all the procedures and processes we have in place because we have a totally new financial situation.'

He tells us that because Fianna Fáil established social partnership, they had to be loyal to it. 'We are the authors of it, and we should stick with it, especially now we were in tough times,' he says stubbornly. 'It doesn't mean you come out with a deal you can't afford, but you must respect the process, because who is going to listen to you if you don't?'

Lenihan and most of his Fianna Fáil colleagues believed social partnership, in the guise that Cowen envisioned it, had to be jettisoned. But it was a matter of honour with the taoiseach.

The proposed deal, to Cowen's great disappointment, fell through. 'In the end we couldn't do the deal, because it involved pay cuts and the unions couldn't accept that.' But he denies strongly some of the claims made against him. 'They [the unions] came up with a proposal for less days at work, and it was portrayed in the media that I was advocating it … it wasn't that I was advocating this, but I was saying we have to discuss it with them. We can't just dismiss it and not discuss it.'

Cowen says that he was the prime mover in continuing the talks, and that subtlety was misinterpreted as his being in favour of the twelve-day deal. The gist of talks was 'let's discuss it and if we don't agree with it and if we don't accept the figures and they don't work then we won't do it'. He concedes that the row was characterised by some of his opponents in the party as a breach with Lenihan. 'But there were some guys, some people, at some levels in the party, trying to create this issue between myself and the minister for finance.'

The following Wednesday Lenihan announced what was his third major austerity budget in fourteen months, revealing €4 billion in cuts and tax increases.

7

El Cid

In the days before Brian Lenihan delivered his third budget in fourteen months, he complained to his colleagues about pains in his back and stomach. Anxious, knowing the kind of stress he was under in the run-up to the budget, which was unveiled on 9 December 2009, they urged him to go to the doctor. 'I had a pain in my stomach for a few weeks before the budget; now I wasn't concerned about it, though, I thought it was muscular,' Lenihan said later.

'He met me one day in the Dáil. He said, "I have this niggly pain in my stomach. I must have eaten something at a dinner,"' says Mary O'Rourke. She told him to get himself checked out by a doctor.

Micheál Martin noticed that Lenihan wasn't himself. 'I was at a Northern Ireland meeting with him, one of those North–South ministerial meetings [in Armagh] and he was limping afterwards … and I remember him saying he was going somewhere to lie down. And I thought nothing of it. And he said, "I need somewhere to lie down before I get the bus back."'

Asked what Lenihan thought his ailment was, Martin says, 'His hip.'

Lenihan, despite his physical discomfort, had that tough budget with cuts and tax increases totalling €4 billion to sell to his party, his coalition partners and the country. He dismissed his aunt and colleagues when they worried he had taken on too much work.

Having delivered the budget and having tended to his considerable media commitments throughout that day, Lenihan arrived back in Leinster House. The financially agile defence minister Willie O'Dea was charged with bringing the VAT aspects of the budget through the Dáil, and the debate concluded at midnight. Lenihan didn't seem encumbered physically. 'Afterwards he says to me we'll have a pint and I says how can we have a pint at this time of night?' O'Dea recollects. Lenihan suggested a well-known pub near Leinster House. '"Go up to Doheny's," he says and he was in the best of form, drank three or four pints. I had a few myself.'

The following morning Lenihan was late for his scheduled appearance on Pat Kenny's mid-morning show on RTÉ Radio 1. It has become the tradition for the finance minister to go to RTÉ's Montrose studios and speak to the public on radio about the budget measures introduced the day before. In the days when Brian Cowen and Charlie McCreevy were in giveaway mode, such encounters were more sedate and easier to navigate. Now, callers instanced the personal pain Lenihan's cuts had caused. The finance minister was empathetic and did his best to explain his actions. Not for the first time, he felt the full force of public anger first hand.

He was feeling more and more unwell and some noticed that he had turned a little yellow. 'Certainly after the budget he was very jaundiced, and he went to hospital,' says his advisor Alan Ahearne.

'A few days after the budget, I had an acute onset of jaundice,' Lenihan later said. His family had noticed changes but were not concerned at first. According to Conor Lenihan: 'We knew he was not well and he was going in for tests prior to Christmas. Yes, he had been losing weight but we were not alarmed at his weight loss because he had actually been through a very assiduous diet period and he lost weight anyway.'

But when symptoms similar to those of Brian Lenihan Senior, who in his later years had contracted liver disease, began to manifest themselves in his brother, Conor became worried. 'Then he started to lose more weight and his skin took on a slightly yellow pallor, which to us did not look very healthy and obviously it created a very vivid reminder of what happened to my father … because the same thing happened to Dad, losing weight and the skin pallor and colour changed.'

Brian Lenihan Senior underwent a liver transplant at the Mayo Clinic in 1989. He died in 1995.

Mary O'Rourke again encouraged her brother's son to see a doctor. 'I said to him, Brian, you had better get yourself right … he told me he had gone to the local doctor.'

The minister attended the Oireachtas Finance Committee Christmas dinner in the Fire Restaurant at the Mansion House on the night of Tuesday 15 December. He appeared to be in good form and headed home early. But the following day, Wednesday, hours before he was due to spearhead legislation in the Dáil to cut the pay of public servants, Lenihan became extremely unwell in his office and was taken to the Mater Private Hospital. Knowledge that Lenihan had been taken to hospital circulated in government circles and the minister's office told journalists that he was due to go in for a minor procedure and that his appointment was brought forward. His press office said that he was being treated for a hernia, as it was understood this was the problem.

Lenihan was admitted to a private suite at the Mater Private. A female garda stood sentry at his door for the duration of his stay. Lenihan was cared for by Professor Gerry McEntee, a consultant surgeon with expertise in the pancreas and liver. There is a long-standing family connection between McEntee and the Lenihans, as the respected consultant treated Brian Lenihan Senior before his liver transplant. McEntee also has political connections. He is the brother of the late Fine Gael Meath East TD and junior minister Shane McEntee and uncle of current junior minister Helen McEntee.

Lenihan underwent surgery, which officially was for a suspected hernia. Even close family members were initially relaxed at his emergency hospitalisation. Mary O'Rourke says, 'Conor Lenihan and I spoke about the 17th or 18th, and I said to Conor I don't think it looks good.' Conor reassured her that it was a hernia. She thought, 'Well that is curable, there is nothing wrong with that. It is not a big thing. But as days went by we got more news.'

O'Rourke insists that statements that it was a suspected hernia were not a cover story to deflect media attention in those early days. 'No, it wasn't a cover story. No, he genuinely thought that's what it was and the doctors thought so, too. No, we never thought of cancer because he was so healthy ...'.

Inaccurate speculation about the minister for finance's medical condition had to be prevented. There was enough uncertainty and chaos around Irish finances without stories leaking haphazardly. Willie O'Dea says at that stage he had no reason to disbelieve the hernia story. 'But I was talking to a guy about a week later, a businessman who had some, well, connections, and he told me, he says it was much worse.'

In reality, Lenihan was told almost immediately that he had stage four pancreatic cancer, a diagnosis that normally means a person would have at most eighteen months to live. 'The doctors examined what was wrong with me and established that there was a blockage in my pancreas,' Lenihan was to tell reporters. 'They inserted a stent so my pancreas is working normally, but the blockage did and does comprise of cancerous tissue which will require medical intervention, namely chemotherapy and radiotherapy.'

In an attempt to provide the ailing minister with the best possible chance of survival, doctors consulted abroad on what their options were. 'The authorities at the Mater Hospital were very good and sought a lot of international opinion on my condition, so there was a fairly wide circle of knowledge in terms of my condition,' Lenihan said. And as a result, the speculation that the finance minister was far more seriously ill than initially thought began to do the rounds.

During the two days he was in hospital, a shocked fifty-year-old Lenihan and his wife, Patricia, had to quickly adjust to the news that he was now battling a fatal cancer which was deemed by his doctors to be inoperable. 'They are not able to operate on it at this stage because it is very close to a blood vessel. So all of that was a great shock to me when I heard it, as any of these things are to anyone who has had a warning of this type.

'I will have to adjust my lifestyle and set my priorities in terms of tackling this illness, but I am in a position to tackle my work,' he said in an interview in the New Year.

Mary Harney recalls speaking to the minister for finance during those days. 'He'd been sick, he was out of action for a day or two and somebody said to me "Brian Lenihan is in hospital, he is unwell", so I sent him a text and he called me up … he didn't tell me what was wrong with him but he said the following: "Mary, you're so right about the cancer centres." First of all he said, "Thanks for your text I appreciate it, hopefully I'll be coming home tomorrow" … he never said "I have cancer" but he left me in no doubt that he had.' Harney had recently launched a policy of centralising cancer treatment to eight hospitals, and showing her his support for the measure, he had avoided mentioning his particular condition. Lenihan left hospital on Friday, after the initial exploratory operation, to recuperate at his home in Strawberry Beds.

It is an unpalatable part of the job for political correspondents, but when a minister for finance is admitted to hospital they are required to compile all available information in advance of writing a story. In the course of phone calls and meetings with contacts it became clear to John Lee that Lenihan had a serious condition. After discussions with the Department of Finance press office, the *Mail on Sunday* ran a story which opened: 'Finance Minister Brian Lenihan has left hospital after a hernia operation but has been asked by doctors to return to the Mater Private hospital for further tests tomorrow and Tuesday. Although tests after a hernia operation are not routine procedure, Mr Lenihan's family is said not to be concerned that there have been any complications. Mr Lenihan's being cared for by Professor Gerry McEntee, a consultant surgeon with expertise in pancreas and liver problems. Prof. McEntee also conducts routine hernia and groin surgery.' There was no question of running a story about a minister's health that deviated from official information provided by his office. It was clear to the reporter, however, that Lenihan was seriously ill.

Lenihan returned to hospital on Monday 21 December and stayed overnight. As he explained, doctors inserted a stent into the entrance of his pancreas. His hospitalisation caused him to miss a Cabinet meeting at which Cowen brought nominations to the board of NAMA on his behalf.

Lenihan asked Cowen for a private word after a meeting in Government Buildings soon after he returned to work on Wednesday. Lenihan told the taoiseach that the stomach pain which had hospitalised him the week before was far more serious than first thought. They went into Cowen's personal office. Lenihan said he had been diagnosed with pancreatic cancer.

'I went to the taoiseach as soon as I was released from hospital and I explained the position,' Lenihan recalled in an interview. 'He was very upset to hear of my bad news but he indicated that he was anxious [that I would] see my way to continue to serve, and I weighed up the options.' Lenihan was touched by the warm and generous support Cowen offered him.

Cowen spoke to us at length, for the first time, about his thoughts and feelings at this emotional time. 'Brian [Lenihan] was typically Brian, he was very matter of fact about it,' he says. 'Obviously he was concerned about Ireland, he was anxious about his family.'

Lenihan told the taoiseach that he wanted to continue. 'He was very anxious about wanting to stay on in the job; his capacity wasn't in any way impaired,' says Cowen. 'He had this health challenge, a serious health challenge. But he felt there were prospects to continue.'

Assessing Lenihan's description of the disease, Cowen was satisfied that the man he had chosen as his lieutenant at Finance must continue the fight. 'It was at the entrance of the pancreas and not in the pancreas itself; he was explaining that it was going to require a lot of attention, but if he was satisfied in his own frame of mind that this was what he wanted to do, then I had no problem with that. He had great capacity,' says Cowen. Though the prognosis was stark, Lenihan's natural optimism allowed him to continue his job unhindered.

Harney says, 'My other memory of him was I don't think he'd any expectation that he was going to die as quickly as he did. He lived ... and he was committed, as if he didn't have the illness.

He got a little bit tired, no more than any normal person would, putting in those hours.'

His colleagues did not see him flag in energy. 'He seemed to work every hour that God would send him. The man was very clever, of course, and he was very much on top of his job. I saw no evidence that his illness was interfering with his capacity for work or his judgement,' Harney says. 'I think it a sense of the decency of Brian Cowen that he didn't even raise the issue. Many others might have asked him to move on … but also it was the right thing as Lenihan was up to the job,' she adds.

Cowen says the thought of asking Lenihan to step aside because of his illness simply didn't arise. 'I have heard people say, "Why didn't you consider changing the position?" That didn't occur to me at all. Particularly given the type of man you were dealing with. He was quite determined, willing to continue on and his capacity wasn't being affected in fairness.'

Cowen's innate decency was to the fore and there was no detailed inquisition of the sick man. 'He came to me and says "Listen, you need to know this." I didn't pry into health records or anything like that. I didn't go any further than that. He told me what the story was and that was it. It wasn't a case of I need to talk to his fella or talk to your doctors or anything like that. I accepted what he was saying, I had no reason to think he was being anything other than completely frank.'

Cowen and Lenihan had a personal discussion and the minister for finance spoke of his religious beliefs. 'We chatted about it, I mean he was a very philosophical guy. He had a good faith, and without going into the ins and outs of it, he had figured it out. He had his own way of looking at these things. He wasn't being in any way maudlin, he was being very straightforward. It was tough, very tough,' Cowen adds.

Cowen was always held in esteem by colleagues for the care with which he dealt with personal issues. 'When Lenihan began to be ill, Cowen was very caring towards him,' says Pat Carey. 'Brian Cowen was and is a very kind man, despite the portrayal, sometimes not helped by himself.'

Many people in the political and media community became aware of Lenihan's condition over the course of Christmas week. The independent television station TV3 had obtained information that made its journalists believe that they should broadcast a story about Lenihan's health. On Christmas Eve the station told Lenihan's press officer, Eoin Dorgan, of their intention to broadcast a report on St Stephen's Day saying that Lenihan had pancreatic cancer. The decision to make public the health condition of a senior politician without his consent was the crossing of a media rubicon. It had not been done before in Ireland.

Dorgan contacted Lenihan and Cathy Herbert, and the minister was forced to break the news to his young children on Christmas Day. Brian's son, Tom, then at school in Belvedere College, later recalled being told by his father of the cancer: 'I found out on Christmas Day, yeah; I think the report was Stephen's Day. There wasn't sufficient time to tell the people he wanted to tell. You tell your immediate family don't you? It was pretty shocking. But it was a matter of public interest, the health of the minister for finance. I was doing training for rugby with the school and we brought Clare in, my sister. We gathered around and he told us he had a growth. I said, "Is it cancer?" and he said, "Yeah." At that time I was quite hopeful that he would make it.'

While granted a short reprieve to tell his young family, Lenihan was not given the chance to tell his wider circle of family and friends. Although a lot of criticism was levelled at TV3 subsequently, Lenihan said that it was not the only outlet pursuing the story. 'A number of news organisations approached my office on Christmas Eve about my condition. Again, I am glad I had some time to explain my condition to my family. I would have liked a slightly longer opportunity to explain matters to my wider family and friends. Clearly I did have an opportunity to explain matters to my own immediate family. I have a son and a daughter as well as a very loving wife. So naturally I was very anxious that all of these matters should be explained to them and I did have an opportunity to explain it to them. But in relation to the wider picture, clearly I didn't have an opportunity to explain matters to the wider Lenihan clan.'

Conor Lenihan reveals that he, too, was present with his brother on Christmas Day, but due to different family troubles. 'I am a separated person or was a separated person,' he says, 'so I had nowhere to go for Christmas dinner.' Because of the pressure from the TV station, Brian wasn't given the opportunity to tell his mother, Ann, in person that he had terminal cancer. 'My mother was actually abroad and normally I would go to my mother's for Christmas dinner. I was invited by Patricia to join her and Brian and the kids and the family for dinner on Christmas Day.' Brian phoned his mother to inform her of the impending broadcast.

Conor sat with the family in their living room as Brian, left with no other alternative, broke the news to his shocked children. 'It was a very difficult situation for him to address. I think it would have been nicer if the media had not gone and done what they did,' he says. That afternoon the two brothers went for a walk along the nearby soccer pitches in the late afternoon dusk. There were four years between them; Brian was fifty then and Conor forty-six. The family had moved from Athlone when Brian was twelve and Conor eight, and they had spent their teens kicking ball together on those pitches in Castleknock.

'He and I had a habit of kind of going out for walks,' Conor says. 'That time at Christmas we went out for a walk at the pitches up the road from him and we wandered around and then got into a car. He drove himself and we drove around the constituency and he was reminising about all of the infrastructure and stuff he had got in the constituency, where he had secured assistance for clubs. So he was kind of reviewing and looking back at things. And he had become a little bit more, how would you put it, nostalgic.'

Conor says he maintained that composure around his family. 'He was very anxious not to be maudlin or emotional because he was aware that that would upset his family members around him. I think his main thing was that he wanted to get on and do his job. There were kind of emotional times.'

On the morning of St Stephen's Day, a Saturday, the Lenihan family braced themselves for the worst. The finance minister himself spoke to Aengus Fanning, a friend and the late editor of the *Sunday Independent*, to discuss the details of his condition. The Sunday newspapers, which go to press on Saturday evening, contacted Lenihan's spokesperson, who issued a statement: 'We are not commenting on the rumours except to say the minister is well and enjoying the Christmas break with his family and does not propose talking to the media about anything until the New Year.'

However, it soon became clear that TV3 was going to report on Lenihan's condition at 5.30 p.m. that day. Shortly before 5.15 p.m., the channel began running a promotional teaser on the bottom of its screen which said: 'TV3 will broadcast a news story of national importance in its 5.30 bulletin'. When TV3 announced details of Lenihan's medical condition to the nation, it unleashed a wave of fury. While an arguably legitimate story of significant public interest, the timing and the sometimes clumsy nature of the TV3 report caused anger, even among family members who were anticipating it.

'It was terrible, but we did know,' says Mary O'Rourke. 'But to see it naked in front of your eyes, visually. Brian was very good about that. He never held it in for them or anything. He was very forbearing.

'I got a call from Ann, his mother, on Christmas night, telling me it was going to happen. It was awful.'

The Lenihan family also questioned the need for TV3 to feature an extended conversation with John Crown, a consultant medical oncologist at St Vincent's Hospital who was later elected a senator. 'They had Crown on,' says O'Rourke. 'I couldn't understand Crown. Crown wasn't his doctor. I thought that was very unethical. What right did he have to talk about him? They didn't have to do it at all.'

While Lenihan's wife, Patricia, and their children were trying to come to terms with his illness, his extended family and political colleagues were furious at the crassness and insensitivity of the TV3 broadcast. 'We were not as forgiving about it as Brian, we were livid,' says O'Rourke, and years later her hurt is still palpable.

Lenihan's junior ministerial colleague Dara Calleary is even more condemnatory: 'TV3 were disgusting. How dare they, how dare they? Really, really disgusting. It was completely unfair on his family, and on him. What they did was put a gun to his head, "tell your family what we know", that is what TV3 did. Nobody ever wants to tell that news, especially over Christmas. He should have been given a few days. You know it was a matter of public interest, but ….' Christmas was a time when confrontational political discourse was put aside in Ireland. The print media had until that point viewed the Christmas season as a period when controversial stories were avoided.

There was genuine shock among Lenihan's Cabinet colleagues. Micheál Martin was in Cork with his family when the news came on the television. The brutality of the broadcast contrasted with the scene in Cork, Martin says. 'I was down with my in-laws. We were watching the TV3 news. We were all shocked at the revelation on TV3, we couldn't believe that, we thought it had broken new ground.'

Martin had been made aware that there was an issue with Lenihan's health but had not been fully briefed on the matter. 'I rang Brian an hour later, and he said, "Look there is nothing to worry about." He said, "I'll deal with it" and he explained the issue.'

Lenihan told Danny McConnell in an interview for the *Sunday Independent* a week later that he would continue in his job. He said he was looking forward to a 'full and vigorous year ahead ... Fortunately in the Department of Finance the first half of the year is quieter than the second and so that will give me a chance to undergo a course of treatment in anticipation of a full recovery.'

The newspaper reported that the minister had been in an upbeat mood when he strolled in Dublin city centre that week. He visited several bookshops; in one he purchased Peter Clarke's new biography of John Maynard Keynes, titled *Keynes: The Twentieth Century's Most Influential Economist.*

'The exchequer returns are out next Tuesday and I expect some slight improvement in the tax returns for the month of December,' said Lenihan in the interview. 'I am glad to see that there was more spending in the retail economy this Christmas than last year, as far as can be judged.'

Lenihan hoped to continue work with the minimum of fuss or interruption.

Professor Crown, meanwhile, engaged in a damage-limitation exercise and sought to clarify the circumstances in which he participated in TV3's St Stephen's Day broadcast. 'I would not have agreed to participate without the assurance that the minister had been informed,' read a statement. 'Raising awareness of pancreas cancer, an important health issue in Ireland, could only be a good thing,' he said. 'I was also aware that the audience would likely include many pancreatic cancer patients and their families, including Lenihan and his family.' He added that the 'reported anger of government press spokesmen at my interview must be seen in the context of the systematic government disinformation campaign on the issue of cancer and other health services in this country'.

The TV3 broadcast led to more than seventy complaints to the Broadcasting Authority of Ireland.

Following that bleak bulletin, there were understandable fears in government over whether Lenihan could continue. The decision to stay on as minister for finance had been made between Lenihan and Cowen, and there was no further discussion in government about Lenihan's ability to perform his duties. Lenihan passed on assurances from his doctors that his treatment would not incapacitate him.

There was no disinclination among Lenihan's government colleagues to discuss with him his ability to manage a disease that was likely to be terminal and at the same time handle the portfolio of the Department of Finance. It was legitimate to ask whether a man with pancreatic cancer could cope with the job of the minister for finance during this financial crisis.

Micheál Martin says that Lenihan was as open and discursive with colleagues about his condition as he was about most subjects. 'He would discuss it with you from time to time. He said to me at one stage later on, he said he was very lucky that the medicine wasn't interfering with him.'

Pat Carey says that he, too, talked things through with Lenihan. Carey asked, 'Brian, are you sure you can carry on?'

Lenihan was adamant: 'I will get through this.'

Whether Lenihan was in denial about his illness or genuinely felt he could beat the odds, his optimism was palpable and he felt he would make it through. 'He genuinely believed that,' says Carey.

Willie O'Dea says, 'It was speculated whether it would affect him. Would he want to keep it on in those circumstances?' Yet Lenihan, a deep thinker on all matters, believed he could be of help to the country and that the work could help him deal with his illness.

O'Dea recalls, 'Once he decided he wanted to go on, he said, "Am I going to be at home listening to Beethoven every day waiting to die?"' O'Dea confirms that the Cabinet, though concerned, was behind him. 'When he decided he wanted to stay on there was no question he'd be allowed to. Obviously we were all worried would he be up to it, naturally.'

Lenihan was alive as always to media and communications requirements, even at this fraught time. He knew in a way that Cowen never did that a senior politician has to explain matters directly to the public, but on his own terms. He decided that RTÉ broadcaster Seán O'Rourke's *News at One* would be the best medium and he got Eoin Dorgan to ring the presenter on New Year's Eve.

O'Rourke, feeling sorry for himself as the inclement weather had caused pipes to burst in his holiday home, quickly had to discard his own woes. 'I remember feeling very small, worrying about burst pipes in Donegal where this was a man who had been handed a life sentence,' O'Rourke recalled. The interview went ahead on Monday 4 January 2010. The broadcaster was assured by Cathy Herbert that there were no 'no-go areas' and he was free to ask him anything he liked.

In the thirty-minute interview, at the Department of Finance, Lenihan set out in considerable detail his hospitalisation, diagnosis and course of treatment. 'Well they have described the fact that there is cancerous tissue at the entrance of my pancreas, beyond that I am not going to a medical textbook to elaborate on that. It is clear it is a growth and it is a growth that I intend to defeat or it will defeat me,' he declared. 'That is the challenge facing my medical advisors and I'll face that challenge and I am confident I can surmount that challenge.'

Lenihan began his chemotherapy later that week and was to face a programme of treatment for up to six months, with regular dosages every fortnight. He conceded that surgery was not possible as the tumour lay on a blood vessel and any attempt to remove it could kill him. 'I think mental disposition is very important with all of these conditions,' he said. 'I was glad to learn that the rest of my body is in a very good shape, there aren't any secondary infections. I have a very good liver, heart, lungs; the different organs are working very, very well. Clearly a body in good shape is in a position to put up a formidable resistance and that is what I am determined to do.'

This government, so ill-starred since Cowen and Lenihan assumed their positions, now had a true human tragedy to add to its burdens. Lenihan's condition contributed to the dark mood that prevailed in the Dáil and in Fianna Fáil over the following year. When the country's finance minister was diagnosed with fatal cancer during such uncertain economic times, the public, as evidenced in radio phone-ins and letters to newspapers, perceived it as evidence that Ireland truly was lacking in fortune.

Lenihan's candour in his interviews, following the public sympathy over TV3's decision to report his condition, saw his support increase markedly. 'When he did Seán O'Rourke, he was fantastic and that gave everyone a lift. That really gave everyone a lift, to see how strong he was, and he wasn't phased by it,' says Dara Calleary.

Amid the sorrow, Lenihan's bravery had a galvanising effect on others. Mary O'Rourke believes, 'He did a wonderful programme. He spoke in detail as to where the tumour was, that it was at the neck of the pancreas and that it couldn't be operated on. I remember listening to that with such horror, real horror. If they operated he could die immediately. He was so honest with Seán O'Rourke. From then on Brian resolved to keep on the path of talking, to tell people what things are like, how bad things were.'

Lenihan's son, Tom, posted a message on Facebook thanking those who had offered their support. 'Hi, I'm Tom, Brian's son,' he wrote. 'I showed my dad the page. Thanks to everyone for your kind wishes, we appreciate it.' So, with the interview over and the country in no doubt about how sick he was, Lenihan got back to work, albeit in a reduced capacity.

'I know when we came back [to the Dáil] in January, he would have spoken very highly of the taoiseach's response and encouragement,' says Calleary. 'I know the taoiseach would have made it very clear to Brian Lenihan that whatever he needed it would be put in place.'

He seemed to spend more time in the department now, which was a bit of a surprise for his staff. 'It did change things certainly, because he was around more. That was a bit of a shock. He wasn't gallivanting around the place, so that was strange,' says Alan Ahearne.

Another welcome effect was that the illness seemed to insulate Lenihan further from the full rancour of the public and the media. He had up until this period been the government's best communicator and now he seemed to get more of a hearing and there was less inclination to shout him down and criticise him. He did not suffer the later intimidation and verbal abuse that his colleagues did.

There were attempts to downplay the toll that was taken on Lenihan while he was receiving chemotherapy and radiotherapy for his cancer during the first half of 2010. He was often forced to cut back to a three-day working week, though this was denied by his officials at the time. 'They gave me a couch,' he told his aunt one day. 'And I lie up on it if I get tired.'

Ahearne recalls the changes to his working regime. 'He had to take rests a lot. There was a couch brought in for him to lie down during the day, and his private secretary, Dermot Moylan, would make sure that he was left alone when he needed to rest. He used to rest for a couple of hours during the day. But he still did long hours, early morning and late evenings. In meetings he was still very focused,' Ahearne adds. 'There were days, yeah, he looked bad. I remember the first day I came up after that Christmas he was diagnosed, we sat together and he looked at me and said: "You look very worried." So, yeah we were always worried about him, concerned about it, given the diagnosis he had.'

At home, his teenage son, Tom, watched his father decline. 'I used to wake up at the same time as him and … he'd be in the bathroom getting sick. The physical deterioration of his body was very quick, he didn't lose his hair but the physical deterioration was quite evident.'

By February 2010 Lenihan had become a familiar figure to the oncology staff at the Mater Private on Eccles Street. They recall him asking, 'Will we be much longer? I have a meeting back in my office in twenty minutes.' Anxious doctors and nurses gently tried to persuade him that he must stay – that his health was the most important thing. They took extra care to protect his privacy as he underwent treatment. Intense bouts of chemotherapy are normally so debilitating that they leave patients unwell for days.

Lenihan rarely went home after treatment. Against medical advice, he was regularly back in his office in the Department of Finance or in the Dáil Chamber for a vote within minutes of concluding his treatment. Racked with pain, Lenihan told staff that he was fine. But the toll on his body was immense. Throughout his treatment he was collected from home by his now retired garda driver and trusted family friend Shay Martin, who lives close to the Lenihan family home in Strawberry Beds, and driven into the Mater Private clinic. On the days he wasn't rushing back to meetings in his department or to a Dáil vote, once his round of treatment was finished Lenihan would ask to be driven to the South Bull Wall in Ringsend, where he would take a brisk walk. He enjoyed the blast of fresh air and the spray from the sea on his walk to the lighthouse and the wall's end.

The fact that Lenihan did not lose his famous head of black hair led some of those closest to him to think that the doctors went light on the treatment, as they knew he was terminal. 'I am convinced since, and no doctor told me, no medical man told me, but I am convinced that they didn't give him huge chemotherapy. They figured, he's only got so much left to live. Because pancreatic cancer is fatal,' says Mary O'Rourke. 'So what is the point of pumping him full of stuff? Sure he didn't lose his hair, you couldn't do that much chemo and not lose your hair. He was able to go about his job. No one told me but it is in my mind that they went easy on him.'

These observations were made by friends and family who were not necessarily briefed on the intricate details of Lenihan's treatment. The effects of chemotherapy on patients vary.

Lenihan's Cabinet colleagues got used to him regaling them with stories about his treatment in minute detail. Pat Carey says, 'He would tell us in grotesque detail about the cancer, where the tumour was, the size of it, that it was the size of a golf ball, and then it had greatly reduced to the size of a marble. He talked his way through his illness. Certain levels of solidarity were very important. How he kept going I don't know.'

Ray MacSharry reveals that Lenihan told him that he had used an opportunity during an official trip to Washington DC in 2010 to seek further expert medical opinion as to his condition. 'The advice Brian got was that the cancer was inoperable. Brian knew he was a dying man, but he was stoic about it and was determined to keep working hard on behalf of the Irish people for as long as he could.'

Mary O'Rourke gained a slightly different impression of the America trip after discussions with her nephew. 'He went to a fine cancer guy there. The guy in America would have done it [an operation] if he wanted it done, but the risk … He could die on the table. The tumour was on a blood vessel.'

His brother, Conor, felt that the illness allowed Brian to prioritise and dispense with the duties that were not directly related to national finance. 'My view is that he did a better job because he had this illness,' says Conor. 'He did a better job as minister for finance because 40 to 50% of an average minister's time is taken up with unnecessary things that he should not be doing or are unnecessary in terms of their core function or mandate as a minister. Brian chose to make an efficiency gain in terms of how he did his job because of his illness. It was a good opportunity to concentrate totally on what he was doing.'

Those close to Lenihan were of the opinion that he believed, or forced himself to believe, that he had longer to live than the eighteen months the doctors had given him. Yet still it was clear to all that his time on earth would be significantly curtailed. This finite amount of time had a dramatic effect on Lenihan's remaining professional life, and a dramatic effect on the internal politics of Fianna Fáil. It was in the months after his diagnosis that Lenihan's attitude to Cowen and his leadership changed fundamentally.

'I don't think it encumbered him. He continued to work and was very motivated by his work. This is one of the reasons why I suspect he was not that keen to move in a very public way against Brian Cowen. I think he was hugely motivated by the kind of work he was doing,' says Conor. 'The fact of his illness made him even more motivated to construct and create a scenario which in financial, budgetary and business terms could never be reversed.

'I think he felt "I can make an impact now. I may not have very long to make that impact so I need to focus on getting these things done." And in effect his four-year plan is the policy of the succeeding government. You know he succeeded at that level. He created a four-year plan which was effectively the template of the Fine Gael/Labour government,' says Conor.

Our interviews have confirmed that towards the end of his period in office, despite the illness, Lenihan did hold genuine leadership ambitions. He began to undermine Cowen's leadership in a more visible way, canvassing recalcitrant TDs and senators for their opinion on the leader in the corridors of Leinster House, meeting rebels away from the Dáil and generally preparing the ground for an eventual challenge. 'My brother was very interested in becoming leader of the party. He believed he could do a better job than Brian Cowen,' says Conor. 'He believed he could communicate the aims and ambitions and goals of the government in a much more coherent fashion than the manner in which Brian Cowen was going about it.'

His illness subsequently forced him to transform his potential candidacy into that of an 'interim leader'. Conor articulates the plan that began to take shape in the early weeks of 2010 as the two brothers, John McGuinness and others attempted to set up the minister for finance as a successor to Cowen: 'He thought, given his illness, that he could provide a kind of leadership in a very limited period of time. He confessed that he might not be around after the election but he certainly could give leadership and hopefully help the party as it went in to that election.'

The Lenihan family, to those who know them well, share a wicked and subversive sense of humour. It is that ability not to take themselves too seriously that made the members of the Lenihan political dynasty so popular with colleagues and the electorate. Conor reveals a family joke that he and Brian, both Hollywood movie fans, used to get them through the dark times. 'He often referred to what he called the El Cid scenario, where in a very famous Charlton Heston movie the hero, El Cid, is actually dead but is strapped to the horse and they send him in against the enemy and they are all frightened of him. So he had some sort of amusing relationship with that particular movie and he used to refer to it for a while and I used to say to him "How is El Cid this morning?"'

But Lenihan was extremely earnest about his own mild messiah complex when it came to the family's beloved Fianna Fáil. He truly believed he could transform the party's fortunes in a way that the 'unlucky general', as Mary Harney described Cowen, could not. 'He was actually serious about that and thought it was a possibility and might have helped both the party and the government. Helped the government in the context of the election, of having someone up front who was laying out the economic choices we had made and had to make. He also felt, and this is an interesting separate issue, that he could repair and get the confidence of the Green Party. Because confidence and patience had been worn out after what had happened under Cowen,' says Conor.

So in January 2010, as the country got used to the news that the finance minister was a very ill man, the internal battles within Fianna Fáil and within the Cabinet were escalating and Lenihan found himself on a direct collision course with his taoiseach.

8

2010 – A False Dawn

The deep financial depression reached its nadir in 2010 and the Irish people vented their wrath on the government. Ministers and TDs from that government told us that this now manifested itself in violence. Such was the aggression that they stopped going out at weekends, and even felt afraid walking the streets because they were being attacked.

Billy Kelleher recalls an occasion in mid-2010 when he and fellow Cork minister Batt O'Keeffe encountered an angry man on a busy Molesworth Street, yards from Leinster House. 'We had just met each other and we were walking back [to Leinster House] together,' says Kelleher, 'and a fella went and caught Batt by the tie. He was trying to swing him onto the road and that sort of thing. I started shouting at him.' The attacker was 'just a very angry individual and he was shouting and roaring'. Terrified that the attacker, who was now swinging O'Keeffe round and round by the tie, would cast the minister under a car, Kelleher alerted some gardaí who were standing sentry outside the Dáil. They intervened in what must have been a slapstick moment. But it could have had nasty consequences.

'He was okay, but I mean it [intimidation] was everywhere,' says Kelleher. 'For ministers, garda security was being ramped up more often … when you went to attend a function there was going to be some hostile crowd there in advance of you. It was just becoming impossible in terms of moving around.'

Kelleher, a friendly and convivial man, was shocked by the

deepening aggression towards the government, and he began avoiding official functions unless they were essential. And socialising in his home city of Cork was off limits. 'We just wouldn't have being going out, my wife [and I]. I just thought it was getting too tricky. Fellas would be causing hassle and you did not want to be in a restaurant or in a bar or put your family in a difficult position.' One day, as he left a funeral home near the quays in Cork, a man approached Kelleher and violently shoved him to the ground.

Ministers say that it became a constant fear that a passer-by would lash out. Willie O'Dea recalled the menace in the air and said he was constantly 'abused in the street' towards the end of his period in office. An instantly recognisable figure, and a constant canvasser of the toughest neighbourhoods in his native Limerick, O'Dea now feared walking the streets of the capital. 'I stay in a hotel in Baggot Street there when I go up to Dublin, and it's only a ten-minute walk to the Dáil. It came to the point where I couldn't walk in any more in the morning; if I had done that ten-minute walk I'd have run the gauntlet of one person abusing me, if not two or three.' The ministerial car became a refuge of safety from the baying public – O'Dea, from mid-2010 on, had to be driven the quarter mile to the Dáil from his hotel.

O'Dea said the dislike for the government became so universal that on one occasion a foreign visitor had to intervene after a security guard in a bookshop left him to his fate. 'One day I went into a bookshop nearby [Leinster House] and I went upstairs to the history section,' he recalls. 'It was fairly quiet,' but the tranquillity did not last. 'The next thing some guy recognised me and he began a tirade of abuse … and there was an overseer, one of those floor walkers or whatever you call them and he just kept his mouth shut and didn't intervene at all.' What unnerved O'Dea most was that he was abandoned, though a good samaritan saved him from what was a rapidly escalating situation. 'In fairness some Pakistani fella came in and he says [to O'Dea's assailant], "What I think you're doing is most inappropriate, this is not the place, not the time." But that was the Pakistani, the Irish guys kept their mouths shut!'

There was certainly no other time since the early years of the state when government ministers and TDs were targets of almost daily random confrontations and assaults. Though ministers in the succeeding government were subjected to hostile demonstrations, there were no incidents like these. Verbal altercations lurked around every corner, and one never knew when they could turn physical. 'It was overtly hostile, I've never gone through a situation like it in politics and I don't think any other minister ever in any government has,' says O'Dea.

Conor Lenihan was another high-profile minister who had grown up in a political atmosphere which, though passionate and confrontational, had never been violent. The change in mood in Dublin was shocking and he was required to institute preemptive measures. 'There was lots and lots of hostility during this period,' says Conor. 'I used to occasionally go out socially and to be honest I had some very good friends who would flank me when I was out … I did not need a formal security detail as I had very good friends who basically acted as a security detail because you would have these angry people coming over shouting and screaming.'

Random people were 'losing it in front of you'. He avoided entering into debate with these people, who must have been suffering terrible trauma in their lives to behave in that fashion. 'You could not respond because if you responded it made the situation worse.'

It became apparent towards the end of 2010 that a general election was imminent and TDs were required to get out into their communities on a more regular basis. On one such outing, in a housing estate in Tallaght in his Dublin South-West constituency, a man came at Conor Lenihan with a weapon. 'There was a moment when I thought this man, who had a screwdriver in his hand and was coming for me, I thought he was actually going to hit me,' he says, eyes widening at the memory. 'He just stopped at the last moment. I suppose I was slightly afraid. I thought the man was going to hit me and as it turned out he didn't.'

Dara Calleary did not fear for his personal safety, but the policy of boycott, which was born in his home county of Mayo, could be just as painful. 'I never felt afraid in fairness but it was difficult,' says Calleary. 'People were going out of their way to ignore you. And I certainly got a bit of gyp in some pubs. You were being accused of destroying the country. And a lot of people were genuine about it as well. They were genuine coming up and saying it as they saw it. And that is fine.'

The most intense verbal invective was reserved for Cowen. Every taoiseach is surrounded by a low-key but efficient garda personal bodyguard and is transported in a powerful state car. Nevertheless, few Irish politicians have been subjected to such a sustained period of media assault and verbal abuse from the public as Cowen. In his interviews with us he downplayed criticism, saying that he led during unprecedented times. 'There was a lot of anger, people were losing their jobs.'

Journalists, and satirists, fed off the public anger, though many, not least us, look back on the period as one in which greater restraint could have been shown. Cowen does not mince his words. 'There was a lot of stuff going on radio and on the telly, it was pretty horrific stuff. It was again a sign of the times.' He feels that some of his political opponents drove the media on to excess: 'That [personal attack] becomes part of the political currency … People can get very personal and over the top.' At no time during our interviews did Cowen become maudlin or self-pitying, nor did he seek to blame those trying times on others.

Cowen understands that his personal style did not encourage sympathy. He was widely acknowledged as an aggressive and effective debater. He couldn't suppress his tribal animosity for Fine Gael and, in the Dáil Chamber at least, he showed particular disdain for Enda Kenny. 'Sometimes the more trenchant you were against a guy, the more you were going to be quoted. So it [his style] encouraged a bit of that … Some of it was over the top, but you have to stand up to that, you have to be thick skinned. It wasn't nice, you take it.'

The former taoiseach plays down any mistreatment his wife and two daughters may have suffered, but acknowledges 'there was a little bit'. 'The family are very resilient, strong and very supportive. I didn't have any real worries about that,' says Cowen. 'The public debate was getting very personal and things were being said that I didn't like being said.

'One of my kids was in college, she was well able to look after herself. One was at home [in school in Offaly]. Of course it was challenging. They may have gotten a bit, a little bit [of verbal abuse] but nothing they couldn't handle. They have to stand up for themselves, it wasn't a systemic thing, it was in the background.' Cowen's voice remained steady as he recalled the difficult time for his family, yet in his understatement it was clear that his family suffered due to the media treatment of their husband/father. 'They would have been reading what was being written, pretty negative stuff.'

All the negativity coming the government's way had not yet

led to loss of senior personnel. But in 2010 ministers began to resign and a government losing ministers spells doom. When ministers resign they can be replaced, but the psychological blow is irreversible. It displays weakness, generates ill-feeling and often sends the minister who has lost his or her job to the backbenches, bitter and hurt. That former minister can become at the least a problem and at worst an implacable enemy of the leader.

Willie O'Dea was one of the most high-profile ministers in Cowen's government. An acclaimed electoral performer who runs a slick political machine in Limerick, he has achieved something of a cult status in the political world. A tough, articulate operator with a rapier wit, he is diminutive and wears a distinctive moustache. He is instantly recognisable – Limerick artists The Rubberbandits wrote and recorded a song about him.

In 2009 the *Mail on Sunday* had published an exclusive front-page story with the headline 'O'Dea Misled High Court'. The sub-heading read 'Defence Minister admits swearing untrue affidavit against political rival. His story changed after tape of what he'd said emerged.' O'Dea, an experienced lawyer, had made a mistake that would end his ministerial career. Early in 2009 he had made a defamatory claim about Sinn Féin councillor Maurice Quinlivan. Quinlivan, during his bid to be elected in the 2009 local elections, criticised O'Dea for sending out letters to planning applicants using Department of Defence paper. Quinlivan also published the cost of the six civil servants employed to help Mr O'Dea with constituency affairs.

A combative and eloquent politician, O'Dea was experienced in the art of replying to political charges within the accepted bounds. On this occasion his reason deserted him. During a late-night, impromptu interview with local journalist Mike Dwane, O'Dea let rip: 'While occasionally we send out letters to planning applicants on the wrong paper, we have never been involved with anyone who shot anybody, or robbed banks, or kidnapped people,' he said. Though pushing it, this was a typical charge against a Sinn Féin member and might not have led to the courts.

In this case, Maurice Quinlivan's brother, Nessan Quinlivan, was a senior member of the Provisional IRA and had escaped from Brixton Prison in London with Pearse McAuley in 1991. They had been awaiting trial on charges relating to a suspected IRA plot to assassinate a former brewery company chairman, Sir Charles Tidbury. Nessan had been described in court as an 'essential cog in the IRA'. McAuley was one of those convicted of the killing of Garda detective Gerry McCabe in Limerick in 1996. The killing of the garda, which occurred in the same year as the murder of journalist Veronica Guerin, led to a crackdown on armed criminals. McCabe's murder aroused particular passions in Limerick. However, Maurice Quinlivan was not connected to any of his brother's crimes.

O'Dea went further, and said to Dwane: 'I suppose I'm going a bit too far when I say this, but I'd like to ask Mr Quinlivan is the brothel still closed?' Nessan Quinlivan had bought an apartment in Limerick, in an area known as Clancy Strand, which was raided by gardaí in January 2009. O'Dea added: 'Do you know the brothel they found in his name and in his brother's name down in Clancy Strand?'

When gardaí raided the apartment, they found three Brazilian women suspected of running a brothel. The three women appeared in court. Nessan Quinlivan was not in court when the tenants of his apartment were convicted of charges relating to prostitution. He was not referred to in court. And he said that he had no knowledge that his apartment was being used as a brothel, a claim which was not called into question.

Maurice Quinlivan was in no way connected to the apartment and he sought an injunction to restrain O'Dea from repeating the false statement. O'Dea swore an affidavit for the injunction proceedings. 'I must categorically and emphatically deny that I said … that the plaintiff was a part-owner of the said apartment.' Yet that was false. He had made such a statement. O'Dea said that he did not recollect making the statement but Dwane had retained his tape recording of the interview and the minister was caught.

O'Dea agreed to pay a substantial cash settlement to Quinlivan and an agreed statement was drafted. It read: 'It is not suggested by Mr Quinlivan that Mr O'Dea acted other than innocently in making such a denial in his affidavit.' The settlement was made out of court in December, after the *Mail on Sunday* story.

The emergence of Brian Lenihan's troubles had pushed all other political news into the background but when the Oireachtas returned from its Christmas break in January 2010 the opposition began to pursue O'Dea. The *Limerick Leader* posted a transcript of the taped conversation with O'Dea on its website and Fine Gael senator Eugene Regan called on O'Dea to resign.

The big problem, according to his political opponents, was not necessarily the defamatory comments but the misleading affidavit he subsequently swore. His spokeswoman told the *Mail* when the story broke that he had not remembered his exact words on the journalist's tape: 'When it was brought to his attention, he said he was mistaken and he rectified it immediately … he didn't recall exactly what was said in the course of the interview.'

Speaking about his resignation at length for the first time, O'Dea says he did not intentionally tell an untruth: 'The thing was fully investigated by the gardaí subsequent to me going and they found they were laughing at the idea at the time [that] I did anything misleading.'

A motion of no confidence in the Limerick minister was tabled by Fine Gael, says O'Dea, 'of course, because the government was so weak and in such a bad position and the economy was deteriorating'. His opponents responded to his misleading behaviour with further dissembling. 'Fine Gael were sort of gung-ho and they went for me, [they said] a whole lot of misleading stuff but who gives a shit?'

The government has the power to replace a motion of no confidence with a motion of confidence; it is mere procedure. But for a minister to be at the centre of a confidence motion for such a serious incident is extremely difficult for a weak government. Then, admits O'Dea, he made further errors in the confidence debate. 'Two things happened. I made a very aggressive speech which I shouldn't have made – I should have played the nice guy.' O'Dea, like his friend Cowen, found it difficult to pull back from confrontational politics when the mood demanded it.

Then the Greens had to speak, and Eamon Ryan delivered a speech full of caveats that was not interpreted as supportive. 'But secondly, which is even worse than that, Eamon Ryan came in to defend me and he did so in such a way that it was the most damning defence I ever got ... I was damned by faint praise and people were just laughing at his performance.'

Ryan told us about the circumstance that led to his lukewarm speech, saying the decision that he speak on behalf of the Greens was taken in a discussion with John Gormley 'literally on the way' to the Dáil Chamber. He asked his party leader: 'What do I say? What do I do? How do we play it?' There was no time for a considered response, so they agreed that Ryan should 'just not whip it up any further'.

The squirming Greens were becoming as damaged by this mess as Fianna Fáil were. Ryan's clumsy and heavily qualified speech did him and the Greens immense damage. He stammered and stumbled his way through the address and he knew he would pay a huge price for his poor performance. 'Politically, for me, it was dynamite, it was desperate stuff. You should never do it because you're battling for something that you can't easily defend. You don't have the full facts at your disposal,' he says. 'So I went in and gave the speech, which was hugely damaging to me personally, but I did it on the basis that I don't want the government to fall on this issue which I don't even know – no one knows – the full details of.'

The shambles kicked off internal wrangling within the Greens. The O'Dea saga was a tricky one for the party, already edgy about life in government. Having to defend O'Dea amid accusations that he committed perjury was not for them. It smelled far too much like the Fianna Fáil of old they detested. Still, as is the way of coalition governments, they voted for the damaged O'Dea. After the vote was taken, and the Dáil formally expressed confidence in O'Dea, the Greens remained edgy. They began to voice their unwillingness to continue to support O'Dea within government. This contradictory behaviour and their inability to hold the line was increasingly exasperating for Fianna Fáil.

'The vote was duly taken and people voted in line with the whip and I went down to the self-service restaurant to have a cup of tea with Derek Mooney [O'Dea's special advisor]. Dick Roche [a Fianna Fáil junior minister] was down there and he came over to me and he said did you hear about your man Dan Boyle on Twitter?' recalls O'Dea. In what was becoming a familiar tactic for the Greens, its ministers would say one thing in public and Green senator Dan Boyle would say the opposite on his social networking account.

Boyle had been watching the entire Dáil debate from his office and he had become angry. His itchy Twitter finger, which had come to annoy the hell out of many in Fianna Fáil, gave in to the temptation to re-ignite the crisis. He tweeted he was 'not happy' with O'Dea's arrogant performance in the Dáil and expressed the belief the Greens had been bounced into the confidence motion.

And so, amid the clatter of teacups, Roche related that 'Boyle said he doesn't accept what you say.' To a bemused late-night restaurant clientele of civil servants and bleary-eyed politicians, O'Dea exclaimed, 'And the crisis still goes on. Jesus!'

'As it turns out I was going home [to Limerick] that night because I was exhausted. The following day anyway I got a phone call at nine in the morning to say the Greens had called a special party meeting about this.'

Fianna Fáil, masters of political defence measures, couldn't deal with coalition partners who accommodated conflicting views. Not only did the Greens' prevarication anger the Fianna Fáilers, it unnerved them. This wasn't politics as had long been practised in the Dáil. The Greens locked themselves into an anguished conclave for most of the day in what they called a 'flash parliamentary party meeting' and that evening O'Dea received a call from the taoiseach. Less than twenty-four hours after expressing confidence in O'Dea in the Dáil, the leader of the Greens, John Gormley, went to the taoiseach's office and effectively threatened to exit the coalition if the minister for defence was not sacked.

O'Dea said, 'Well look, I'm not going to be the cause of running down the government. If that's the case I'll go.'

Cowen said meekly, 'It's a pity.'

'So … I went,' O'Dea tells us. He is unambiguous – the Greens demanded his head.

O'Dea is less than forthright about his feelings on Cowen. 'No, I understood his position was extremely … weak.' Cowen had cast aside a minister seen as personally loyal to the taoiseach, a man who had enthusiastically participated in the 2008 Offaly homecoming, who had vocally defended the government and all its dysfunction since.

In party lore Cowen himself was the ultimate Fianna Fáil man, someone who saw coalition as a nasty compromise. In the days when the party was new to the concept of having to share power, he told the party's 1992 ard-fheis: 'If in doubt leave them [the Progressive Democrats] out'. Now he was leaving out a Fianna Fáil minister to satisfy a political party with far fewer similarities to Fianna Fáil than the PDs had. Cowen was perhaps more damaged by the O'Dea controversy than anybody else bar the man who lost his job.

Gormley then claimed that he had not demanded O'Dea's head, stating that he was not in the business of issuing ultimatums. He claimed, in the crucial twenty-four hours between the confidence vote and the meeting with Cowen, that several things had happened, including an overly robust Dáil performance which had altered the position of the Greens. However, it is believed that Gormley sought the head of O'Dea in an attempt to belatedly restore some sense of credibility to the Greens.

O'Dea still harbours deep resentment towards the Green Party for forcing the end to his ministerial career. 'My feeling towards the Greens is that they behaved very unfairly and very dishonourably, that was my feeling then and that's still my feeling,' he says, despite his own actions in the affair.

'I went up to Gormley to discuss it with him in the government offices,' he continues. Gormley told him that he understood that there was another newspaper story about O'Dea coming out the following day. He had been told that O'Dea contacted journalists attempting to stop the original story being printed. This is not factual. But given the false affidavit, sympathy for O'Dea within the government and the now coalition-inured Fianna Fáil party was limited.

'I just remember it was difficult for him personally, it was difficult for him at the time, but there were far bigger issues,' says Dara Calleary. 'We were in a far bigger situation, like everyone had to keep their eye on the game of getting the country through the mess … I am not being cruel to anyone, but you know a coalition government has to work on trust, and the most important thing in 2010 was that we had some sort of stability. And you know it was incredibly difficult for Willie, the stability of the government and getting us through that period was very important.'

O'Dea resigned on 23 February.

At the beginning of March the government suffered another blow when former Green Party leader Trevor Sargent resigned as minister of state in the Department of Agriculture after accepting that he made 'an error of judgement' in contacting gardaí about a case involving a constituent. There remains a strong suspicion that Sargent's contacting of the garda came to light as a result of some Fianna Fáil operatives acting in revenge for O'Dea's departure.

Without much fanfare, in a brief statement to the Dáil, Sargent said he had contacted gardaí in relation to an alleged assault on a constituent in September 2007. This person had come to see him in June 2008 in anger at the slow progress being made with the case. The constituent alleged he had been headbutted after reporting vandalism to the parents of a child he had seen trying to remove a road sign.

Given Sargent's pristine political persona, the details of his resignation shocked many in government circles. The timing, being so close to O'Dea's resignation, led to opposition claims that Fianna Fáil had a hand in the leaking of the letter that prompted Sargent's resignation. The taoiseach said he presumed the information came to light because of its link to a recent court case.

Then came a third resignation. On 23 March Minister for Arts, Sport and Tourism Martin Cullen, a controversial figure, informed Cowen of his intention to resign because of ill health. In a letter to the taoiseach, Cullen said that he was retiring from public life on medical advice. 'I have always been a fighter and optimistic in both my personal and political life ... However, my consultant's advice is that my condition is deteriorating further and options for treatment and recovery are narrowing.' Cullen's health condition stemmed from a serious car accident some years previously in which he injured his neck.

Cullen had been subjected to savage, and often ill-conceived and unfair, press attacks over the years. He requested that his resignation be effective from a date of Cowen's choosing – it was accepted immediately. The resignations, coupled with a desperate need to reassert control over his party, spurred Cowen to announce his intention to conduct a Cabinet reshuffle.

This was to mark yet another occasion in which Cowen as taoiseach, when presented with an opportunity to advance his cause, ultimately ended up on the back foot. He promoted Tony Killeen and Chief Whip Pat Carey into Cabinet to replace Cullen and O'Dea. Next Cowen jettisoned the most controversial member of his praetorian guard from the Department of Enterprise. Mary Coughlan swapped places with Batt O'Keeffe and took over the Department of Education.

Leinster House cynics often refer to the Departments of Education and Social Welfare as convenient portfolios to give to women: for chauvinists they are considered more suited to females. Coughlan had been one of the few women in the history of the state to hold a major economic portfolio as minister for enterprise, trade and employment, but it is fair to say that the Coughlan experiment in Enterprise had failed. Just as his party had not adequately assessed Cowen's qualifications for leadership, he had not adequately assessed Coughlan's qualifications for deputy leadership. She lacked subtlety and nous and had endured a torrid time.

Mary Hanafin, by then firmly disliked and distrusted by the Cowen camp, was demoted from Social and Family Affairs to the Department of Tourism, Culture and Sport, which was renamed Arts, Sport and Tourism. Éamon Ó Cuiv was moved to Social and Family Affairs. Carey was given Ó Cuiv's old role at the Department of Community, Rural and Gaeltacht Affairs, which was renamed the Department of Community, Equality and Gaeltacht Affairs.

Another of Cowen's allies, John Curran, was appointed chief whip. Curran was a leading member of the so-called 'bar lobby' of Cowen's inner circle of drinking pals.

Wexford TD Seán Connick was promoted to a junior ministry, as were Greens Mary White and Ciarán Cuffe.

Though the opposition criticised the two promotions to Cabinet, they were accepted by most of Fianna Fáil. 'They were popular, they were experienced, they were safe hands, and you know the thinking, the thinking was stability,' says Dara Calleary. 'What you needed was experience, experienced parliamentarians; Pat Carey had been a very good whip.'

Carey knew the thinking of the parliamentary party, and his experience would now be at the Cabinet table.

Calleary says that Clare TD Tony Killeen was 'a very strategic kind of a guy, a very good guy.

'You know if the government is going to run five years, that would be the time to put new blood in, but this was not normal.

And stability was very important.' Calleary himself was assigned as a junior minister to both the Department of Finance and the Department of the Taoiseach. Cowen had also announced the setting up of a Public Service Board, which would aim to accelerate public service reform in consultation with the unions. Calleary was assigned to push through change in the public service. Lenihan was suspicious of Calleary, whom he suspected of being a spy for Cowen.

The hope Cowen had of a lift from his new team didn't last long. Lenihan, the following week, announced that the taxpayer would have to put another €18 billion into the financial carcass of Anglo Irish Bank. This was on top of the €4 billion already committed. Defending the cash injection, Lenihan said that allowing the bank to fail at that stage would cost even more. 'In terms of the banks, of course the people are shocked, absolutely shocked, I am shocked at the figures at Anglo and Nationwide. But there is really no other choice. In reality, Ireland can't afford a default because half of what is in Irish banks belongs to Irish people, so it just can't be entertained … a major default would have [a] catastrophic impact on the Irish economy. The only solution at Anglo is to work it out over a long time, minimise the exposure to the taxpayer and try and recoup whatever we can along the way.'

The shocking news, naturally, dominated the news agenda for several days, both at home and internationally, and led to a charge being made against Cowen which wounded him deeply. In the Dáil on 31 March Fine Gael leader Enda Kenny set the tone at the start of the day. He held Cowen responsible for all events since he became finance minister in 2004. He also referred to a private dinner that the then minister for finance attended just a month before he became taoiseach, along with Seán FitzPatrick and the board of Anglo Irish Bank in Dublin.

Cowen responded to Kenny by accusing him of an attempted smear. 'I do not accept the contentions made by Deputy Kenny and I treat them with contempt.'

But Labour Party leader Eamon Gilmore upped the ante. He was a stronger performer than Kenny during high-profile Dáil debates. He suggested that the bank guarantee scheme in September 2008 was a ready-up to save the bacon of a number of individuals connected to Fianna Fáil and Anglo Irish Bank. 'That decision,' said Gilmore 'was an act of economic treason for which this country is now paying very dearly.'

Gilmore's powerful charge visibly stung the attenuated Cowen, who responded with indignation. 'I consider that to be beyond the pale,' he said, insisting that nobody should doubt the motivation behind his actions. 'They were the very same, laudable motivations that would have moved him [Gilmore] had he been in my position. I would never come into this House to accuse another Irishman of what he accused me [of],' Cowen said to applause from his backbenchers. It was a highly emotionally charged affair and the exchange was one of the most memorable of that Dáil.

Even if it was prefaced by the use of the word 'economic', Cowen was clearly deeply insulted by Gilmore's use of the word 'treason'.

Yet somebody had to take the blame politically for the disastrous collapse of the Irish banks. Cowen was minister for finance between 2004 and 2008 when the banking–property developer axis was allowed to run riot, and as taoiseach he introduced the bank guarantee scheme. Even though he and his government had shown considerable bravery in tackling the crisis, once it had woken up to it, political responsibility for the crash fell squarely on Cowen's shoulders.

Lenihan's Anglo announcement also drained confidence in

the banking system at an awfully disadvantageous time. There was now speculation that the total cost of dealing with the banks would top €100 billion. Certainly that figure was not contemplated on 29 September 2008. Repeated expressions of reassurance uttered by Cowen and Lenihan when the guarantee was introduced were beginning to ring hollow, as were the assurances made when NAMA was established that the agency might even show a profit.

The atmosphere in Dáil Éireann during this period was deeply depressing, even poisonous. Cowen knew that his backbenchers were not maintaining discipline. A group known as the Lemass Group was formed with John McGuinness and Noel O'Flynn as its leading members. They were a backbench group, formed along the lines of the British Tory party's 1922 Committee and they met to discuss 'Fianna Fáil values'. It served little purpose bar giving those openly critical of Cowen's leadership an official standard to follow. Like many initiatives in Fianna Fáil during this period, they were overtaken by events, as criticism of Cowen became more open within the party during 2010.

In the weeks after O'Dea's resignation, government and opposition figures began to spin against Lenihan, calling into question his ability to continue in office given his illness. O'Dea remembers: 'Well somebody did [spin] … Jesus, dreadful! Well it was pretty bad, yeah it was pretty bad, somebody certainly started briefing against him very strongly.'

Concern about whether a man with terminal cancer could endure the workload Lenihan did as minister for finance was legitimate. But while Cowen continued to show compassion for his finance minister, Lenihan's condition didn't deter either man from engaging in another venomous clash over the Croke Park Agreement.

The pair had disagreed again before Christmas on the wisdom of a further social partnership deal, with Cowen strongly advocating an arrangement to keep the unions happy. Lenihan had stressed that he felt that such deals could no longer be afforded given the scale of the crisis. The December budget, more by accident than design, allowed Lenihan to be more radical in terms of the scale of the cutbacks than Cowen was ready to accept. The desire of the taoiseach to come to a peaceful agreement with the unions, and Lenihan's feeling that there was no place for such an agreement, continued to cause extreme tension between the two men.

Following the collapse of talks with the unions in December, at Cowen's behest, and against the strong wishes of Lenihan, talks with union leaders were re-opened in March 2010. Agreement to re-enter talks was reached after Cowen called the bosses into his Government Buildings office. Lenihan was furious. This was an irretrievable disagreement, according to John McGuinness. 'They came apart on Croke Park. There was a concession given to the secretary-generals about certain issues to do with their pay, and those concessions were given by the direct intervention of Brian Cowen. And Brian Lenihan said that he did not want to sign off on it but he was told by Brian Cowen that he had to.'

The government performed a U-turn on proposed pay restructuring for the most senior civil servants – the department heads or secretaries-general. 'And therefore a certain pay aspect of the payment of secretaries-general was protected. And everybody thought that that was absolutely fucking disgusting. And Lenihan was disgusted by it. Now there were other issues, too, that negatively impacted on Lenihan,' says McGuinness.

Mary O'Rourke says her nephew was deeply hostile to the talks, saying the move by Cowen saw the two men diverge in a manner that was never really reconciled. 'Brian Lenihan knew it [a pay deal] wasn't sustainable, and I think most people in Ireland knew it wasn't sustainable. I always thought it so odd that the unions knew we were in so much difficulty, screwed, but you see Cowen had been schooled in the Bertie tradition and to Bertie the unions were most important.

'It was like a fork in the road. It struck Brian Lenihan that surely the taoiseach must see we can't go into this deal,' says O'Rourke.

The talks commenced under the auspices of the Labour Relations Commission with the lead being taken on the government side by the Department of the Taoiseach. Dara Calleary, who was the government's lead negotiator, says, 'I was dealing with it at that stage, Croke Park was well underway. It was definitely being driven out of the Taoiseach's, no doubt about it.'

But the depth of Lenihan's anger went much further than the public was aware of at the time. Pat Carey says, 'Lenihan didn't want anything at all to do with Croke Park, he felt it absolutely made no sense to be doing a deal with anybody. He would get quite exercised about that. Things were bad enough without making them worse for people. But Lenihan felt you have to do the right thing, to do whatever is necessary no matter what the cost.'

As for Conor Lenihan: 'One of the most difficult and credibility-destroying decisions made for that government was the decision to re-open the negotiations around the Croke Park Agreement … Mr Cowen and Tánaiste Coughlan were going helter-skelter for an agreement on those lines. And this came as a huge shock to backbenchers, to members of the public and indeed to the minister for finance and everybody else in government.'

Conor agrees that Croke Park marked the point where the

two Brians went their separate ways. It sent them on a course which would ultimately see their working relationship descend into open hostility. 'That was the beginning of what I would call the separation of ways between Brian Lenihan and Brian Cowen. That more than anything else was the end.'

Mary Harney says the relationship between the two had started well but ran into difficulties: 'Certainly at the start it was excellent.' She acknowledges that Lenihan was beginning to brief against the taoiseach. 'It wasn't evident at Cabinet but it had to be difficult when he [Lenihan] got involved in the leadership issues. It didn't affect the work and Brian Cowen never said to me that he was angry or anything like that.'

Lenihan was negatively canvassing his Cabinet colleagues about the labour agreements, and he could be persuasive. He might have thought he had a willing ally in the former Progressive Democrats' leader. Harney knew that she had to pick a side and was in agreement with Lenihan's view on Croke Park, but she believed the Cabinet had to back its taoiseach.

'Yes, I agreed with Brian Lenihan that we shouldn't have paid them. But actually because Brian Cowen had taken over from Bertie, and him being the consensus person, he didn't want to be the one to break the social partnership agreement … the Cabinet always backed the taoiseach, there is no other way. If it comes to a dispute between the minister for finance and the taoiseach, then back the taoiseach.'

Micheál Martin says the Department of Finance ultimately was happy to go along with the Croke Park Agreement, even if the minister wasn't enthusiastic. 'I think Croke Park was a one/two in many ways. While Brian Lenihan was saying he was negative about some aspects of Croke Park, my assessment and observation of the Department of Finance is the Department of Finance ultimately sided with public partnership, sided with benchmarking. They'd go to war with you on a €20 million extension to a school or an IT spend, but when it came to the unions and the public service benchmarking, Finance were never far behind.'

Martin plays down the level of disagreement between the two men and says that the Department of Finance sometimes feigned the intensity of its protest. 'But Finance were ultimately [in favour of the Croke Park Agreement] in the name of stability and all that would concede. And what you get with Croke Park, again, the unions in many ways were playing games.'

There were no mass strikes or periods of industrial strife during the term of this government, which was quite an achievement in Martin's eyes. 'To me that's what Croke Park ultimately was about, and you didn't have all-out industrial war.'

In March 2010 John McGuinness, who had lashed out at Cowen and Coughlan in 2009 after his sacking as a junior minister, went public on his intention to call on his leader to resign. Ahead of a meeting of the parliamentary party at the end of that month, McGuinness made it known he was going to confront Cowen over his failure. The Carlow–Kilkenny TD said he had not approached any of his colleagues to ask them to back him at the meeting. Repeating his call for Cowen to consider his position, McGuinness said to reporters before the meeting: 'Hopefully those that are interested in the leadership might step into the space that I have created and indicate their interest in the leadership at that stage, put their case, and let's see who's interested.'

McGuinness had been in constant contact with Lenihan, and he saw his outburst as a means of clearing a way for Lenihan to make a move against Cowen. But McGuinness was left with egg on his face. Lenihan made no such move, saying the time wasn't right. 'I felt I gave him the sword to slay the dragon, but he couldn't draw it on Cowen,' says McGuinness.

At the private party meeting, McGuinness spoke for twenty-eight minutes but was not supported by anyone else. At the same meeting, Cowen spoke passionately to his colleagues and appealed for party unity. He said he was proud to be taoiseach and that every member of the party was important to him. He accepted there had been problems, most notably with communications and also the party's poor standing in the polls.

Despite the failure of the McGuinness clarion call to gather any support, between it and Gilmore's wounding charge of treason, it was Cowen's worst week since taking office. He was nervous, too, knowing his standing was diminished. He was sufficiently worried about his position that he did a ring-around of his TDs to shore up support.

Despite the mounting disquiet amongst his own party's ranks, Cowen clung to power desperately as the country's fortunes continued to decline.

9

THE TWEET IS MIGHTIER
THAN THE SWORD

The taoiseach's interview on RTÉ Radio 1's flagship show, *Morning Ireland*, shortly before 9 a.m. on 14 September 2010 at the Ardilaun Hotel in Galway, was the first Irish political crisis to be started by a tweet. A few minutes after the interview conducted by Cathal Mac Coille, Simon Coveney, the Fine Gael front-bench transport spokesman, via the nascent social media website Twitter, posted the sentence: 'God, what an uninspiring interview by Taoiseach this morning. He sounded half way between drunk and hungover and totally disinterested …'.

This simple sentence sent an already tired and emotional press corps into turmoil. Conflicted newsrooms, uncomfortable breaching the legal and uniquely Irish cultural boundaries that prevented them from forcefully asking questions about the taoiseach's social life, now cast aside their doubts.

Cowen's real sin was timing. With the nation outside the confines of the Ardilaun Hotel fearful and suffering, the annual Fianna Fáil think-in was perhaps the most ill-timed social evening a frontline politician had ever participated in.

There was sympathy within the press corps, and across the Irish political spectrum, for Cowen because this kind of hard-drinking get-together was, and to lesser extent is, a mainstay of the political diary. Like so many innovations in modern politics, Bertie Ahern came up with the idea of the off-campus parliamentary party meetings, or 'think-ins', that now mark the return to work of the political parties in September. John Lee attended the first Fianna Fáil jamboree in Inchydoney, Co. Cork in 2004 and every one since. He also made it to as many of the Fine Gael and Labour think-ins as he could, but the Fianna Fáil parties were far and away the most outrageously enjoyable events.

Over a hundred Fianna Fáil ministers, TDs, senators, MEPs and around forty journalists would find themselves secluded in a country hotel for two days. In Ireland, that combination can mean that a lot of drinking takes place. In what now seem like far-off days, it certainly was fun.

One of the many incongruous features of the long nights at the Ardilaun Hotel, Taylor's Hill in Galway city on 13 and 14 September, was that Cowen had just learned from putative rebels that they were calling off the dogs. At around 7 p.m. in the main ballroom Lee met leading dissident Noel O'Flynn, the Cork North-Central TD, who said plans for a heave were off.

Cowen seemed to relax, as did the rest of the parliamentary party. Even Lenihan's revelation that the government might seek still deeper cuts in the forthcoming budget than the previously flagged €3 billion didn't dampen the mood. O'Flynn said jovially, 'We're not doing anything now, there won't be any more stories, and there will be no move against the taoiseach. The message has been passed and we're unified again, there's a general election coming, probably next year.' He said that the taoiseach could 'relax' that evening.

Cowen addressed the group on the economy and the government's plans to pull the country out of recession. The politicians then went to Blazers Bar for pre-dinner drinks, and Cowen, according to Mary O'Rourke, had a pint of beer. 'I was in Ardilaun, somebody brought me down and we went in and settled in that night. The next thing Terry Leyden, I and Brian Cowen were in the bar at 7 p.m. … I bought Terry a pint and I bought Brian Cowen a pint and I had a glass of white wine. And they were settling into the next round when he offered me one but I said no, I wanted to get ready for dinner.'

The dinner was in the large function room, the Connacht Room, and Cowen sat at a table with Lenihan, Mary Coughlan and John Curran. Cowen was drinking beer. The meal was a five-course affair, with seafood vol-au-vents followed by a choice of sea bass or beef. Cowen had the beef. Red and white wine flowed.

Parliamentary party chairman John Browne gave a short, unadorned address encouraging unity and this was followed by a long speech by former GAA president Joe McDonagh. What many thought would be the highlight of the evening came when McDonagh roused the hall with a rendition of 'The West's Awake', the song he famously belted out from the Hogan Stand in Croke Park when Galway won the All-Ireland Hurling Championship in 1980. The mood for song took hold.

After dinner, Cowen stayed around the function room, chatting and drinking with Lenihan and others in the main banqueting room. Lenihan drank red wine, and remained seated, looking exhausted and pale. Cowen then drifted slowly through the lobby to Blazers Bar. A group of journalists stayed at a smaller bar in the function room, where Coughlan, true to form, had bought them a round of drinks.

As the night seemed to be drifting away, sounds familiar to any veteran of a Fianna Fáil gathering emanated from Blazers Bar. The sing-song started at about 12.30 a.m., with Proinsias Kitt – a brother of TDs Tom Kitt, Michael Kitt and Áine Brady – singing songs and doing skits of musicians Van Morrison, Daniel O'Donnell and Tommy Makem. A packed bar-room listened to Tom Kitt tell a funny story about a Connemara man who goes to New York and brings his bike. A section of the bar, raised up a few steps from the main room, had become a makeshift stage. Cowen's eyes sparkled as he sensed an opportunity to bring his well-honed act to a wider audience. The taoiseach moved to an area to the right of the bar as you faced it; he was surrounded by the usual group of Batt O'Keeffe, John Curran, John Cregan and Darragh O'Brien, and he seemed in good form.

Pat Carey recalls, 'I have a key recollection because after the dinner I would go back to the bar. I had no drink at all. I left early. It is unfortunate Brian Cowen didn't follow me. But walking out I bumped into Cathal Mac Coille, who was on his way to bed as well. And then someone came up beside me and it was Brian Cowen. He said he was going to bed early.'

The taoiseach didn't go to bed early.

The group of Cabinet ministers who had been in the function room, some sensing fun, some smelling trouble, headed for Blazers, but there were so many in the bar some were forced to stand outside in the lobby looking in.

Cowen then began a twenty-minute monologue where he impersonated former GAA commentator Micheál Ó Muircheartaigh. The story was set on the train bringing the Kilkenny hurling team to Croke Park for the All-Ireland final, and consisted of a series of interviews with characters, culminating with the driver, who claimed to know nothing of GAA and instead to be an ardent soccer supporter from Inchicore. Peter Sellers would have been proud of the multi-character performance – it was funny.

At this stage it was heading for 2 a.m. and Cowen decided to tell a few silly stories featuring the Ryder Cup-winning golfer Philip Walton from Malahide in north County Dublin. John Lee was standing at the door between Micheál Martin and Dermot

Ahern, and noticed that they had begun to look nervously at each other. Ahern turned to Lee and said, 'What's he doing there?'

Lee replied, 'He's impersonating Philip Walton.'

Ahern, bemused, asked, 'What's he doing that for?'

'I don't know.'

As Cowen stepped off the makeshift stage to applause, the singing continued.

The wheelchair-bound MEP Brian Crowley, better known as quite a handy banjo player, took to the piano and belted out Billy Joel's 'Piano Man', a song about broken, unfulfilled dreams. Junior Minister Seán Connick sang Bagatelle's 'Summer in Dublin'. Áine Brady and Bobby Aylward did a turn, and John Cregan sang 'Raglan Road'.

At around 3 a.m. Cowen could resist it no longer and decided to step up for a song. Quietening the bar, exclaiming, 'Whisht up lads, this is a classic!', he launched into 'The Lakes of Pontchartrain'. The traditional American folk song about a lost Creole love is associated with singer Paul Brady and has also been recorded by Christy Moore. Cowen made a good stab at it.

TDs and journalists were now flagging. There was a day's work to be faced into the following morning, a Tuesday. Cowen hung around for a while longer, listening to more songs, and then left the bar at about 3.40 a.m. He was not the last to leave, with Lenihan deep in conversation with TDs – about twenty people remained. The last of the stragglers left at 4 a.m.

Gene McKenna, a former *Irish Independent* political editor, had been replaced as Fianna Fáil's communications director during the summer. Armagh man Pat McPartland, who had come from Northern Ireland Water, where he had been director of corporate affairs, had stood in to what was considered a prestigious position in Irish politics. This was pretty much his first day on the job.

Following established protocol the taoiseach's regular coterie of civil servants did not accompany him to these party events. The post-Ardilaun spin from Government Buildings was that had Eoghan Ó Neachtain or one of the more established civil servants been there, the following morning's interview would not have been allowed to go ahead. This was an unfair dig at McPartland, as Cowen's chef de cabinet Joe Lennon was there, a fact that was unnoticed by the press corps.

Veterans of Fianna Fáil hooleys hadn't been troubled by the early morning fun. 'I wasn't there for the "Lakes of Ponchartrain" … and I heard it the other night and I roared laughing … But lots of sessions end with a sing-song,' says Mary O'Rourke. She was, however, appalled at the taoiseach's lack of guile when it came to RTÉ. 'I don't think the fault was necessarily the drinking but it was that he had undertaken to do *Morning Ireland*.'

'If you are a morning person, then *Morning Ireland* is your best time but if you are not and you have been drinking, then … if Eoghan Ó Neachtain was there it wouldn't have happened,' she adds.

The *Morning Ireland* crew were in Galway on Monday night, in preparation for the interview. Presenter Cathal Mac Coille was at the dinner but went to bed soon after – a schoolmasterly sort, there could not have been a greater contrast to Cowen in what was to become easily the most infamous radio interview in Irish politics. *Morning Ireland* interviews with the leaders of all the political parties are normally done the morning after the main dinner at think-ins, and Cowen's had been arranged weeks in advance. He was scheduled to go live on air at 8.15 a.m., which is the prime slot on *Morning Ireland*. He eventually went on at around 8.50 a.m. The interview took place in the hotel restaurant, with the clatter of cutlery and plates clearly audible in the background.

'The next part of the episode I recall was I was in having the breakfast, in the dining hall. Mary Wallace [former minister] was with me and somebody else,' says O'Rourke. 'Brian came in and the taoiseach was approached by a waitress who asked him "Taoiseach, what would you like?" and he said, "Will you get me a pot of tea?" … I said, "He hasn't even had a cup of tea." But that was him, he didn't do fuss, he doesn't do fuss.

'But somebody should have said he had a sore throat and is not able to talk. I don't mind the drinking so much, because in Irish life lots of things like that go on. But it was the stupidity of going on *Morning Ireland* thinking he could have done it … well one look at him was enough.'

Pat Carey says he got up the next morning and went down to breakfast where he joined Ned O'Keeffe and Tony Killeen. They were sitting beside where the *Morning Ireland* crew had set up. 'After a while we were looking around and at our watches.' People began asking, 'Where is Brian Cowen?'

Cowen sounded distant from the start of the interview, and his voice was muffled. Any Irish citizen who lived through those fearful times, the many of *Morning Ireland*'s 450,000 listeners facing into that September day not knowing if they could pay their bills or keep their job, will remember that interview with anger. Mac Coille welcomed Cowen, and then either unintentionally, or intentionally, did him no favours: 'Thanks for coming over before your breakfast.' It was clear to the listenership that the taoiseach had not been awake for long and it was nearly 9 a.m.

The contrast between the gravity of the issues Mac Coille was asking questions about and Cowen's disinterested demeanour was marked. Mac Coille asked of Lenihan's €3 billion cuts: 'What's going on?'

'There's nothing going on,' Cowen replied testily.

He made some mistakes. He referred to Croke Park and said, 'the implementation in many ways of the Good Friday, ha, sorry, the Croke Park Agreement'. Then he said, 'That is legislation that is in place; sorry, that is legislation that is in preparation.'

Cowen actually improved. Listening back now it doesn't seem strikingly bad, but listening to the interview in 2016 lacks the crucial element of context. In 2010, speaking to a nation that was already two years into austerity, many of whom were fending off creditors, banks and bills, it was a very careless interview. Those of us listening in Galway knew there would be trouble – Cowen had given bad interviews before, but the timing of this would loosen the hounds.

As a senior civil servant listening in Dublin told us in an interview for this book, 'He sounded very – as if he had a cold. I was a bit surprised that he got certain things mixed up, like that he called Croke Park the Good Friday Agreement … because actually, he was good on those kind of things. I spoke to him about it, after it, he told me he didn't have a cold. The next thing [was] people that watch Twitter. I heard about the Simon Coveney tweet immediately and then it was actually Fianna Fáil that were dealing with it [the controversy] for the rest of the day.'

It was the post on Twitter from Coveney that allowed the botched interview to become an enormous media story. There are a couple of misconceptions around the tweet. Coveney said later that it was a 'gut' reaction. However, he posted it at 9.15 a.m., a good fifteen minutes after the programme had finished and twenty-five minutes after the interview began. So it is safe to say he gave the move a good bit of contemplation, if not some consultation.

Opposition figures as senior as Michael Noonan, a man not shy of a pint himself, were to come out later in the day condemning Cowen's behaviour. As the senior Fine Gael people no doubt understood, this move now allowed the media to go for broke and attack Cowen. It forced political correspondents at the event to finally confront a senior Fianna Fáil figure about drinking at these gatherings. Newsrooms are still full of senior journalists who came up through the ranks in the 1980s, 1990s and early 2000s when extremely heavy drinking, on and off duty, was the norm in public life. Even by Irish standards, the boozing was excessive. This was something that the political correspondents and editors just didn't know how to handle without tailspinning into hypocrisy.

Cowen has not given his full account of the night before, and the morning of, the interview until now. 'There would have been no controversy about it if Mr Coveney hadn't issued a tweet – "it *sounds* like the taoiseach is under the weather. It *sounds* like",' paraphrases Cowen. 'And then everyone reacted to that.'

He is clearly still hurt by what he felt was a subversion of Irish political convention. 'And as regards the social event part of it, we had our day-long meeting, we had our dinner that night as you know, Joe McDonagh spoke at it.' He maintains that the night, which was kicked off by McDonagh, was not a wild night. 'He [McDonagh] came back that night. It wasn't raucous or anything like that, it was just a nice little social occasion. Okay it turned into a bit of a ... but it wasn't raucous or the way it was portrayed,' he haltingly relates.

We put it to Cowen that there had been far more boisterous events. 'Exactly, exactly,' he says, 'so in my opinion it sort of became ballooned into something it wasn't. People were sort of chasing back [reviewing it in hindsight].'

Nevertheless Cowen is not oblivious to the public relations damage that the event caused. He says with understatement: 'Obviously it was a PR faux pas for us. That is true.'

Cowen also points out that none of the people he met that morning implied he was drunk. The morning of the interview he met John Trethowan, of the Credit Review Office, who was to speak at the event later that day. 'In fairness to your man John Trethowan, it hasn't been commented on, he met me before I went on that programme and he makes the point [that] we had a normal chat, and he said, "Oh this idea that you went on the programme jarred is not true."

'I don't think Cathal Mac Coille has ever suggested that I was jarred,' continues Cowen.

When Coveney tweeted his review of the interview, a number of journalists approached Cowen to ask him for a response.

'So what was that about? That was really Coveney, it was sort of a political opportunity to throw that in there, and next thing, everyone was around it,' says Cowen. 'And of course within fifteen minutes of it happening I had cameras in front of me and I was explaining to them, "Here guys, I'm not jarred, you know."'

Cowen believed then that he gave a substandard interview and he believes now that his medical condition contributed to the standard. 'I wasn't at the top of my game obviously because, in a sense, you can't say that throughout your career that every interview that you did was great, and I listened to it afterwards and I do sound clogged up to be honest with you ... Unfortunately that's sleep apnoea.'

Coveney was entitled to comment on what he heard but Cowen, a most political of leaders, maintains that he was stitched up by an ambitious Fine Gael opponent. 'It sounds clogged up when you listen to it. I do have that sleep apnoea problem, but anyway that's regardless, that doesn't matter. Because it is not the reason at all why it happened, it happened because of the Twitter, if there was no Twitter there wouldn't have been a word about it.'

It was put to him in our interview that the media capitalised on it. He responded: 'Of course they did, it was a story.'

Micheál Martin, who was becoming increasingly sceptical of Cowen's leadership, says of the night's events that there should have been no platform in the first place. 'My observation of that is that we shouldn't probably have actually had the event in the way we had it.

'My brother said to me afterwards, "I meant to ring you." "Why?" I said. "Well I heard Mattie McGrath on TV," – who had just been expelled from the parliamentary party – "and do you know what Mattie said? He said I'll miss the social side of it."

'And the brother said, "Oh Jesus, that means it's business as usual, the lads are going to go down and do what they did in previous years." And he said the economy has changed, people are in a different space, and they won't get this at all.'

Martin, who attended all the previous events, says that the timing 'was the big mistake'. 'Because, I was at previous ones [parliamentary away-days] at Inchydoney and others during the Celtic Tiger and the idea of being up until two in the morning was not unusual for any political party in my recollection.' Martin believes it was a mistake to have a social event at all 'given the circumstances' the country found itself in. 'And most of the journalists would say the same. In fact, what was interesting the morning after is that there was divided opinion among the journalists.'

Martin was blissfully unaware of the emerging furore when he walked out of a boardroom meeting. He was memorably caught on the hop in front of TV cameras. 'I took the stampede if you remember the following morning,' he recalls, laughing. 'There was the famous incident with [TV3 journalist] Ursula Halligan. Ursula questioned me with an apple in my hand, or was it an orange? I'm not sure.'

As he finished his healthy breakfast he looked stunned, and appeared to run for cover. 'And I was saying, I'll be back to you in two seconds, and I went in to find out what had happened. The tweet you're talking about, she was hanging it [her questions about Cowen's interview] on the tweet.'

Martin and Coveney share the Cork South-Central constituency, and Martin, no less than Cowen, is firm in his assessment of the Fine Gael frontbencher's intervention. 'I went back and I replayed the interview, and I actually didn't think the interview was bad. It wasn't a great interview but it didn't suggest anything that Simon Coveney had suggested. And I was kind of angry at Simon at the time and I thought it was wrong of him to do what he did.'

Some of the politicians there that day are, with some justification, still sore about the media's role in the debacle. 'I also felt there was an element of an ambush there. A lot of the journalists present didn't really want to report too much about it, because they had been there previous nights, but when the [news] desk rang, some journalists didn't agree with all that,' says Martin, referring to the less compromised reporting of drinking at the hotel that night.

He states categorically: 'I don't believe he was drunk at all.'

The frontline politicians who recall those incidents at the Ardilaun seem conflicted; they believe Cowen was unfairly treated but understand that he needlessly exposed himself to criticism. Mary Harney, who couldn't attend this event because it was a purely Fianna Fáil occasion, believes Cowen courted disaster through the company he chose that night.

'I think the problem was that the journalists were aware that he was drinking with them the night before, and if they hadn't been aware of that, would the interview have caused the problem it did? I don't think so.' She believes, too, that timing was the issue: 'But anyway, look, we were in difficult times. I think it was more the context of that, when it was and how it was, and the fact that the media were there and they were aware.' Nonetheless, Harney empathised with her colleague, and was emotionally intelligent enough not to exacerbate his embarrassment: 'I was just sorry. I don't think we discussed it, no, it's not the kind of thing you'd discuss.'

It is an unwritten rule in Dáil Éireann that one must not accuse a fellow TD of being drunk in the Chamber. Excessive consumption of alcohol could often occur during late-night sittings. And certainly no TD had ever accused a taoiseach of being 'half way between drunk and hungover' in public before.

After the interview Cowen eventually ambled into the lobby and, chatting to hotel guests, he seemed extraordinarily chipper. TV3 political correspondent Ursula Halligan led a group of journalists who approached the taoiseach as he made his way in for a closed session. As the cameras rolled, she asked Cowen had he been drunk or hungover when he gave the radio interview. In what was not to be the last occasion that a senior Cabinet minister was gobsmacked in front of the cameras that morning, he responded with shock: 'I'm sorry – absolutely not,' he said. 'That's ridiculous.' Looking at the large number of journalists around him he gathered something was up and continued, 'That's uncalled for.'

The New York Times, BBC, Reuters, Press Association and Fox News all filed reports on the taoiseach's performance within hours of his appearance on *Morning Ireland*. Amid the roaring controversy, Cowen, advised by Ó Neachtain, offered a 'mea culpa' by way of *RTÉ News* the following day, insisting he meant no disrespect to the Irish people but accepting it wasn't his best interview. He was also very contrite when the Cabinet met that day, apologising to his ministers. 'I remember vividly him coming in kind of looking like the bold schoolboy whose dog had eaten his homework. The head down, I won't do it again. He was very contrite all right and apologetic. But it did a huge amount of damage to himself and the government,' says Pat Carey.

Eamon Ryan, too, recalls the apology Cowen gave to his ministers, and how it was, to say the least, an uncomfortable moment for them all. 'He was upfront about it, but not in a long, dramatic way, at the start of the Cabinet meeting.' Yet Ryan recalls his annoyance at how Cowen's poor interview had dominated the Green Party's conference in Dundalk, which coincided with the Fianna Fáil event. 'I was in Dundalk at the time, speaking to a conference, and then I heard the *Morning Ireland* tape and I hightailed it back from the meeting in Dundalk to the Dáil for our own parliamentary party meeting. I remember at the time the loss of confidence from it.'

Cowen had not spoken at length about the reputation he feels he unfairly obtained as an overzealous social reveller until he did so in an interview for this book. 'This thing came up, too, about the drink. I don't think any journalist in all the time observing me, and I'm twenty-seven years around the place, [said] I performed a public duty where I wasn't able to perform that duty. I never mixed that.'

Many ministers have a drinks cabinet or a fridge in their office. Political correspondents invited in for an interview would often be offered a beer, though it is a rare occurrence now. It never happened in Cowen's office. 'When I was a minister I made a point of never touching the drinks cabinet in an office or a department. I wouldn't go near it, I had no interest in it, I never offered drink to anybody who would be coming in to see me or anything like that; I'd never have a drink, it never happened in my time.'

Cowen says he did like to socialise with colleagues in the bar. As quoted earlier: 'At the end of the day, there is no doubt I'm a gregarious type of fella, you know what I mean? If I have a long day or a hard day I relax by talking about other things. I sit down and have a couple of pints with a couple of people.'

Cowen believes that he was unfairly judged in a way that his immediate predecessor, Bertie Ahern, wasn't. When asked why it became an issue, he said that there was an effort to imply he wasn't doing his job properly. 'It's back to the stereotype, it's back to the suggestion that you weren't doing your job. I sent in my diary to the [Banking] Inquiry, it's there for all to see. If anyone wants to suggest that I wasn't working twelve hours a day then they should look at my diary.

'You don't do jobs like that without working hard,' he adds.

And he believes, like many Irish people, that after a day's work he is entitled to a pint. 'I enjoy sitting down and chewing the fat with guys and having a couple of drinks. But not in a way that would in any way affect me doing my job, it never happened.'

He heard, many times, the criticisms about the optics of his appearing to be an enthusiastic socialiser. 'It would have been better, it would have been better looking back … It's all about perception, you're better off …' he trails off, considering how to word what follows. 'I was trying to be authentic, being myself. Doing my job but being myself, trying to be authentic with people. Not putting up a face that is not "him" at all. And in that sense, I'm probably comfortable with myself in the sense that I know I don't allow things like this to impinge on me doing my job.'

It might come as a surprise to both his supporters and his

critics that Cowen admits he could have handled the whole question around socialising and his image better. He should have changed his ways for public relations purposes, 'but unfortunately it's like everything, and if someone thinks that is the case, or if people are putting it about that that is the case, you're better off saying well, "forget about it we won't be doing that", and that would probably be a better response to avoid that sort of stuff.'

We ask if he is specifically referring to socialising.

Cowen stresses that what he should have said while he was taoiseach was 'leave it so, leave it so, leave it there for a while'. It is clear he is referring to alcohol for he continues, 'and I could do that – I've done that after Christmas this year, there is no problem'.

Cowen remains relaxed, but he is self-reproaching as he refers to what he now clearly perceives as a mistake, to have publicly complied with an embedded stereotype. But he just would not, or could not, bow to the pressure from handlers and the media to be something he was not, and admits 'you can get a bit stubborn about something'. He says he resisted calls for him to conform with the wishes of his PR handlers and commentators, saying to himself, 'I'm not going to succumb to that now, that's OTT stuff.'

He says he realised in hindsight that he should have changed his habits to kill exaggerated stories about his drinking. He asks rhetorically, 'But by the same token, what do you do?' And then answers his question: 'If there are people putting that about, you are better off killing it.'

He was determined to be authentic to himself: 'And I allowed myself to be myself and not to submit to it … I always sort of had an antipathy towards this political correctness, people telling you how to behave.'

Fianna Fáil is a social institution, a large club, in a way that Fine Gael, Labour and Sinn Féin are not. Fianna Fáil members enjoy the company of other Fianna Fáil members. And Cowen had successfully built up a political support base that saw him cruise into the taoiseach's office by fraternising with the party's grass roots. He stresses that he had built up the reputation in the party for helping others and he felt, at the time, that he should not torpedo that for a soft image make-over.

'I've represented this constituency for twenty-eight years. You can go around here, any part of it, people know me. I'm a hard worker, I worked diligently for my people, I worked in government, I worked hard for the party, and I never had a problem. That was another thing, maybe, where some of this came from. I never had a problem whether we were in opposition or in government going and doing functions for colleagues. Not many guys were doing that.'

Throughout this interview Cowen remained quietly spoken, but clearly felt intensely the importance of what he was saying.

John McGuinness' assessment of Cowen's performance in Galway is unsparing. 'That blind loyalty, that tribalism. And then it was expected that he had a group around him that were by and large associated with the Dáil bar lobby, that's what they referred to them as.'

The 'bar lobby' was the nickname given to the group of TDs who were Cowen's friends. It was claimed by some that he spent too much time in their company in the Dáil members' bar. McGuinness believes that from 2008 to 2011 Fianna Fáil was more closely associated with this activity. 'Essentially they were people that liked to take a few pints and enjoy themselves, and during that period there was a big number of Fianna Fáil TDs that drank in the Dáil bar and that added to the whole public perception of the Dáil bar and Fianna Fáil.'

McGuinness was one of those who thought Cowen would

become more aloof from his friends when he became taoiseach. 'It was expected that Brian, when he was made taoiseach, would leave all of that element behind him, as you have to do when you're in a position like that. And you begin to reward people for their ability and you put them in places that they're going to serve the country. And it became evident over a period of time that that was not going to happen with Brian Cowen. He just found it, in my opinion, extremely difficult to force himself from that group that had been so friendly with him during the time that he was on the backbenches and during the time that he served as minister previous to being appointed taoiseach.'

Though McGuinness can be strident in expressing his opinions on Cowen, we can confirm that his views on this particular issue were echoed by a number of Cowen's colleagues from the time. He continues his criticism of Cowen and his friends: 'In fact he did not leave them behind and continued in the same vein as if nothing had happened, as if he was not the leader of Fianna Fáil, as if he was not the taoiseach of the country, and he just became more and more reliant at a very early stage on the false comfort that they were giving him in relation to his leadership and in relation to the problems of the country.' McGuinness identifies Cowen's main cronies as 'Batt O'Keeffe, Mary Coughlan, Bobby Aylward, Liam Aylward [before he was elected an MEP], John Cregan, John Curran and basically the Country and Western set as they were described previously – they served with him.'

Cowen understood distance, but he felt a politician should enjoy the company of people. The ordinary members interested him and he points out that this is not always the case with his colleagues. 'I liked to go to Roscommon and meet a guy in Ballyforan,' he says, 'or I'd like to go to East Galway and meet a guy in Ballinasloe, or go to a function and get to know the people.

Part of what I thought about politics was … there needs to be an enjoyment in it too … You know the way people who say "ah I like meeting people" but they don't mean any of it,' he laughs. 'But they don't like meeting people at all. I was actually comfortable in the milieu if you like. I liked meeting the guys who were out there working for us on an ongoing basis, who do it because they just love the old party and they love the activity.'

Again Cowen had Bertie Ahern's ghost hovering over his shoulder. Ahern, one of the most personally charming men in politics, was at the same time slightly aloof. He understood the value of separating himself from the parliamentary party and didn't socialise with them. Cowen would have heard the criticisms that Ahern had gone too far and was too distant.

Cowen's grandfather Christy, a cattle dealer, served Fianna Fáil as a member of Offaly County Council from 1932, the year that Éamon de Valera first formed a Fianna Fáil government. Brian's father, Ber, replaced him on Offaly County Council when Christy died in 1967. Ber was elected to the Dáil in 1969 and was re-elected five times. So Brian Cowen's family had been immersed in Fianna Fáil almost since its foundation, and he appears to lament a different era in Leinster House.

'Look, it's like being in the Dáil. When I went in there first, there were what I call good characters in all parties,' he says. 'When I mean a character I don't mean people involved in clownish behaviour, I'm talking about people who were interesting people. They were very happy in their own skin, they had their own way of expressing themselves. This diversity that you see in society you need to see in there as well. And some people look down on a certain type of politician because they don't fit an identikit that they feel should be the ideal politician. And I don't buy that … and I saw them in all parties. I remember men that socialised together: Frank Cluskey [former Labour leader] and Brian Lenihan Senior. And they were interesting people to be in their company and converse … They weren't people who were saying "I don't talk to you because you're over here and I'm over there", you know that sort of nonsense that is going on … I was never of that conscience.'

He recalls, 'I remember I got a great bit of advice when I was very young in the Dáil, probably the best advice I ever got, and it was from a colleague who was a friend of my dad's, a social friend of my dad's. But he wasn't in the same party, and he said to me, "Can I give you a little bit of advice?"

'And I said, "Fine, I'd like any advice I can get."

'And he said, "Don't judge your friends by politics."'

Cowen asked him what he meant.

The man replied, 'If you do you will end up only talking to half the country.'

'That would be exactly my way of looking at things,' Cowen concludes.

For many, the abiding image of Cowen is of him going head-to-head with Enda Kenny or Eamon Gilmore in Dáil Éireann, fingers pointing, arms sweeping. Cowen acknowledges this, but says he didn't get personal. 'I could be very pugnacious, you know, in my style in the Dáil or whatever, but I never engaged in personal attacks on people. I had a strong political view but I would always be able to talk to the people I was conversing with or debating with. I'd never have a problem sitting down with people and having a cup of tea or a pint. You know, talk about other things,' Cowen adds.

He believes that the discourse in the Dáil has changed, that it has become nastier. 'And I think that is important, there has to be a certain *esprit de corps* in the place and I don't believe that there is the same *esprit de corps*. My impression is that that *esprit de corps* isn't as good as it used to be and that's not good for politics generally. It's not about people being "palsy walsy", it's just about that mutual respect … you know there are a lot of things we have in common that we could discuss.'

Many will have sympathy with Cowen's fondness for a less politically correct time. However, others won't, just as they didn't at the time. Politics is a pitiless game and Cowen's opponents in Fianna Fáil and beyond saw an opportunity. Conor Lenihan was one of those who shared the chagrin of many Fianna Fáil members over the Ardilaun interview: 'Unfortunately the taoiseach lost an awful lot of credibility as a result of the incident in Galway.'

There was a seismic shift in the Fianna Fáil party in its attitude to Cowen. He had opened himself up to ridicule, always a deadly move for a politician. 'So if you are to pinpoint a time and a place where the tensions became more open and obvious I think you would have to talk about that period. This incident caused great difficulties for the taoiseach and for his continuing authority and credibility as a leader,' says Conor. 'I think progressively the possibility of a replacement and a leadership contest started immediately after Galway.

'People were talking about a potential replacement of Brian Cowen and the reason for that was there was a very strong perception in government and in the parliamentary party, as there was in the country, that he was not communicating effectively through this particular crisis.' Conor Lenihan says the Galway event was 'absolutely vital in terms of the erosion of trust in the authority and credibility of the taoiseach, Brian Cowen.' His brother, for several days, refused to publicly criticise Cowen over his poor interview, but he was weighing up a run for the leadership.

Mary O'Rourke agrees that the Ardilaun event cemented the

need within the party for a new leader and confirms that Brian Lenihan was being called on to mount a heave: 'The desire for a new leader began to be embedded in Ardilaun. It was ready-made and the incident, "Garglegate" as you [the media] call it, intensified it. There was a clear desire for him [Brian Lenihan] to run.'

On the Thursday night after the Ardilaun debacle, John McGuinness left the Dáil in his black Mercedes Benz and was halfway home to Kilkenny when he received a call from an agitated Lenihan. The finance minister was upset about the recent turn of events and requested that McGuinness meet him immediately. McGuinness pointed out his geographical dislocation, but Lenihan asked him to double back and return to Dublin. 'I came back, because if the minister for finance asks you to come back you do … he wanted to talk about something serious.'

They agreed to meet in the Merrion Hotel an hour later. 'I spent hours with him that night in the room behind the reception.' Lenihan and McGuinness talked over pots of green tea. The Kilkenny TD said that Lenihan's concerns about the Fianna Fáil party flowed out that night. 'He expressed the view that Brian Cowen was difficult to deal with, hard to talk to and he, Brian Lenihan, couldn't influence Cowen.'

McGuinness and Lenihan had danced around the issue of leadership in the preceding months, but now the finance minister spoke of his belief that a heave against Cowen was necessary. 'He knew the very serious step that had to be taken and he also knew the unwillingness of some within Cabinet to take that step,' says McGuinness. 'So the only thing for him to do was to rely on the backbenches and some of the Cabinet and go for the leadership.'

During their lengthy discussion, Lenihan put the case forward that the country needed a national government which would bring most if not all sides in government together in the national interest, given the scale of the crisis. He alluded to the national government, featuring Labour and the Tories, that Britain had established in the 1930s to face the crises leading to the Second World War. 'He said to me, "You know, John, if I did take over the leadership of Fianna Fáil I would have to consider a national government, how do you think the Fianna Fáil parliamentary party would take that?"'

McGuinness said he believed that the TDs and senators might back such a plan. 'He [Lenihan] said in order to achieve that he would have to be leader … I told him that then was the time for him to contest the leadership.'

This was not a mild discussion about an unpopular boss. It was the plotting of a treacherous move that Fianna Fáil had prided itself on avoiding since the dark Haughey days – the ousting of the leader. They discussed the mechanics of a heave against Cowen. McGuinness said, 'No Lenihan has ever wielded the sword against the leader,' and he offered to initiate the move on Cowen to facilitate a Lenihan heave. 'I don't mind doing that provided you're willing to step in and take on the contest,' he told Lenihan.

Lenihan said he would consider it. As far as McGuinness was concerned, the move against Cowen was on.

The 'incident' and its fallout was now being referred to in the press as 'Garglegate', the rather tiresome tribute to Richard Nixon's Watergate scandal whereby every controversy now has 'gate' tacked on the end. The Friday after this so-called Garglegate, Lenihan gave an interview to Danny McConnell to air concerns about the recent events and make it clear that Lenihan had a big problem with his taoiseach. The pair spoke on the record for almost twenty minutes, and for over an hour afterwards.

Lenihan admitted that the *Morning Ireland* interview and the fallout from it were highly damaging to the government. He told McConnell the taoiseach's poor performance did 'real damage' and had been an 'unwanted distraction'. 'The taoiseach apologised to his colleagues over the matter,' said Lenihan. 'That shows his assessment that there was damage done here. I agree with that assessment. Yes, it has been damaging and yes, precisely, it has been an unwanted distraction. But look, I'm not going to be drawn any further on this issue.' Lenihan added that the controversy and ongoing speculation over Cowen's position was a real difficulty at a critical time, especially as Ireland's rate of borrowing hit record highs. 'We have more important things to address as a country, far more important. We have seen the nervousness in the financial markets in recent weeks. I am working full time to ensure we bring finality and certainty to the problems at Anglo Irish Bank.'

But once the tape stopped, Lenihan questioned McConnell about Cowen's position. 'What are you hearing?' he asked off the record. A long discussion ensued about those who were believed to be in favour of him replacing Cowen and others who would back the taoiseach. The *Sunday Independent* ran a front-page story: 'Lenihan prepared to lead', based on McConnell's discussions with Lenihan, as well as the minister's briefings to Aengus Fanning, the editor of the paper.

Willie O'Dea, who did not become significantly involved in briefing against Cowen, nevertheless had also become convinced at this stage that a change was needed. 'There was anticipation that Brian Lenihan would make a move. Lenihan wasn't exactly discouraging them, I'd put it like that. People were going to him you see, he was the alternative focus.'

There is a peculiar set of signals and feints that occur when a leadership heave is underway, and often what is not said by a candidate is important, according to O'Dea. 'People who were really pissed off, and there would have been plenty of people who were pissed off because of the situation, were going to him and complaining loudly and he wasn't exactly saying to them, "You can't say that, shut up, go away."'

Political correspondents from the period will confirm that most of the briefing against Cowen and promotion of Lenihan as an alternative leader was done by Conor Lenihan and John McGuinness. As Brian's brother, Conor's actions can be understood on one level, but it was damaging for Cowen to have a minister of state in his government briefing and plotting against him.

McGuinness, a former minister, was extremely eloquent in presenting an argument. 'Yes, he [Brian Lenihan] was actively seeking support. At that stage, he was exhaustive in his trawl of the numbers, to see if he had the support. He certainly gave everybody the impression he was going to challenge.'

In September and October Lenihan spent a lot of time sounding out the backbenchers, wondering if there was room for a challenge and if there was room thereafter to take on what would be a whole new construct of government – a national government. Mary O'Rourke insists that Lenihan's considerations of a move were driven by a growing sense that Cowen had lost the confidence of many within the party: 'Brian had done the numbers.'

He asked his aunt at this time: 'Do you think if I became taoiseach, it would make a difference, Mary, for the forthcoming election?'

She replied, 'It might, but we are into the land of iffery.'

O'Rourke says that she and her nephew did discuss the possibility of him becoming leader, but there was something holding him back from knifing Cowen. 'Well there were two things, first he was grievously ill and he would have known that, and also there was a Fianna Fáil loyalty to the taoiseach of the day. I remember he said that the boss, Brian Cowen, was very good to him when he got sick. He had a fellow feeling. He was tugged, he was.'

Lenihan had begun a deliberate policy of talking one-on-one with as many Fianna Fáil TDs and senators as he could in a bid to court their support. He knew he was dying and only had a short time left, but felt he could offer Fianna Fáil a better chance in the pending general election if he was leader. He would discuss the state of the party with some of them, one-on-one; others were invited to the Department of Finance for some purpose, but inevitably the conversation led to the leadership.

A Dáil vote is one of the few occasions when all TDs are gathered in one spot. Lenihan used the ten-minute periods between votes being called and cast to lobby and sound out the people. 'When there is a vote called in the Dáil the numbers of TDs would show up to cast their vote and Lenihan would be there and he would often use those occasions to chat to people, he would often reach out to you and talk to you as an individual about representations that you were making as a TD. But inevitably again that led to issues around the leadership,' says John McGuinness.

Lenihan told McGuinness that he would be an interim leader and then would pass the leadership on to somebody else when the inevitable happened – his death in 2011 or 2012. 'In late 2010 he said that he had only a limited time left. And that he would see himself as a leader who could lead the party into a general election, that could make all of the changes that were necessary, do it with a greater degree of freedom because he knew that there was an end to his life on the way.'

Cowen could sense the increased unhappiness over his own performance following the *Morning Ireland* debacle, yet seemed unable to seize the momentum away from his detractors. Six days after the disastrous interview, and a period of intense speculation of a Lenihan coup, he arranged to join his minister for finance for a press conference on the steps of Government Buildings. It was meant to be a Lenihan solo event, but the taoiseach insisted on attending. Cowen understood the symbolic importance of the two men standing side by side.

Lenihan confided in his brother that Cowen had railroaded him into a public display of unity. 'Brian Cowen came down to my brother's office and asked him to come out with him. He was on the plinth being cajoled into speaking in favour of the taoiseach a few days after the Galway incident.' Conor Lenihan claims that his brother spoke in support of the taoiseach almost accidentally. 'And next minute he was there in front of the media. He couldn't but assert support for the leader so you know that type of thing was happening.'

Before the press conference two Fianna Fáil Dublin-based TDs – Tom Kitt and Michael Kennedy – had called on Cowen to resign. Cowen was asked questions about his leadership. He told reporters: 'I'm not a taoiseach on probation. I'm the elected leader of our party. I have the full support of my government colleagues.'

It was also at this time that Cowen was coming under pressure from a number of those close to him within the party to remove Lenihan. O'Rourke insists that the 'bar lobby', or at least some of its members, were 'at Cowen to get rid of Lenihan'. 'They had gotten the whiff that the PP meeting were egging Brian on and they didn't like it. They claimed they could all have done better as minister for finance. The cuts were beginning to hurt … I am not sure he did listen to the bar lobby, but I do know Cowen was never going to get rid of Brian Lenihan, how could he?'

Lenihan was convinced that his decision to plot against his leader had been the right one. Still, he held out hope that, if he could only talk man to man with his taoiseach, he could convince Cowen to change his ways. Yet, according to O'Rourke, this was no longer possible – Lenihan told her that he was encountering difficulties in meeting Cowen alone. He had sought meetings with Cowen in Dublin but every time he wished to see the taoiseach, Mary Coughlan would be present. In O'Rourke's account, Lenihan would phone Cowen to say, 'I have to see you boss, for an hour.' She explains, 'Cowen would say, "Come on over, come on over", and when he went over Mary Coughlan would be there beside him. Now she was the tánaiste and was entitled to be there. But he always had her with him.'

'When Brian would turn to budgetary matters, Coughlan would say, "Oh, Brian, you couldn't do that, you couldn't do that, Brian."'

Eventually, after several weeks of this farce, of trying but failing to get Cowen alone, he got in his car and went to Cowen's home in Tullamore, County Offaly. The frustrated finance minister told O'Rourke he had to confront Cowen on familiar ground: 'Well I have so many things I need to discuss with him.'

O'Rourke continues her account of the minister's mission: 'So he told me, "I rang the boss this morning, Sunday morning, and I said to Cowen I have to see you." So he went down [to Offaly]. He spent an hour or two hours with him but he was utterly frustrated so things had gone very bad.'

There was further frustration for Lenihan. Cowen would not comply with his pleas to change his policy course and his public style. 'But that was Brian Cowen, couldn't face up to it. He would shut the mind off and bury the head.' O'Rourke is a wonderful storyteller and skilfully creates in the listener's mind images of those whacky, frantic days. Her account would be hilarious if such serious matters were not being discussed. It does illustrate that Lenihan, and his family, at this stage believed his relationship with the taoiseach had become totally abnormal.

Though there was exhaustive discussion amongst the party members, the process would lead towards a simple conclusion: the counting of numbers. What Lenihan was trying to do was establish whether he had a sufficient number of people in the parliamentary party who would vote for him.

'There was some low-level canvassing all right, some sussing out,' recalls Billy Kelleher.

Micheál Martin, the man who eventually succeeded Cowen, had far greater frontline political experience than Lenihan. He also had a more finely tuned political sense and he could count. Thus he was more realistic when Lenihan approached him about the leadership. 'He did come to me in November at one stage and asked was I interested and so on like that. And it was kind of, how would I put it, kind of a "what if" scenario type thing.

'I indicated that if there was ever a vacancy into the future … but I wouldn't be pushing for it, that I would be a candidate,' he says. 'I think he wanted to suss me out if there was a vacancy would I be going for it. But I said I wasn't moving in any shape or form against the taoiseach, but if there was a vacancy into the future I would be throwing my hat at it.'

Martin believes there was an element of 'make believe' politics going on with the conspirators. He had been a Fianna Fáil member before being elected to Cork Corporation in 1985 and had first-hand experience of the trauma the heaves against Charlie Haughey's leadership had caused in Fianna Fáil. 'I'm not so sure a lot of the people going around touting for a change knew what they were involved in,' he says. 'I think there were approaches made to Brian Lenihan, of that there's no doubt, but to what extent they constituted a real heave or not I'd be [doubtful]. I think there was a lot of exchanges of views going on, and all the rest of it.'

Martin knew the time was not yet right to move on Cowen. 'But my own view was he [Cowen] would have won. He had a very solid centre support in the parliamentary party; there's a historic reluctance of the party to vote against the leader of the day.' And Cowen, with twenty-seven years in the parliamentary party behind him, had a lot of personal capital to draw on. 'But also people liked him in the parliamentary party, people were fond of him, and he had a lot of support at all times within the parliamentary party. So that was my sense of it.'

In the end Lenihan did not move against Cowen. This was to his discredit. He allowed others to put their political careers on the line to do the running for him and then he failed to plunge the knife, despite his deep unease and anger at Cowen.

The excuses, according to Conor Lenihan and briefings from Brian Lenihan later, were manifold. Brian Lenihan was gravely concerned about the destabilising impact any heave would have on Ireland's already battered international reputation. 'He, too, was ultimately unsure about his health. Swayed by these factors, Lenihan ultimately decided against challenging Cowen. Like his father, Brian just couldn't stick the knife in when he had the chance,' says Willie O'Dea.

And when it came down to it, Lenihan simply didn't have the numbers. Cowen did. But Lenihan continued to plot and machinate.

10

BAILOUT

On 21 September, the day that Brian Cowen and Brian Lenihan appeared at that tense, post-Ardilaun press conference at Government Buildings, the cost of Ireland's borrowing hit its highest level since the euro currency had been established. Lenihan's plotting against Cowen was temporarily put on hold as the whole focus of the government shifted to staving off bankruptcy. Since the spring of 2010 Ireland had found it more and more expensive to borrow on international financial markets.

The financial crisis had tightened its grip on Europe and some countries, notably Greece, Ireland and Portugal, were finding it more difficult to borrow money. Governments borrow by issuing government bonds which are purchased by investors. As an economy deteriorates a government may have to borrow from large financial institutions. Eventually it becomes more of a risk for a large bank or investor to lend to that country. So the lenders charge more for loans. The cost of borrowing becomes so extortionate that the country can be forced to seek financial assistance from organisations such as the International Monetary Fund (IMF).

As the crisis worsened, a committee was established by the European Commission with the ECB and the IMF to organise loans to embattled countries. It became known as the Troika – the Russian word for a sled pulled by three horses. The arrival of the Troika in a country to take over its finances meant it had hit financial rock bottom and could no longer adequately administer itself. Greece had become the first eurozone country, in April 2010, to require external loans by way of what became known as a Troika bailout. Greece no longer had the confidence of market lenders. International perceptions were not helped by a consistent pattern of Greece falsifying data it provided to the EU and other international bodies. Once Greece had taken the Troika assistance, confidence in other troubled EU countries, already at a minimum, fell further and borrowing costs increased further.

Throughout 2010 the besieged Irish government struggled to maintain confidence in its efforts, while those outside Ireland's borders struggled to find anything to feel confident about. The hits kept coming for Ireland. Standard & Poor's, a credit agency, gave a very unfavourable rating assessment for the country that autumn and Irish government bond yields increased steadily. The yield is the amount of money a lender makes when purchasing a government bond to cover their risk – the higher the yield, the higher the cost of borrowing to Ireland.

Former Central Bank governor Patrick Honohan says that when the rating agency downgraded Ireland it indicated that international financial opinion-makers saw NAMA as a serious liability to Ireland. 'I think Standard & Poor's must have had some kind of sense, even before they were announced, that the NAMA valuations were coming up worse. And they had started to realise in their mind that NAMA was implicitly an obligation. They started to add all the sums together and they were getting very big.'

Cowen, to this day, maintains that the government, in the autumn, felt it could have struggled on without assistance for some time longer. 'At the start of 2010, though in deep recession, Ireland was able to borrow at rates that were only slightly higher than normal,' he says. 'At the end of September 2010, the government announced its intention to withdraw from the markets as a tactical move since we were fully funded until mid-2011.'

Elsewhere, the decision of the Irish government to stop borrowing money was interpreted as it being forced out of the markets by the international financial wolves encircling Ireland. All the time, the international pressure on Ireland was mounting and, yet, Lenihan still did not believe a bailout was certain. Eamon Ryan shared that view. 'I did not think a bailout was inevitable, we still had €20 billion in cash. The numbers were horrific but at least in my mind they weren't hiding anything, and ultimately that was important,' he says, in a pointed reference to the chicanery of the Greeks.

Then, on 30 September, Lenihan revealed the full cost of bailing out the Irish banking system – €50 billion. Many who worked in Leinster House during those days recall this as perhaps the darkest of days. Labour's Joan Burton dubbed it 'Black Thursday', and paraphrasing the words of US president Franklin D. Roosevelt after Pearl Harbour, she described it as a 'day of infamy'.

Dara Calleary remembers vividly the shock when he heard the figure: 'I went, "What the fuck?"' He had been sent to Brussels to deputise for Lenihan at a meeting of EcoFin (European finance ministers), which he believed was a mistake. He told Lenihan, 'There is no sense in me going over – a junior minister that they have never met – to explain this.'

It was decided that Lenihan should participate in a conference phone call with EcoFin. 'I could not get over that day, the respect that was there in the room for Brian Lenihan, particularly from Christine Lagarde. Massive respect with all his colleagues.' Calleary got an up-close view of some senior players in world finance – Ireland's *bête noire*, Jean-Claude Trichet, and the since disgraced IMF boss Dominic Strauss-Kahn. 'Trichet was a prick, and Dominic Strauss-Kahn was a bigger prick.' Calleary states of the ECB boss: 'Every word he said there was a lie, Trichet, that day at EcoFin.'

When news of the €50 billion cost to the Irish banks was revealed at the meeting, those enemies of Ireland went in for the kill.

'Strauss-Kahn was actually the worst that day, they were going around saying Ireland is fucked, Ireland is fucked,' says Calleary. 'And if they were doing that at EcoFin, they were feeding the markets. I have absolutely zero doubts about it.

'Strauss-Kahn was in agreement with Trichet: Ireland, little Ireland can go piss,' was Calleary's interpretation of what he observed there that day.

Calleary, a level-headed young minister, not usually given to hyperbole, was the man on the ground at that crucial meeting. He believes that in addition to the pressure cooker of the Troika, the United States was using its influence.

'But, the other element in this is [US Treasury Secretary] Timothy Geithner, like they're [the US administration] getting away with it in terms of their role in this.' Fearing Ireland could destabilise the world economy, Geithner was to intervene in the Irish saga again in the coming weeks.

The points being put here by Calleary have been repeatedly rebuffed by the former bank president.

The fears of contagion, the fears that countries which were in financial freefall would drag down other European countries, were very real in late 2010. The USA, China and other global superpowers were fearfully watching the European troubles and all eyes were increasingly focused on Ireland. And conversely, the economically strong countries didn't seem to care how their statements could adversely affect the weaker nations.

On 18 October, in Deauville, France, German chancellor Angela Merkel and French president Nicolas Sarkozy declared that a new permanent euro-area financial rescue fund to be set up by 2013 would require private sector creditors to accept some debt restructuring. This would mean that those financial institutions lending to sovereign governments would face losses, big losses. It could only mean that the risk was much higher with countries like Ireland, and so the cost of borrowing increased again – at the worst possible time. 'This was known as the Deauville declaration,' says Cowen, adding that they tried to clear up the mess too late. 'It was clarified afterwards that the debt restructuring provision would only apply to new debt after 2013. The original statement had caused further market jitters: the damage was done and bond yields jumped further.'

The Irish government was working on a recovery plan. 'We had indicated to the EU Commission and the ECB that we were preparing a four-year National Recovery Plan to be published in November, prior to the budget,' says Cowen. 'It would show that we were committed to an adjustment programme that would bring the budget deficit down below 3% by 2014.' The EU now required countries to get their budget deficit below 3% of GDP by 2014. But Cowen believes Deauville scuppered the confidence that the four-year plan would engender.

Mary Harney says the likelihood of a bailout grew significantly after the Merkel–Sarkozy deal. 'You felt it in your bones it was about to happen, particularly after Merkel and Sarkozy made the comments. Remember they were in Deauville and they said that in a "peripheral country, the bonds won't be honoured". After that the money started flying out of the place.' Harney also says Ireland was treated differently by Europe's major powers. 'We weren't treated the same; on the one hand people were very supportive, but I tell you all around that time we were very much on our own. There is no doubt about that. I'm very supportive of Europe – there are huge advantages to a small country being in Europe; Ireland's advantages overwhelmed the negatives – but one thing was certain, there is no doubt that the big boys called the shots.'

By October low-level meetings and discussions were taking place between Irish officials and the EU, and to a lesser extent the IMF, about the country's fiscal and banking difficulties. That month the ECB began to turn the screw on Ireland. Lenihan received a pre-emptory letter in October from the ECB president expressing concern about the Irish banks. More letters and messages would arrive in the coming weeks. Weeks of spiralling interest costs, mounting concerns over the government's banking policy and the Deauville declaration meant funding avenues for Irish banks were being closed off.

Irish financial institutions were totally reliant on the ECB for funding. The level of ECB emergency funding that had been put into Ireland now topped €130 billion. It was unsustainable.

Yet on 4 November Trichet tried to shore up confidence in the government's economic plan as Irish borrowing costs spiked to a new record. He told reporters that the Cabinet's decision to front-load the €15 billion four-year austerity plan with a €6 billion package in 2011 was of 'extreme importance'. He emphasised the requirement for the Irish authorities 'to be alert permanently' as they tried to balance the books.

Then, on Monday 8 November, EU commissioner Ollie Rehn visited Dublin. The hard-faced Scandinavian gave an address to the Institute of International and European Affairs on

Dublin's north side where he concluded that it might be a 'small consolation' but he had 'no doubt that Ireland, too, will overcome this crisis. You are smart and stubborn people.' He added that Ireland's €15 billion target for adjustments required to meet the 2014 deadline was negotiable depending on Ireland's economic performance. Rehn's careful speech was not interpreted in Ireland as an endorsement of Trichet's positive words. The Finn insisted that Ireland would have to abandon its 'low tax' principles. The EU maintained a campaign to force Ireland to increase its 12.5% corporation tax rate in the coming years. Many EU figures believed that the regime was giving unfair advantage to Ireland in attracting foreign, particularly US, investment. The campaign failed.

In a statement that was interpreted as patronising, Rehn departed saying, 'Europe stands by you.' The price of Irish ten-year bonds, according to Bloomberg, stood at 7.902% as Rehn began his address, but had risen to 7.938% by the time he had finished. He then left for a G20 meeting of world leaders where it is believed he gave a damning report about Ireland.

On 11 November the bond yield rose to 8.6%. The ECB, concerned that it had now lent one-fifth of its entire stock of reserves, €130 billion (including almost €40 billion in September and October), to Ireland, decided enough was enough. On Friday 12 November, following another week of record-high interest rates of well over 8%, intense pressure came on Ireland to accept a bailout, amid growing fears of contagion spreading into Spain and Portugal.

The ECB and others in Europe began briefing the press, principally the international financial media, in what was interpreted by the Irish government as a dastardly scheme to push them into a bailout. 'The ECB Governing Council decided it could not sustain its large exposure to Irish banks,' says Cowen. 'ECB and EU sources commenced off-the-record media briefings leading to reports that Ireland would need a bailout and that discussions were underway.'

As Central Bank governor, Patrick Honohan also sat on the board of the ECB alongside other European central bank chiefs. He has confirmed that ECB sources briefed against Ireland, but says such leaking was ill-advised. 'I don't think they should have briefed carelessly,' says Honohan. 'There was no collective decision, but one or two senior people definitely briefed investors, probably journalists, saying, "Ah, Ireland is going to be next." That was very unwise and unhelpful.'

Under immense pressure, Cowen insisted all was well and no plans for a bailout were afoot. 'We have made no application whatever for funding. As the minister for finance outlined, we have funding up to mid-year because of the pre-funding arrangements done by the National Treasury Management Agency,' he told reporters as he canvassed in Donegal ahead of a by-election. The government had been forced to hold it after Sinn Féin senator Pearse Doherty took a High Court case. Doherty won the case and won the by-election.

Despite Cowen's denials, during a tense call with Trichet, Lenihan agreed to the opening of talks in Brussels to explore what a possible programme for Ireland would look like. The next day, Cowen and Lenihan met with their key officials to discuss the next move. 'There were internal discussions with myself, Minister Lenihan and key officials. We were clear that if discussions were to take place it would be "talks about talks". In other words we made no commitment at that point to formally apply for assistance until we were satisfied with what the authorities had in mind and the conditionality attached to it,' says Cowen.

It was next to impossible to keep such conversations quiet and the financial establishment in Europe continued to encourage press speculation. The Department of Finance denied that discussions were happening and rejected suggestions that any request for assistance had been made.

Cowen severely criticised the off-the-record briefings against Ireland. 'The off-the-record briefings were clearly trying to create a situation where a formal Irish application for assistance was being portrayed as a *fait accompli* by those informed sources, without prior agreement on conditionality. This was unacceptable to us,' says the former taoiseach. 'We were not against exploring the issues with the EU authorities, but neither should they presume nor anticipate what decision the Irish government would make. We wanted to know what they had in mind before we would indicate what position we intended to take. We were looking to explore what possibilities there were before giving our considered view.'

The Sunday newspapers on 14 November carried renewed speculation from Brussels and Frankfurt about a potential programme and the pressure intensified on the government to clarify what exactly was going on. Despite the pressure, the Cabinet denials persisted. Batt O'Keeffe said on RTÉ Radio 1 that he was 'absolutely unaware of any moves from Europe. It's been a very hard-won sovereignty for this country, and this government is not going to give over this sovereignty to anyone else.'

In the most explicit denial, on RTÉ Television's *The Week in Politics*, Dermot Ahern said speculation that Ireland was about to seek financial aid from Europe was incorrect. 'It is fiction because what we want to do is get on with the business of bringing forward the four-year plan. There is nothing going on at the direction of government in relation to this.'

On Monday 15 November EU chiefs in Brussels still held out hope this rampant conjecture would end. However, their hope dissolved when Vitor Constâncio, an ECB vice-president, said, 'The banks are at the centre of the problems in Ireland and considerations have to be pondered.'

The stonewalling and dissembling by ministers in Dublin, in the face of unprecedented press briefings from Europe, had become farcical. Some Irish politicians saw their reputations permanently tarnished. Lenihan was responsible for the awkward predicament Noel Dempsey and Dermot Ahern found themselves in that Monday. The two ministers were at an event in Dublin Castle when they were interviewed by reporters. Eoghan Ó Neachtain had insisted that Lenihan brief them directly. The minister for finance had spoken to Ahern before he went on TV the previous day and they spoke again minutes before they faced reporters in the courtyard of the Castle. Dempsey, too, spoke to Lenihan, who reiterated that there were no talks about a bailout. But talks were occurring at that very moment in the Department of Finance.

Dempsey and Ahern stood side by side, grim-faced and earnestly shaking their heads: 'I'm not aware of it [pressure], nor is Noel,' said Ahern. 'I have spoken to Brian Lenihan today and he will be going to the [European Council] meeting and articulating Ireland's position and will be part of any initiative that the Council takes in conjunction with the Commission.'

Lenihan believed that a denial of talks was essential to negotiation tactics because if a deal was publicly confirmed Ireland would have to accept that it be dictated on Europe's terms. Refusal to confirm there would be a bailout meant that Ireland still had the option to reject a deal if the terms were too punitive.

Dempsey said in a subsequent interview that he was 'livid' with Lenihan for allowing him to continue the obfuscation. 'The one thing that we had to try and avoid was saying "we're going into a bailout" without knowing what was involved in that,' he said. 'There was nobody either in the political system, in the civil service, or apparently in the banking or regulatory authorities, that knew exactly where everything was or what was going on … [Brian Lenihan] hadn't the absolute trust in anything he was being told, probably by anybody, because he felt nobody knew the full picture, and I think that was a fair enough assessment.'

When the bailout was eventually confirmed, the two men looked ridiculous and the image of the two ministers shaking their heads became an emblem for the dysfunction of the government of that time. Pat Carey recalls how he narrowly avoided being one of the fall guys. 'I was almost the one. I was asked to do that interview, and I said to Eoghan Ó Neachtain that I shouldn't, that Lenihan should be doing that. He said, "He can't do it." And I said, "I can't do it either." And only later did I discover that the two lads ended up as real Laurel and Hardy stuff.' The double act attracts comparisons from their colleagues with another great comic duo. 'They were like the two old fellas up in the balcony in *The Muppets*. Statler and Waldorf,' says Willie O'Dea.

The tragi-comedy was very damaging to the government's already rapidly diminishing credibility. 'It was just absolutely devastating, devastating; it gave everyone the clear impression of a disjointed government, total incoherence, total incoherence,' recalls O'Dea. 'Because I mean anybody watching the thing, and I watched it over and over again, knew the boys used the line given to them from Lenihan.' The duo's government colleagues are damning of their performance, but, since they were working off a briefing from the finance minister, it is difficult to believe any of the other ministers would have done things differently.

Eamon Ryan believes the two men were unfairly exposed. 'I think in the end what happened in terms of Dermot Ahern and Noel Dempsey kind of being left out in the yard in Dublin Castle looking really stupid probably did more damage to that sense of collegiality ... It was "wait and see how it pans out". Noel Dempsey and Dermot Ahern were less lucky, and I think they were not well served in terms of the way they were left hanging out there.' He believes that it was of little value to deny the bailout talks on Monday 15 November. 'At that stage it was very late in the day.'

Ryan was careful not to put himself in front of the cameras – he had checked with other government figures to find out what was going on. 'Ringing Kevin Cardiff, ringing John Corrigan, various people, I think it became very clear to us immediately that there were talks taking place, that it [the bailout] was likely to happen ... So we, the Green Party, said to ourselves that weekend, "Shut up and say nothing."'

Those close to Lenihan have defended his actions. 'Brian was trying to play a lone hand, lone hand ranger, and he was on his own playing his hand. Because at this stage his confidence in Cowen was kind of gone,' says Mary O'Rourke. 'He was still trying to get the best deal possible from Frankfurt, and when you are on your own you don't tell anyone, you don't even tell your other hand. He had hoped that he would still be able to avoid a bailout. So you keep your cards close to your chest.'

Lenihan had absolutely hung his ministers out to dry, but a more holistic media management process might have kept Ahern and Dempsey out of the firing line. O'Rourke puts the blame for the outright denial at the door of Ahern and Dempsey, who she suggests were ill-prepared to answer the questions being asked. 'I know and I feel sorry for Noel Dempsey and Dermot Ahern, they were long-time ministers. But were they not reading the newspapers? Hadn't they advisors? Could they not have gone cautiously? But they said "no, no, no",' she recounts. 'And I know they feel very sore about it, deadly sore about it.' However, O'Rourke stresses that the dysfunctional communication was a by-product of a collapse in trust between Cowen and Lenihan. 'But it is clear the relationship between the two Brians had deteriorated, well I must tell you.'

O'Dea, for his part, says that Cowen was not happy that two colleagues were made to look so foolish: 'He wasn't best pleased, no.'

In a statement, the government announced that its four-year plan for multi-billion euro savings would be released within the next seven days. On Tuesday 16 November the Cabinet met and was briefed by Lenihan. His colleagues berated him for misleading his fellow ministers. 'The Cabinet was brought up to date about the situation that was developing. I did not like the continuous anonymous briefing against Ireland, which I saw as an attempt to bounce us into a decision before we had further clarification,' says Cowen.

Following the meeting, Lenihan travelled to Brussels, arriving late because of fog. Faced with overwhelming pressure, Lenihan resisted calls for Ireland to surrender its 12.5% corporation tax rate. 'The pressure was intense [on Lenihan] at those meetings. The ECB were at all times pushing for this position of Ireland being in a programme without explicitly confirming it would continue to support the Irish banking system,' Cowen recalls. Trichet was backed by EU Council president Herman Van Rompuy and German finance minister Wolfgang Schauble in taking on Lenihan, who refused to accept an immediate bailout.

Schauble put considerable pressure on Lenihan to attend a press conference after the meeting to announce a deal was being requested. Lenihan stoutly refused. 'I said I would not, reminding him that Ireland has a sovereign government elected by the people,' Lenihan recalled. He did accede to fresh talks with the EU and the IMF about a bailout. The Eurogroup of ministers released a statement confirming that negotiations had taken place, making a mockery of the government's weekend strategy of denial.

Cowen recalls the decision to commence talks in Dublin and how he misjudged the impact of the arrival of the Troika officials. 'At the EcoFin meeting, it was included in the Council's published conclusions that an EU delegation, with IMF staff joining them for the first time, would travel to Dublin to continue the consultations ... I underestimated the impact of the IMF coming to town element, which immediately sent a message that this was now a done deal rather than a genuine continuation of existing discussions up to then.'

The following day, Wednesday 17 November, Lenihan remained in Brussels for yet another EcoFin meeting, where he battled calls for Ireland to make cuts in excess of the €6 billion that would be detailed in the forthcoming four-year plan. It was confirmed publicly that the IMF and the EU crack team of officials would be arriving in Dublin the following morning.

Mary Harney told us in an interview, however, that all this cloak-and-dagger brinkmanship had been a needless circus. Amazingly she, and presumably other senior government figures, had long known that a bailout was imminent. 'I was aware, even from the summer, that there were discussions at an official level going on. People in the public service were talking about it.'

EU Commission chief José Manuel Barroso told reporters

that the Irish banking crisis must be addressed: 'This must be done speedily and decisively to pave the way for full confidence to be restored.' British chancellor George Osborne declared his willingness to come to Ireland's assistance if required.

Patrick Honohan, too, admitted to us that he had known as far back as early summer of that year that international power-brokers believed a financial programme should be imposed on Ireland, and that he was under pressure to get the government to seek help. Honohan was in favour of Ireland accepting help, and as a member of the ECB board he was conflicted in his loyalties. He reveals that there was huge apprehension at ECB level over Lenihan's stubborn refusal to request help.

They communicated this to Honohan on 17 November. 'On Wednesday night, I called [Lenihan] because the ECB guys were jumping up and down … they thought this was very destructive to Ireland because they did not think Ireland was going to go into a programme, because Brian Lenihan had said in Brussels, "I am not going to go into a programme, I am not going to apply for a programme."'

Mary O'Rourke had arranged to meet Lenihan in the Dáil self-service restaurant at 9 p.m. The Dáil sits late on Wednesday nights to accommodate votes, often until after midnight. The food in the self-service restaurant, which is usually of a fine standard, inevitably deteriorates as the night stretches on. When Lenihan arrived his aunt called to him: 'That auld rabbit food is still there.'

Before Lenihan could begin his meal, his private secretary, Dermot Moylan, interrupted and said, 'The boss is on the phone.'

O'Rourke asked, 'Is that the taoiseach?'

Lenihan replied laconically, 'No, Honohan.'

With extraordinary stress and tension being imposed on a critically ill man it is understandable that Lenihan would resort to sarcasm. But he now appeared to be in significant conflict with his Central Bank governor as well as his taoiseach. 'Brian was very angry, fulminating when he came back,' says O'Rourke. 'Brian didn't like the way it was done.'

Lenihan told her that Honohan wanted him to call a Cabinet meeting to seek a bailout and he had replied that it was not within his power to call Cabinet meetings. That was the responsibility of the taoiseach. According to O'Rourke, Honohan had warned Lenihan that he was to go on radio the following morning.

Honohan's recollection of the phone call differs from O'Rourke's version. He agrees that Lenihan was angry: 'It would confirm my view that he was cross.' But he adds, 'I would not have asked him to call a Cabinet meeting, that is not my place.' He also disputes O'Rourke's claim that he told Lenihan he intended going on radio the night before his interview. 'No, no. I had not come up with that idea,' the former governor says. 'I was only passing on a message from the ECB, they were all upset.'

Lenihan told him, 'Why don't you go? Why don't you apply? I have no authority.'

Honohan believes that Lenihan was shirking his responsibility and wanted to avoid being the man who rubber-stamped the bailout. Honohan then speculates, 'But did he have no authority because he had not told anyone?'

On Thursday 18 November, at 8.13 a.m., Honohan blew the government's increasingly futile strategy out of the water when he rang RTÉ to try to get on the *Morning Ireland* radio programme. He phoned RTÉ from his hotel room in Frankfurt. He says he made up his mind to break ranks with the government's continued denials because of a damning *Financial Times* article he had gotten wind of the night before. He decided that 'I needed to try to stem the uncertainty and the panic. I think *Morning*

Ireland is the obvious place and I had been on it before and I knew what the audience was.'

He struggled to make contact with the programme, having realised he had no idea what number to ring. 'So then, could I find a telephone number for them? I think Neil [Whoriskey, Honohan's press officer] gave me a number to call and I just called them.' Des Cahill, the well-known sports presenter, answered the call, took a number for Honohan and got a colleague to ring him back. He was put through to presenter Rachael English. And he announced that Ireland was in talks with the EU and IMF about a bailout. 'I know that these talks are serious talks, that the IMF and the European Union Commission and the ECB would not send a large team if they didn't believe, first of all, that … they could agree to a package, that there is a programme that is fully acceptable to them, that could be designed, and is likely to be acceptable to the Irish government and the Irish people,' Honohan told English.

Lenihan and Cowen were as one in their reaction to this intervention – they were incandescent. O'Rourke says, 'Then, of course, Honohan became Mr Goody Two Shoes and everyone loved him. He had blown the cover and that was it. Brian [Lenihan] was desperately trying to hold the line. I'm sure Cowen was furious, but Brian [Lenihan] was furious, he sure was.'

Eamon Ryan was more understanding of Honohan's predicament. 'I think the ECB put an enormous amount of pressure on Patrick Honohan and he would have been very sensitive about what was going on because he would have seen the figures and where they were going out.'

Few other senior government figures were as magnanimous. The governor may have thought he was being helpful, but he was not a politician and according to Alan Ahearne gravely misjudged the ramifications for elected representatives: 'It made it politically more difficult. There was criticism because it wasn't the taoiseach or finance minister announcing it, it was someone else … Lenihan was not happy. It made it much harder for him. While it didn't change the outcome, Lenihan was certainly wrong-footed politically. Politically, it was tough.'

Mary Harney, the most experienced politician in Cabinet, felt Honohan didn't understand negotiation as the elected TDs did. 'It accelerated the crisis I suppose, but then again he had responsibilities to the ECB of which he was a member. But clearly it was a time when we were trying to play our best hand when in negotiation.' It was all about the deal for her: 'We're trying to get debt written off. We're trying to negotiate the best possible deal. When those things come into the public domain it weakens your position, the inevitability of it.' And she felt it unduly upset citizens hearing the interview on the country's most listened-to current affairs show. 'I respect the fact that he felt he had to do it, but at the time it caused a lot of upset, it added to a sense of panic for the country.'

Dara Calleary is one of those who believed that Honohan was conflicted by his position on the ECB board. 'I am old-style in many things, and I just did not think it was a good idea. I thought, my God, this is the governor of the Central Bank, what team is he on? Is he on the Irish team? Is he on Team Ireland or is he on Team ECB? And I firmly believed it was Team ECB.'

Cowen reckons Honohan put the government 'in a bad light because of the interpretation given to events that we were keeping what was going on away from people. In fact, we were trying to put ourselves in the best position we could, before formally requesting assistance.'

Honohan denies the charge that he was favouring the ECB. 'It is simply not true. Because first of all what did the ECB have to gain from that? Why would I do that to please some people in the ECB? Am I going to get a bonus? Are they going to think I am a good fellow because he came around to our point of view instead of his own country's point of view? It is absurd. They would despise someone who would behave like that.'

Completely wrong-footed and with his strategy now in ruins, a dejected Lenihan rang Honohan an hour after he came off air and said, 'Patrick, I can't contradict anything you said.' Honohan wasn't exactly contrite and the former bank governor says, 'I thought it was a very funny thing to say and I said, "You certainly can't." But he was actually restrained.'

That afternoon the IMF spokeswoman in Washington, Caroline Atkinson, said the focus of the discussions was 'to look at whatever measures might be needed to support financial stability'. She said talks would take into consideration the IMF's views 'on the government's budget plans … on tax and spending measures'.

Under fire from the opposition, Cowen denied that the rescue plan would lead to a loss of Irish sovereignty. He also dismissed suggestions of failure. 'I don't believe there's any reason for Irish people to be ashamed and humiliated.'

The following day a dozen-strong team from the IMF, staying at the Merrion Hotel, walked fifty yards across Merrion Street to negotiate the rescue package. There were also twenty officials from the ECB and the European Commission. The Irish government, too, had a large negotiating team, with many senior officials including Department of Finance Secretary-General Kevin Cardiff, Chief Executive of the Financial Regulator Matthew Elderfield and, later, Patrick Honohan.

Years later the contents of a letter from Trichet warning Lenihan that he must enter a bailout were released. Cowen described it at the Banking Inquiry: 'On 19 November, ECB President Jean-Claude Trichet sent a letter to Minister Lenihan threatening withdrawal of ECB funds in the absence of a formal bailout request. This was not well received by us.'

Sent from Frankfurt, the letter was stamped 'Secret' and addressed from the ECB and the 'Eurosystem', the term used to describe the collective of the ECB and the group of national central banks in the euro currency. Trichet wrote that the governing council of the ECB 'needs to assess whether it is appropriate to impose specific conditions in order to protect the integrity of our monetary policy'. He said that the 'exposure' of the Irish and European financial systems to the dysfunctional Irish banks 'has risen significantly over the past few months to levels that we consider with great concern'. He added a long list of requirements he believed the Irish government needed to fulfil in a short time. Chief among these was an order that Ireland should immediately enter a funding programme: 'The Irish government shall send a request for financial support to the Eurogroup.' He continued, 'I am sure that you are aware that a swift response is needed before markets open next week, as evidenced by recent market tensions which may further escalate, possibly in a disruptive way, if no concrete action is taken by the Irish government on the points I mention above.'

Trichet's bellicose language was a clear threat to Lenihan, with the subtext that if he didn't enter a bailout programme he could be responsible for bringing down the European financial system. Honohan rather undermines his contention that he wasn't overly influenced by the ECB when he confirms he had a role in drafting the letter and concedes that it would have been interpreted as a threat. 'Obviously this letter is going to be taken as a threat, that is obvious to me anyway. And I told him so,' says Honohan. But he defends Trichet's right to send it. 'Trichet regards himself as entitled to send that just from the point of view of stating the facts. What are the facts? We have lent an enormous sum of money, we are at our limit, we cannot in our mandate lend any more money. It is not a threat it is just a fact. I do think he is within his rights, I do not think it is dishonest. It reflects the legal basis on which he sent that letter. And I don't think it was a hostile letter.'

Honohan believes that Trichet took the attitude of somebody dealing with 'a recalcitrant child'. That Trichet was saying to Ireland 'if you don't do your homework you will not get any more sweets'.

That weekend, much to the annoyance of the French and the Germans, Lenihan reiterated that Ireland's corporation tax rate was non-negotiable and said talks were still at a 'preliminary stage'. The government met to sign off on its four-year plan of cuts that would be implemented into 2014, which had been agreed upon by the EU and the IMF in broad principle. Lenihan would announce €6 billion in cuts in the budget.

On Sunday 21 November the Cabinet met to formally agree to seek help. Cowen said during the negotiations, which were to continue for a week, that he attempted to get Troika agreement for burden-sharing by unguaranteed senior bondholders – that would allow Ireland to default on huge debts to private lenders. He said that the IMF personnel in Dublin were sympathetic but that when it was referred to a higher level within the IMF the proposal was rejected.

Cowen claimed at the Banking Inquiry that the United States vetoed the plan through Timothy Geithner, US treasury secretary. 'He was opposed [to the default option] because he claimed it would totally undermine market access for those European countries that were in trouble. We also understand that the ECB were opposed to it for the same reason,' said Cowen.

'Without the EU Commission, ECB and IMF all being in agreement, it was not possible to have the burden-sharing issue included in the programme. It was made clear to us that any attempt by us to burden-share with senior bondholders would mean no programme for Ireland.'

Burden-sharing, or 'burning the bondholders', became a populist general election proposal for Fine Gael the following year and was to remain a politically explosive issue for years to come. There was also much criticism of the interest rate for the loans being set at 5.8% when it was clear the cost of lending the money was substantially lower. Honohan, who had played a role in railroading the government into the deal, was deeply critical of the final agreement. 'We could have got much lower interest rates, I didn't like the interest rates, and they were too high, the whole thing was barely sustainable and I said this to the government.'

Cowen remains deeply critical of the role of the ECB in Ireland's bailout.

For Lenihan, the bailout represented a shattering and demoralising defeat. He poignantly described his feelings in his last major interview with the BBC. 'I have a very vivid memory of going to Brussels ... being on my own at the airport, looking at the snow gradually thawing, and thinking to myself: "This is terrible." I had fought for two-and-a-half years to avoid this conclusion. I believed I had fought the good fight and taken every measure possible to delay such an eventuality, and now hell was at the gates.'

Micheál Martin had been away from the white heat of the bailout negotiations, spending time with his family as they had suffered the tragic death of their daughter Léana at this time.

He concedes that the government had badly handled the lead up to the bailout. 'It was a very low moment for the government. Terrible, these were very difficult days, nobody likes to be in a situation where the country has to go into that scenario.' But, ultimately, he welcomed the programme. 'I couldn't get over the opposition to the bailout; to me the bailout was about getting in a three-year loan to pay your education, to pay your welfare, to pay your public salaries, at rates that were better than the market could ever hope to give you at that particular moment of time.

'Maybe one of the errors we made was that we didn't go earlier and embrace the concept of the bailout in a more proactive way and sort of say look, this is inevitable, let's go and do it. I knew electorally and politically it would sink us. But … what was going to run the country? So it was necessary. Also, in time we felt it would be changed down the line.'

Cowen and Lenihan experienced a final defeat on Sunday 21 November. By agreeing to go into the programme they had committed Ireland to an unconditional financial surrender. Then, the following day, Monday 22 November, came political hae-morrhage when the Green Party TDs announced that they had finally had enough. They announced their intention to withdraw from government, calling for a general election for the second half of January 2011.

At a press conference in Leinster House, John Gormley said, 'The past week has been a traumatic one for the Irish electorate. People feel misled and betrayed. But we have now reached a point where the Irish people need political certainty to take them beyond the coming two months. So we believe it is time to fix a date for a general election in the second half of January 2011.' The Greens said they still intended to complete bailout negotiations (the programme was agreed on 27 November), help produce a credible four-year plan to balance budgets by 2014 and deliver a budget of €6 billion in cuts for 2011 on 7 December.

The Greens had decided to pull out that weekend. Eamon Ryan relates: 'Our parliamentary party met and politicians have antennae in terms of what goes on – we could not continue.' Ryan, asked when he knew that the government had reached the end of the line, replies, 'You know when you are spit on.' He claims that some of his party suffered this disgusting indignity from members of the public. The unpopularity of the government was reaching its nadir, and Ryan says Green Party colleagues 'felt afraid to walk down the main street of the village and the town, that is what we were aware of, in terms of public reaction'.

Before holding a press conference they informed the senior Fianna Fáil men of their decision. 'John [Gormley] was ringing Brian Cowen, I was ringing Brian Lenihan, I got through to Brian Lenihan fairly close to our press conference. Brian understood the political logic, they are astute enough politically, their own political antennae told them that this is not credible.'

Though the Greens wanted to delay an election until the financial measures were passed, Ryan was worried that Cowen would travel to see the president in the Phoenix Park and dissolve the government. 'I was nervous. Would he run to the Park? But he didn't.'

Micheál Martin was put in charge of negotiating with the Greens a timeline for the wind-down of the government, and says his party colleagues were in conflict over their next move. There was a tense meeting in Government Buildings that Monday. 'Then there was a meeting of the Fianna Fáil ministers in the Sycamore Room. Some ministers wanted to pull out and say we should call an election.' There was a feeling among some in Fianna Fáil that the general election should be a form of referendum on the bailout and that the people should decide who should implement it … I did intervene and said under no circumstances [should we pull out]. We had three things to do: we had to get the bailout agreed, we had to get the six-billion budget out of the way and we had to do the four-year plan,' says Martin, 'because if we learned anything in the 1980s, successive governments had diddled around, they had not faced up to decisions and they prolonged the recession.'

Martin says that the two senior men backed him: 'Lenihan was 100%, he was relieved, and Brian Cowen was absolutely clear, that's what we had to do.' Martin recalls Cowen saying 'the party is important, but the country comes first'. He admits that going into a general election in those circumstances was 'the ultimate in electoral hari-kari'.

'If there was an election that October we would have saved another twenty or thirty seats,' says O'Rourke.

11

END GAME

By the time the Dáil rose for Christmas on 16 December 2010, a weary Brian Cowen had negotiated a bailout, stewarded another €6 billion in budget cuts and brought in the four-year plan. But his party and his government were in tatters and a large rump of the Fianna Fáil parliamentary party decided he had served his purpose and should fall on his sword.

Looking back, Cowen concedes that there were members of the parliamentary party pushing Brian Lenihan into revolt. 'I won't say he encouraged it, but there were a couple of guys who could be bolshie. I don't think he encouraged it.'

Cowen agrees there was movement against him. 'Now there was a bit of promotion of that [plotting] going on with some guys, a very small number of people, not in the government actually, but in the party, a couple of lads, but it is irrelevant now.'

Until those TDs – John McGuinness and Conor Lenihan and the twenty or so other dissenters – had a publicly declared figurehead, Cowen could not acknowledge the impending revolt. The rebels hoped it would be Brian Lenihan who would step forward but, for now, Cowen had to concentrate on maintaining order. 'I never succumbed to it, I never acknowledged it. The important thing is that we [he and Lenihan] had a good professional relationship.'

Cowen always veers away from any temptation to criticise Lenihan, and he claims that they remained on good terms to the end of the government. 'In fact, we had a good relationship, there is no minister for finance who can operate without the support of the taoiseach. I know that myself,' says Cowen. 'You have to have the support of your taoiseach and you can't have the two guys at the top of government, when it comes to finances, at odds with each other.'

However, Lenihan was briefing against his boss and agitating with a view to taking over the leadership so as to see the party through the pending election. And Lenihan canvassed members of his party, overtly outlining his plan. 'He was seriously going for the leadership and got quite a few deputies running and making the running for him on the matter,' says Conor Lenihan. He describes how, at this delicate time, Lenihan's backers wanted him to keep his powder dry. 'We just wanted him to stay silent … we believed at the time that if he were not to offer public support and was conveniently missing in the run up to that particular contest that many people would have made the working assumption that he wanted the leadership.'

Hearing of how those backing Lenihan outlined their plans, these years later, it is difficult for Micheál Martin's claims of 'make-believe' politics not to reverberate. It certainly sounds like their standard bearer was a deeply conflicted plotter. 'He was available and wanted people to vote in a particular way,' says Conor, 'and that would have been very good and probably would have succeeded.'

Billy Kelleher says Lenihan sought his backing for a move against Cowen. 'When it did become a leadership issue he canvassed me on my support. He told me that he was very sick at the time but he would be able to campaign.' Lenihan's attempts were brave but to many observing them they seemed futile and rather deluded. He promoted to Kelleher the idea he had discussed with McGuinness on a number of occasions – his ousting Cowen to become interim leader. 'He met me for a cup of tea,' says Kelleher. 'He felt that he could give the party credibility, that he would lead us through the election itself and he was very clear that it would be short term.'

The key, Lenihan believed, to his proposed candidacy was that he could stave off what many now feared was impending electoral disaster. 'He was upfront that it would be for a very short period but that he could save some seats, particularly in Dublin and things like that,' says Kelleher.

Martin had already been approached by Lenihan and he was very much against any heave led by the minister for finance. He did not think it was viable. 'I think when Brian became ill, the idea that Brian could then become leader, from my perspective, was something that I couldn't quite comprehend and I didn't think it was sustainable either,' he says. 'I think that Brian did have an idea that he could maybe be a bridge within the party in the pre-election – I just didn't think it was a runner.'

Martin is a pragmatist, a politician who knew that a minister taking the huge step of challenging the leader of the party should have a cogent campaign message. Lenihan's proposals were, in his eyes, utterly ill-conceived. Martin thought that Lenihan encouraged a lot of talk but was not willing to follow it with decisive action. 'There was a lot of noise going on, there was a lot of angst,' says Martin, 'and look, the nature of Brian was, people kept going to Brian. There was a certain element of the younger backbenchers who were very, very concerned about it all. Jaysus, could you blame them?'

Many of the ministers and veteran parliamentary party members had been through hard scrapes down the years, but Fianna Fáil's younger TDs were unable to cope with the thoughts of a general election in this tumultuous political climate. 'Because this was torrid stuff for a backbencher in terms of an election,' says Martin. Many of the more experienced politicians thought that Lenihan and some less grounded TDs were encouraging each other in their delusion.

Mary Harney, too, thought that the idea of Lenihan as interim leader was 'impossible'. 'I never understood that, it just didn't make any sense.' That formerly rational politicians were considering that a man with terminal cancer could run for and secure leadership of a national party in these political conditions shows how out of control everything had become. 'My understanding is people like John McGuinness and these [were pushing him],' says Harney.

She did not believe that Lenihan's condition was causing him to have these considerations. 'I think it might have been a bit of the barrister in him rather than the health, he was super confident. And because Brian Cowen wasn't communicating I think that was the frustration.' She says the contrast in styles between the two exacerbated the heave talk. 'Whereas Brian Lenihan, if you contrast the two, he was out there, he was doing interviews, popular with the public, he hadn't been long in the Cabinet. He was perceived as the guy coming in to sort it all out.'

Over the Christmas break it was realised that Fianna Fáil needed to change if it was to avoid complete disaster at the pending general election. Martin was coming around to the view that a change at the top of the party was needed. He told us that he realised this when 'moderate' ministers and backbenchers approached him over the Christmas break and implored him to take action. 'And some moderate TDs who wouldn't have been part of the noise were saying, look, something has to happen, we can't go to the electorate and there are issues – and whether Brian [Cowen] should lead us into the general election.'

The Dáil was not due to return until 12 January 2011, leaving a gap of four weeks. Amid seasonal festivities, rebellion was allowed to fester. Such a hiatus, in these charged times, was to prove fatal for Cowen.

Martin, having thus far remained loyal, was now approached to move on Cowen. The path to the eventual change of leader began in Cork over Christmas. Junior Minister for Trade Billy Kelleher had decided a new leader was needed for the good of the beleaguered party. 'There was this almost existential discussion among TDs whose grandfathers had been ordinary members of the party,' says Martin. 'People like Billy Kelleher and those were saying things like "We owe it to our forefathers to try and save the party."'

Kelleher confirms that he made the first move. He asked Martin for a meeting as the New Year opened. 'I met him in my house in early January. It wasn't at his prompting or anything. I said there is no way, I believe, that we can go into the election with Brian Cowen as leader. I said to Micheál, this cannot continue … We have no credibility as a party, we have no credibility as a government.'

Kelleher felt that Fianna Fáil had to do something quickly as it was inevitable that an election would happen that February or March. 'We will be destroyed as a political party if we don't do something about the leadership,' Kelleher recalls candidly saying to Martin that January. 'I just felt at this stage that with Cowen as leader we could not credibly campaign. At that stage the public anger towards the taoiseach meant … the party was in freefall in terms of headquarters level and the taoiseach. I could sense that we had no manifesto developed and there was drift.'

Headquarters was the catch-all term for those permanent employees of Fianna Fáil who run and administer the party in tandem with the party leader and his staff. Cowen had, some would say understandably, allowed the structure that would prepare for a general election to deteriorate.

The party was at just 14% in the polls, an almost unfathomable low for Fianna Fáil. Over Christmas, TDs had been announcing their intentions to retire. By early January, when Meath TD Mary Wallace said she was not standing again, the number of TDs who would not contest the general election stood at fourteen. 'The key thing in the party was when all the resignations happened,' says Martin. The decision of those TDs not to run and the subsequent withdrawal of ministers hurt those who decided to stay on and fight.

Pat Carey remarks, 'I had said all along that no matter what happens I am going to defend my record before the people. I think I was critical enough of those who did stand down. I thought it was a selfish approach.' The internal strife in Fianna Fáil was intense, and patience with the Green Party was evaporating. 'With the Greens, it had gotten to the stage "would you make your fucking minds up one way or the other",' says Carey.

Cowen is more forgiving of his junior coalition partners. 'In fairness to them they're honourable guys in many ways,' he says. 'Their own internal processes, how they make decisions, is their own business and not for me to comment on. But it didn't make things any easier, for them I'm sure, or for us. But overall, once they had the facts of the situation and could see what needed to be done, they were prepared to make the decisions, in fairness to them. They were prepared to come into government all right. It was just again a difficult time for them. I have to say on a personal level I have no real complaints, we had our few little differences as you'd expect. A few little tiffs on policy and things but that was for me to manage and the Cabinet.'

Cowen reveals that, contrary to perception, he and John Gormley had a good working relationship. 'John and I met every Tuesday morning and dealt with a lot of the stuff, so all in all, I don't think they have much complaint about how I dealt with them: upfront and straightforwardly and let them get on with their job.'

Cowen's sympathy for the Greens was not shared by many others at the top of Fianna Fáil and, as Christmas turned to New Year, the taoiseach's own position was attacked. Martin had made up his mind – Cowen was toast in the eyes of the public and had to go. 'The whole stuff around the imagery [attached to Cowen], the momentum, you know the media attack on him was fairly severe, there were attacks coming from all sides, to a certain extent it wasn't him personally but it had come to the point where [we asked,] "What would it be like during an election campaign, how would he cope with this, and what were the prospects?"'

And then, just as Martin was beginning to agitate, Cowen was dealt another devastating blow. On Sunday 9 January 2011, three days before the Dáil returned, Tom Lyons and Brian Carey of *The Sunday Times* revealed Cowen's 2008 game of golf with Seán FitzPatrick and the subsequent dinner at Druids Glen. The opposition immediately went on the attack. The story helped to strengthen the perception that the controversial bank guarantee was a bailout by Fianna Fáil for their developer and banking friends. Cowen, already battered and bruised, teetered ever closer to the edge. The following day, Monday, Martin met with Cowen in the taoiseach's office to tell him he thought he should resign. 'I went privately to meet Brian, and I put that view to him that was there.'

It was to be a rare thing in politics: a courteous, acrimony-free party split. Martin recounts that he said to Cowen: 'I'm no messiah,' and that he did not have all the answers. 'I don't think it was anything to do with you, Brian, in some respects. I think this is because of the extraordinary economic crisis that we are in, the bailout situation that has happened. We've done all the heavy lifting on the economy … that has to be done, the budget and all the rest of it.'

Cowen recalls the meeting and gives his account of a discussion that was to throw Fianna Fáil into conflict. 'He said he wanted to see me. And he saw me and he made the point … that it was a question of having a different leader [of Fianna Fáil] and I'd stay on as taoiseach.' Cowen says he dismissed the idea. 'I said I don't think that is sensible. So obviously he had made up his mind to challenge for the leadership, and in fairness we conducted that well, it wasn't personally bitter or anything like that. If he wanted to challenge for the leadership there is a process and "you challenge for it".'

There were no histrionics from the two men, different characters but lifelong party men. Cowen was polite says Martin: 'He was very nice about it and we discussed it. He thanked me.'

Martin, having made his point to Cowen, decided to stay quiet for the time being about the face-to-face showdown. 'I didn't go public, I told nobody, I didn't even tell the TDs who had come to me, and I left it at that.' Martin offered his own resignation but it was not accepted. 'And then the following week the febrile stuff started. I didn't actually lobby anybody or do anything at that stage. TDs came back [from the break] and there was all the usual – when TDs come back into this place the rumour machine starts.'

He wasn't the only one contemplating a challenge. Two days after Martin's meeting with Cowen, word spread among the taoiseach's supporters that a Lenihan heave was underway. It rippled through the Dáil bar that a meeting of Lenihan-supporting rebels was taking place in Buswells Hotel. The meeting, which has since achieved urban myth status, never happened. Two meeting rooms, one in Buswells and one in the Shelbourne Hotel, had been booked by national executive member Jerry Beades, following conversations with McGuinness and Lenihan. Beades was an outspoken critic of Cowen. At the last minute, on Lenihan's orders, the meeting was cancelled. 'He got windy again,' according to Beades.

Even though the meeting had been axed, the news that something was afoot added to the strained and chaotic atmosphere around the Cowen government. Martin had no involvement in this strange incident: 'To this day I can't fathom it. I'm told it was [a] phantom meeting that was called deliberately to create the climate of you know [confusion].'

The following morning, Lenihan was at Stormont in Belfast. A Fianna Fáil party meeting was postponed from 11.30 a.m. to 3 p.m. Given how far his stock had fallen, and with a mood of open rebellion in the air, speculation mounted that the taoiseach would step down. Having received regular updates all morning, Lenihan quickly returned to Dublin in the belief Cowen was about to resign and that he would then be free to make his move. He had failed to initiate a heave against Cowen on several occasions, but were the leader to remove himself, then he would be prepared to go forward. By the time he arrived back in Dublin and walked into the party meeting, his mind had changed. A bullish Cowen faced his colleagues, urging them to stay the course. He was staying. He was clinging on, Lenihan realised. The finance minister once again had to suppress his own ambitions.

As TDs left Dublin for home that Thursday, Cowen knew his position was precarious. He held a press conference on Sunday 16 January and, flanked by Mary Coughlan and John Curran, said that he would hold a motion of confidence in his leadership at a Fianna Fáil parliamentary party meeting the following Tuesday.

Within minutes of that press conference, Martin held a separate press conference nearby to announce he would not be supporting the taoiseach and said a change of leader was required. For so many years Martin had been characterised as a ditherer. 'Indecisive, that is Micheál's biggest problem, he can't make a decision and won't make a decision and he analyses everything to the point of almost having to bring in a consultant to analyse his analysis,' says Pat Carey. At this critical stage, he showed his mettle.

In an instant, Lenihan, who for so long had been the front runner to succeed Cowen, found himself out-manoeuvred. He also had another problem since the bailout: Fianna Fáil TDs were becoming increasingly exasperated with Lenihan on nuts-and-bolts issues and they believed that he had an inability to level with them or tell them the full truth. There was a breakdown in trust after many felt he misled them on a matter during the budget in December – the extent of the controversial universal social charge (USC).

Lenihan had portrayed the USC as a mere merging of existing levies and assured TDs that there would be no additional charge to people. But when it was realised that the rates would in fact be higher and applied to so many low-paid workers, TDs and senators felt betrayed. John McGuinness recalls: 'We were told it was not going to be higher anyway – just one single description for payments that were coming out. And the opposite was the case, but we were sent out to sell that whole USC thing and the rest is history.'

Dara Calleary's anger over the USC is palpable. 'Brian Lenihan was in his element trying to describe it all as no major changes. Just a merging of the health levy, PRSI. Then it kicks home at the end of January, as we were out canvassing. I actually believe the USC cleaned us: the USC cleaned us in Dublin. I think the USC cost us between ten and fifteen seats,' he fumes. 'Brian always sugared things, Brian could always deliver bad news with sugar. And you know, and as we all pointed out subsequently, he continued to do that in terms of the USC.'

Calleary also accepts that Lenihan's options were limited given how poor the public finances were. 'Equally, we are responsible. We knew in our hearts, we knew it had to be something horrible. And then you go out and it's carnage. It might as well have been called a Troika tax.'

On Tuesday 18 January, the day Fianna Fáil would vote on Cowen's leadership, Lenihan ruined his leadership hopes and his political credibility during a radio interview with Seán O'Rourke on RTÉ. On air to discuss the internal wrangling in Fianna Fáil, Lenihan was forced by his interviewer to deny he had been agitating against his leader. He declared he would be backing Cowen. 'I haven't had time to organise a coup, I have been in the engine room,' he protested on air when asked had he been orchestrating a move against his leader.

John McGuinness, unbeknown to Lenihan, was waiting on another phone line listening to this. He had been asked to follow Lenihan on a separate issue. 'So he [Lenihan] came on and one of the questions Seán O'Rourke asked was "Was he canvassing for the leadership of Fianna Fáil, had he an interest?" And he immediately said [impersonating Lenihan] "No, No, No". You know the way Lenihan says,' McGuinness recalls of Lenihan's interview.

McGuinness was gobsmacked that Lenihan could so casually dismiss their campaign. 'He was gone then and I couldn't believe what I was hearing. So when I was questioned by Seán O'Rourke after Lenihan I had to say, "That's not true." He did encourage dissent, he did encourage us to look at the numbers.

'The way he presented it to us was that he was interested, that he was canvassing, that he was gauging support for himself. So I completely contradicted Brian Lenihan. But I couldn't let it go, otherwise the backbenchers who were happy to support Brian Lenihan and talked to me about it, I would have let them down. They might have felt that I was telling a lie, when in fact he was telling a lie. Because the *Evening Herald* had written that day – "Brian Lenihan liar liar".'

Lenihan, naively, had been caught out. 'People said that I rang in, but I didn't, he rang in because of a different reason altogether and got caught in the crossfire,' claims McGuinness. 'So there was that naivety about him that we could all play that game of smoke and mirrors and the facts didn't matter, you could bend them and twist them. I suppose that's his barrister's training, you know, presenting different sides of the case.'

With only hours to the crunch meeting, Lenihan's credibility was shot. Conor Lenihan concedes that his brother had made a mistake in speaking on the radio. 'If my brother had stayed silent as opposed to giving positive support for Brian Cowen by way of a media interview, then that motion may in fact have succeeded.'

Conor also says that a failure of his brother and Martin to co-ordinate efforts meant Cowen's chances of holding on as leader were strengthened in those critical hours before the vote. 'There were enough people there but they weren't prepared to [go against Cowen] on the basis purely that Micheál Martin was involved rather than my brother. I had spoken to Brian about combining with Micheál Martin but obviously there was some difficulty between Brian's and Micheál Martin's part to co-ordinate what they were doing. It might have led to a different result had either party had the foresight to talk to each other and informally co-ordinate their activities.'

Others agree that things got very chaotic, which bolstered the position of the leader. 'It just got messy at that stage between them all within government,' says Mary O'Rourke. 'Was Brian Lenihan going or was Micheál Martin going? All the TDs were getting edgy. First of all they were going to lose their seats, well, three-quarters of them. So it all got messy. Brian Lenihan was going through it all and was telling me stuff. At the last minute, Brian seemed to pull back and not run.'

As party members gathered for the crunch meeting, they were faced with a stark choice. Cowen had called a vote of confidence in his leadership, which meant it was a Yes or No vote. It wasn't a choice between Cowen and Martin. Many felt they had to be loyal to the leader, even at this late stage. In politics, uncertainty is a killer and the lack of a Martin–Lenihan pact stymied the anti-Cowen charge. Cowen did not repeat the mistake of British prime minister Margaret Thatcher in her time of crisis – he personally canvassed in advance of the vote. 'I met everyone and spoke to everyone,' he says.

One of those whom Cowen contacted was his old friend Willie O'Dea, the man he had watched resign a year earlier. 'Cowen rang me himself and he said, "What do you think? Be honest with me."'

O'Dea replied, "'I'll be absolutely honest with you, I think you should go." He thanked me for my views and that was it.'

O'Dea didn't really see the purpose of the strategy. 'It was like a bloody wagon train, and yer man wants to go the shortest route through with the wagon train and there's 57,000 Indians up there on the hill.'

Billy Kelleher stood by the view that his fellow Corkman Martin would be the best person to replace Cowen. 'I just felt that there was no way we could have campaigned with Brian Cowen as leader of Fianna Fáil. Going into the election, I just thought that there was too much drift. [The ability] to actually mount a campaign was evaporating before my eyes.'

As the meeting began, Cowen stood up to address his party. 'The taoiseach spoke and outlined the whole lot. Then Micheál Martin spoke and outlined no confidence in him and told him he could no longer continue with him,' recalls Kelleher. Cowen sought to defend his actions, saying he was attempting to do the right thing by the country, even if it was at the expense of the party's fortunes.

Kelleher took to his feet: 'I think I was the first person [who spoke against the taoiseach staying on] to stand up at that parliamentary party meeting. I said in the interests of the party and the country he should go. That he was no longer tenable, and I would not have liked to have said it because I would have been friendly with Brian Cowen for many years. At that stage you had to do what you thought was right. The party was in disarray, the government was in flitters, we were facing into a general election. So for all those reasons I said he should go. And I expressed no confidence in him that night.'

In past heaves against Charlie Haughey, the issue of a secret ballot became a contentious one. That was not the case here. Cowen had learned from the bloodletting and vengefulness of that period and felt the damage it had done to Fianna Fáil. He wanted no repeat of that now. 'I had put down a motion of confidence and I wanted a secret ballot. I would have voted for secret ballots myself in previous times. I'd no problem with secret ballots, people didn't have to do anything except vote for me if they wanted to vote for me.' Ultimately, Cowen had the support of his colleagues. 'And I won the leadership and that was it,' he says.

Cowen has been praised in Fianna Fáil for putting aside sectional interests and sacrificing the good of his party to help position Ireland on a path to recovery. We put this to him. 'I'd like to have been able to do both,' he says, laughing quietly. 'There's a quote by Frank Aiken that I mentioned at a parliamentary party meeting one time because it sort of encapsulated my view, given the size of the difficulty we were contending with, and that was "the party is important but the state is paramount".'

Mary O'Rourke admonishes herself and others for supporting Cowen in that vote. 'There was war, that's right. Cowen then called a vote and won the vote quite handsomely. But what was the vote?' she asks rhetorically. 'It was a secret ballot and it wasn't a Cowen-versus-Martin or a Cowen-versus-Lenihan, it was Cowen "my leadership" and we followed him. We all voted for Cowen. I remember trooping in, marching in to vote and voting for Cowen. You see we followed him to the end … When I think of it now, what was I doing?'

Cowen held the support of the middle ground of the parliamentary party, and this saw him win the vote of confidence. Just after 9 p.m. he emerged victorious.

Billy Kelleher could see how the gravity of events was weighing on Cowen. 'There is no doubt that there was huge pressure on him in terms of what he had been through … the country was teetering on the edge.'

A short time later Martin resigned from the Cabinet with immediate effect, but did so without rancour. Speaking to reporters on the plinth, Martin said, 'One has to make a stand. I came to my personal conclusion after Christmas that a certain course of action had to be taken. One has to make a stand. One has to force the issue. It has been a very healthy debate and good debate.'

Speaking to us about how the vote affected his relationship with Cowen, Martin says the debate took place without the bitterness that had marked so many previous battles in Fianna Fáil. 'We kept in contact. I felt, given what I had said and done, that I couldn't support [him]. And then I felt that you couldn't stay on as minister in good faith. In fairness to him, he didn't want me to resign. And he contacted me and asked that I wouldn't resign when I announced that I was voting against him,' he says. 'And I think that most people in the parliamentary party were relieved by how that was conducted because it was a very gentlemanly event. I had no stomach for any divisive campaign or anything like that.

'You know, looking back on it you would have some misgivings about it. Would you have done certain things differently? I think certainly I was motivated by a sense of what the moderate ground were saying to me. That something had to change.' With his resignation, Martin was out of Cabinet for the first time in fourteen years.

The day after the vote, the Wednesday, Cowen was in great form, and joviality returned to the Dáil for a brief moment. When Enda Kenny said that a Labour Party motion of no confidence in the government was 'ill-judged and ill-timed', Cowen threw his arms back and bellowed, 'I couldn't agree more', then beamed upwards at the press gallery.

Though this victory kept him in the leadership, there was still a general election coming. Government Buildings had assumed something of the atmosphere of Saigon as the Americans pulled out. 'I felt really this was only a matter of time, people were cleaning out offices and gathering envelopes,' says Pat Carey. 'I arrived in one day and all I could hear was shredding going on, right along the bloody corridor, the ministerial corridor. I looked out and there was Noel Dempsey's office churning documents at a great rate.

'Éamon Ó Cuiv was in the office next to me and he said, "This is the end." And Tony Killeen and I used to laugh we were only around a wet weekend and they were writing us off already.'

Then came an extraordinary event in Irish political history. Even at this eleventh hour, with his government in disarray, but emboldened from his victory the night before, Cowen decided he would undertake a major reshuffle of his Cabinet. From early that Wednesday morning, the taoiseach made it clear he wanted to exercise his prerogative to appoint people to Cabinet positions, given the number of retiring ministers. The two government parties met in Government Buildings early for an hour and a half. Cowen was flanked by Chief Whip John Curran and Minister for Defence Tony Killeen. John Gormley came in with Eamon Ryan and Dan Boyle.

'At the meeting there was talk of legislation and Brian Cowen, after having succeeded in the vote against Micheál Martin, had drafted something along the lines of "we are thinking of doing a Cabinet reshuffle",' says Eamon Ryan. 'I said, "How could you possibly go to the Park with new ministers? That is not credible."'

Cowen said he wanted to refresh his government front bench. He pressed his desire for a reshuffle and mentioned Micheál Martin and three ministers who had announced their intention not to stand in the election – Dermot Ahern, Noel Dempsey and Tony Killeen. They would be replaced by younger Fianna Fáil TDs.

'The Greens were not overly enthusiastic about the idea,' says Killeen. Gormley and Ryan raised two main objections. The first was that this was a cynical 'jobs for the boys' exercise. The second was that it would be seen as a blatant attempt to prolong the life of the government. Cowen believes he was entitled to take the action. 'I said, "John, some of our lads won't be standing and I need to change the Cabinet."'

There was no mention of Mary Harney or Batt O'Keeffe, even though Cowen knew both wanted to go. Harney has told us that when Cowen formed his government in May 2008, she informed the new taoiseach that it was her intention to retire in mid-2010. 'I had actually intended on standing down from the government around then but because of all that was happening I just felt I couldn't … my plan always was to step down sometime around the middle of 2010. I thought that the government was going to last until close to 2012, which wasn't to happen as it transpired subsequently.'

So Cowen, aware of Harney's desire to resign, then requested she do so that night. 'We were coming into an election and Brian Cowen had said that people not running in the election shouldn't stay in Cabinet,' she says. 'I'll tell you what happened – he was going to demand of his own party people that they would stand down, and I felt that I couldn't, with any sense of honour, stay on when I know I'm not running in the election either.'

She thought the reshuffle was not wise. 'That was his decision – I think it was an error. I don't think at that stage the government had, or he had as taoiseach, the authority to be nominating new members of the government. But, however, it was his wish.'

John Gormley later recalled his reaction to the taoiseach's plan. He said he was not aware that the taoiseach intended to press ahead with the reshuffle after the meeting. 'We were told that Cowen was taking Martin's duties, and that it would be left at that. We had no idea about the other resignations and then it was presented to us as a *fait accompli* almost,' he told journalist Mary Minihan for her book *A Deal with the Devil: The Green Party in Government.*

Ryan, with subtle understatement, describes the episode as 'inelegant'. 'Subsequently it was messy, very messy, inelegant to say the least. So that evening in the Dáil, Mary Harney resigns. And it was just, feck it, where did that come from? We did not think it was going ahead.'

The word was out in Leinster House that Cowen was planning a reshuffle. Yet many still didn't believe it.

Billy Kelleher now knew the plan would go ahead and he had had enough. 'I rang Micheál Martin and said I am tendering my resignation.' Martin urged him not to, but Kelleher persisted. 'I feel I have no choice. I have expressed no confidence in the taoiseach and I must tender my resignation … I cannot serve with him or I can't serve at his behest if I have no confidence in him.'

Martin said that others would have to follow his lead and if he went he would cause huge difficulties. He told Kelleher: 'Mary Hanafin has also expressed strong views about the taoiseach in terms of confidence. And if you resign she will have to resign and that will bring the whole government down.'

Kelleher was conflicted and decided to meet the taoiseach. 'So Tuesday I thought about it and on Wednesday evening I went across and met the taoiseach at around five o'clock and I handed him my resignation.' Cowen apparently said, 'Don't do it Billy, I won't accept it. Give me twenty-four hours. Don't do it now, Christ, the whole thing is under huge pressure.'

The odd encounter ended without Kelleher's resignation being accepted. 'He just asked me not to do it, he said tear it [the resignation letter] up,' says Kelleher. The junior minister, shaken by the encounter, left the taoiseach's office and walked across the

Leinster House courtyard, known as the plinth, out the gate and across Kildare Street to the splendid art deco building that is the Department of Trade and Industry. 'I put the letter up on the desk,' he says. Soon afterwards he retraced his tracks and headed for Leinster House. In this most oppressive of times Kelleher needed a drink. 'And I actually bumped into the taoiseach again, it was half-past six and we had a chat together. I know there were other TDs around also in the members' bar. We had a pint. There were not that many in the bar at the time.'

The two men sipped pints of lager. Cowen did not refer to the earlier unpleasantness, able, as always, to compartmentalise. 'He did not mention it, he said nothing,' says Kelleher. 'He said, "Look lads, I will see you later." I think he had something on in Ferbane in Offaly. And then some time later rumours went around of a bad reshuffle and the whole announcement of ministerial resignations started taking place.'

Mary Harney announced her resignation at 9 p.m. John Gormley claimed he passed Harney in the corridor at around the same time and she didn't mention her impending departure. Gormley said he heard about it when his wife, Penny, told him it had just been on the TV news.

Batt O'Keeffe had handed Cowen his resignation at 10.30 p.m., but his departure would not be confirmed until the following morning. Then, at 11 p.m., the resignations of Dermot Ahern, Noel Dempsey and Tony Killeen were announced.

Cowen had gone to Offaly for a local theatre event and, there, he made a series of phone calls. Junior Minister Barry Andrews received a phone call from Cowen after midnight to discuss a potential Cabinet position – it was inconclusive.

'Sure enough the ministers were going to go and there was going to be a reshuffle,' says Kelleher, 'and later on that night, around half eleven, Batt O'Keeffe rang me and said, "Where are you? I heard you were going to resign, you have not resigned have you?"

'No, I haven't Batt.' But he told O'Keeffe that he had intended on resigning. O'Keeffe, though one of the taoiseach's closest friends, was as confused by the fast-moving events as everybody else.

Kelleher told O'Keeffe, 'There are rumours you are all resigning.' O'Keeffe told Kelleher not to do anything 'stupid'.

But events were developing rapidly. 'Then another TD rang me and said that the taoiseach was making appointments to a new Cabinet and it was highly likely that you were going to get a call.' Embattled, yet seemingly emboldened, Cowen clung to the hope that the usual electoral rules applied and that a group of fresh faces in Cabinet roles would give Fianna Fáil a boost.

'So I was a bit disbelieving but it seems to have been the case. There was a high chance I was going to be approached to become a minister,' says Kelleher. 'There were rumours going around that I might get a ministry because Micheál Martin had resigned, Batt O'Keeffe was gone and I think I was the only minister of state in Cork at that stage. So there would have been no Cabinet minister in Cork going into an election, that would not be a great thing. But there were discussions with the Green Party at the present time that were not going too well.'

Cowen was lining up junior ministers, and even TDs, to move into the Cabinet roles. Dara Calleary was told by Cowen on Thursday morning that he was not being considered: 'I got a phone call at 7.30 a.m. that morning, I wasn't going in. He acknowledged the work I had done … the usual sort of stuff, you are going to be an important part of the team.' Calleary is not sure what he would have done if he had been offered a post. 'I don't know … what could you do in six weeks when four weeks of the six weeks are going to be focused on a general election campaign?'

Conor Lenihan was the most vocal opponent of the plan. 'And then we had this ridiculous situation which just robbed Cowen of any shred of credibility,' he recalls. 'He announced or started ringing people from the taoiseach's office offering them ministerial jobs. In fact one of my colleagues came up to me in the Dáil bar on the night in question and said, "I have been offered your job." I thought it was slightly hilarious and funny because at that time so much credibility had been lost in this particular government that many people were not prepared to accept an appointment as a minister from the backbenches because they felt that it would do more damage to them in the election than being an ordinary deputy.'

Conor best illustrates the madness that seemed to have gripped the entire Oireachtas that evening. 'As it happened on the night I had a friend in with me in the Dáil who had actually just gone through a divorce and I was sort of counselling a little bit on how to handle his marital breakdown issues. I was in the visitor's bar counselling this chap. I went back to the member's bar for some reason that escapes me. I ran into Eamon Ryan in the visitor's bar and he said "Have you heard about this reshuffle thing?"'

Conor answered, 'No, I haven't, but obviously you are not serious.'

Ryan said, 'Oh yeah, the taoiseach is up there ringing people.'

Conor replied, 'This is off the wall. This is just a nightmare.'

Eamon then asked him, 'Do you think we should support this reshuffle?'

The junior minister replied: 'If you want my candid opinion I think it is complete and utter madness to even attempt a reshuffle at this late stage in the government's life. If I were in your shoes, as a coalition partner, I would put the kibosh on any such idea.'

What Cowen would have said if he became aware of this conversation at the time can only be imagined.

It truly was surreal. 'Half of us were hoping that we would be fired, myself included, as I had been somewhat dissenting in my approach to a number of things, however obliquely,' says Conor. 'We were all hoping that we would be sacked because that would then give us some possibility of getting elected. But the whole thing in general was regarded as a piece of madness.'

Cowen had assumed Micheál Martin's duties temporarily since his resignation. The Departments of Foreign Affairs, Health, Justice, Enterprise and Employment, Transport, and Defence were now without Cabinet ministers.

John Gormley still hadn't been briefed on what was going on. Cowen awoke to a curt phone call from Gormley at 7 a.m. On *Morning Ireland*, the Green Party's Paul Gogarty dismissed the reshuffle idea as 'crazy'. The Greens were totally opposed to replacing the six departed ministers.

'They were questioning my right to do what I wanted to do. What I was doing wasn't affecting the Green Party,' says Cowen.

At 9.30 a.m. on Thursday it was leaked that Batt O'Keeffe was also resigning his Cabinet post. Mary Coughlan was in charge of the Order of Business. Pat Carey was there that morning: 'I suspect I was [ordered to be] there because they needed two or three bodies to fill the benches. I think it had also gotten to the stage that the opposition had begun to make fun of Mary Coughlan and were not going to treat her like a serious politician.'

Faced with the tánaiste, Enda Kenny immediately demanded that the taoiseach appear in the Chamber: 'It is a cowardly, disgraceful act of the taoiseach … in refusing to come in here today to tell the people of his country what is happening with a government that has imploded, is dysfunctional, has disintegrated and let our people down.' He also pointed out that there were no Green TDs in the House.

When we put it to Cowen that disorder broke out in the Dáil, he blamed the lack of pragmatism of the Green Party. 'Because, unfortunately, they had sort of indicated to me around half eight or a quarter to nine that morning that they had a problem [with the reshuffle] … I said, "What do you mean you have a problem with it? It's not your problem."'

In that early morning phone call, Gormley had frantically told Cowen, 'We've to go in and vote on this.'

Cowen answered, 'Of course you have, the same as if you were making changes we'd go in and vote for your man, or woman, or whoever it was.'

Even with distance, Cowen does not see why the Green Party was cracking. Laughing wryly again, he asks incredulously, 'What's the issue here? … I couldn't understand what they were doing.'

Those of us who worked in Leinster House for those madcap hours remember an unprecedented feeling of chaos and drift among politicians. Perhaps to his credit, Cowen was the only man not cracking under the pressure.

Back in the Dáil, Coughlan tried to say that the resignations weren't confirmed until they had been handed to the president, but she was shouted down. The Dáil had to be adjourned.

Gormley then told Cowen that the reshuffle could not take place and demanded that he name the date of the election. If he didn't, the Green Party was pulling out of government. With the reshuffle idea dead, the Greens were asked if they would support appointments to the key ministries of health and justice, given their legal and financial importance. They said they were not willing to accept that proposal and they were pulling out of government.

Preparations were made for a press conference to announce they were going. Amid the chaos, the Dáil was suspended until 1.30 p.m., at which stage the taoiseach was to make a statement.

Shortly before the Dáil was due to resume after its two-hour break, Gormley and Ryan had a third and final meeting with Cowen. In addition to securing a veto on new appointments, they were given a date for the general election. Gormley's earlier suggestion that the resignations be rescinded was no longer possible and it was then that the option of doubling up ministries came on the table.

All of this happened only minutes before Cowen entered the Dáil at 1.30 p.m. He announced that the six vacant positions at Cabinet would be assigned to existing ministers, and that the election would be on 11 March. He had been forced into a humiliating climbdown and had had to re-allocate the portfolios to the ministers who stayed on. Since Martin had stepped down, Cowen held the foreign affairs portfolio as well as being taoiseach. Brendan Smith became agriculture and justice minister; Mary Coughlan was education and health minister; Éamon Ó Cuiv was social protection and defence minister; Mary Hanafin was sports, enterprise and employment minister; and Pat Carey became transport and community, equality and Gaeltacht affairs minister.

Lenihan was left at Finance. According to Carey, not much science was applied to the allocation of portfolios. 'It was in order that basic housekeeping be done. I got Noel Dempsey's Transport because his office was across the ministerial corridor to mine and why did I get Eamon Ryan's [when Ryan resigned]? It was next door. So I had a vague idea of what had been going on previously.'

The absence of the Greens from the Dáil Chamber was stark.

When Cowen finished speaking the Dáil broke up again. For all the political tension and soaring egos in Leinster House, normally disagreements are unfailingly kept in offices and party rooms. On this occasion the entire personnel of the government benches burst through the main doors of the Chamber and congregated on the landing, ending up directly under the huge painting of the 1919 Dáil. The entire press corps came out of the press gallery at the same time. They stood and watched as Brian Lenihan, Conor Lenihan, Micheál Martin and others talked animatedly, the chagrin showing in their faces. Others shouted and gesticulated. 'Go back to your constituencies and canvass,' were Brian Lenihan's parting words as the group broke up. The tension in the air was palpable. The government was visibly unravelling before our eyes.

At 5 p.m., at a press conference in the Merrion Hotel, John Gormley and Eamon Ryan emphatically stated their opposition to the idea of a reshuffle.

Within two days of Cowen winning a motion of confidence from his parliamentary party, Martin was being urged to move again. 'He had been in a strong enough position coming out of the parliamentary party with a vote of confidence, but unfortunately that created its own firestorm,' says Martin. 'I understand it, politically; he was advised that this could create a fresh beginning, for new ministers to face the electorate. But of course the firestorm was enormous, the Greens balked big time … and it was inevitable then that people were going to resign.

'And then we had the election for leadership and I declared I was going to go for it, and my only motivation was back to what the TDs had said to me: "Somebody has got to go." The land was quite doomsdayish, this wasn't an anti-Brian Cowen thing. People were saying, "Like, Micheál, our forefathers fought to establish this party. You've got to look at reality: you've got to do something to save the edifice, to save something." Everyone felt they were facing electoral doom at that stage.'

The government was on life support with a view to getting the Finance Bill through the Dáil. Overtures were made, says Pat Carey, to Fine Gael and Labour, to shore up enough support to pass the bill through the House. Cowen went to Armagh on government business on Friday. When he'd finished, he did not return to Dublin but went straight to Tullamore to talk to his family. He knew his credibility and authority were gone. Still there was loyalty but Cowen was finally coming to accept reality.

'We had a history and that history with the party is one of great loyalty to the serving leader of the day,' says Conor Lenihan. 'My father very much believed in that notion of supporting the leader of the day. I, unfortunately, believed that this whole innate concept of loyalty to the leader is a flawed concept and has led to a certain extent to Fianna Fáil's demise in recent years because that absolute loyalty shouldn't be absolutely given. Certainly at that point in time we would have been much better positioned as a party if we had changed our leader at an earlier point.'

A press release went out to newsrooms at around 1 p.m. on Saturday 22 January to announce that the taoiseach would hold a 2 p.m. press conference at the Merrion Hotel. There could only be one possible subject for discussion. Such was the importance of the event, RTÉ decided to break from its regular programming to broadcast the press conference. Cowen, flanked by his wife, Mary, Tánaiste Mary Coughlan and Chief Whip John Curran, resigned as leader of Fianna Fáil but said he would stay on as taoiseach until 11 March, which he said would be the election date. (That date would change.) 'Therefore, taking everything into account, after discussing the matter with my family, I have taken, on my own counsel, the decision to step down,' he told the assembled media. 'At this crucial time the focus should be on policies of parties and not on personalities.'

With Cowen's exit now confirmed, Martin immediately became the clear front runner to take the poisoned chalice that the Fianna Fáil leadership had become. He was also the first to announce his intention to stand. 'I will be putting my name forward before the party,' he said from his home in Cork. 'Over the next couple of days, I will be entering into discussions with my colleagues and setting out my vision for the party and for the country.'

Within hours of Cowen's resignation, it became clear that Brian Lenihan, Éamon Ó Cuiv and Mary Hanafin were also to enter a contest which was to be held the following Wednesday. However, it was all the more clear that Martin had stolen a march by being the first heavyweight to publicly challenge Cowen before Tuesday's vote of confidence in the taoiseach. By Saturday night ministers Peter Power and Seán Haughey and TDs Seán Power, Michael Ahern, Michael Fitzpatrick, Noel O'Flynn, Chris Andrews, Timmy Dooley, Billy Kelleher, Michael McGrath, John O'Donoghue, Ned O'Keeffe, Michael Mulcahy, Seán Ardagh and Willie O'Dea had all declared their support for Martin in advance of a vote for the new leader.

The Greens held their own press conference on Sunday night. In the wake of Cowen's decision to resign, John Gormley finally announced that the Green Party was to pull out of government but would support the Finance Bill to give effect to the measures announced in Budget 2011. Gormley said the 'ongoing saga' in relation to the Fianna Fáil leadership had been a total distraction from the business of government and was still not resolved. 'The Irish people have begun to lose confidence in politics and in the political process.' Always an evocative wordsmith, he expressed the feelings of many: 'The Irish people ... have watched aghast the conduct in Dáil Éireann of political parties ... The Irish people expect and deserve better ... I am proud of our many achievements in the areas of planning, renewable energy, energy standards of buildings, water conservation and other environmental areas.'

Although Martin was now the man to beat, Lenihan was still adamant that he could play his El Cid role. At his own press conference at the upmarket Westin Hotel in Dublin, he said that he believed he could 'maximise' the party's vote, remembering Charlie Haughey's old trick of connecting himself with as much of the country as possible. 'I'm a Dublin-based deputy from a family who originated in the midlands and the west. I have strong connections with the whole of Ireland,' he said. 'I have discussed the matter with Micheál Martin and, of course, we will accept the result and work together for the good of the party.' He also downplayed his health troubles, insisting his doctors had cleared him to compete and that he was more than up to the job. But everyone in the room knew his day was gone and he was a beaten docket.

The deadline for nominations closed at 1 p.m. on 24 January, and the new leader was elected at a special Fianna Fáil parliamentary party meeting on 26 January. When the votes were finally cast, Martin was elected as the party's eighth leader, winning on the third count with fifty votes. With just eighteen votes, Lenihan finished third behind Ó Cuiv, having been eliminated in the second round. It has been suggested that, in a final act of vengeance, Cowen's team ensured that their support would go to Ó Cuiv in order to humiliate Lenihan.

With the election won, the new leader was then left with a matter of days to organise a general election campaign. The once mighty Fianna Fáil election machine was a pitiful sight. 'The campaign itself, I just threw the kitchen sink at it personally, knowing …' Martin trails off. 'The issue was how many seats could we save. And I had very little time, days I think – we had to try to get TDs to stand down, get people to switch constituencies. Like we couldn't get a high-profile person to go into Dublin South. We felt that would have gotten the 16% or 17%.'

There were efforts to get Mary Hanafin or Barry Andrews to move from Dun Laoghaire to Dublin South. 'No one would move,' says Martin. 'Poor Conor Lenihan was even contemplating [moving out of Dublin South-West]; we asked him and he said yeah, and then he came back and said no. Conor would have won in Dublin South. Anywhere we had two in Dublin we were saying, "Lads, you're going to split the vote."'

The election was eventually held on 27 February 2011. Amid the chaos the Greens couldn't hang on until 11 March. Fianna Fáil faced a wipe-out in Dublin, where only Brian Lenihan was returned. Cowen was not to stand again. He watched his brother Barry take the seat he had held for twenty-seven years.

The election delivered a historic defeat for Fianna Fáil, which lost fifty-seven seats, coming back with just twenty. Fine Gael and Labour were the big winners, coming back with 113 seats between them. They went on to form a government with the largest Dáil majority in history.

Ultimately, Cowen says, his decision to resign was driven by the final, chaotic revolt of the Greens over his planned reshuffle. 'I just felt that's it for me, my authority has been undermined. I was constitutionally entitled to do what I was doing. People might have a view about the timing of it and all the rest of it or the personalities, that's their own business. I was left in a position where I couldn't do what I wanted to do: you can't lead a government on that basis.'

Cowen, reflecting on the defeat for his party, is pragmatic. 'There comes sometimes a point where the party has to take a hit or there is a hit coming that can't be avoided.' He believes that Fianna Fáil could not avoid the catastrophe.

He insists that the actions he and his government took, while deeply unpopular, saved the country. 'Certainly I would have hoped that it was not as hard as it was, but there was no political capital to be gained in doing what we had to do. There is no doubt that for the state to continue, for us to have some prospects of recovery, I'm absolutely convinced that we were on the right track.'

Cowen continues to be active with Fianna Fáil in his constituency, and has taken on a number of company directorships, including Topaz and the Beacon Hospital. He is relieved that his Banking Inquiry evidence was well received. He appears happier in himself these days. But still, we asked him if he misses politics. 'Not as much as I thought I would. I think having been in the top position there is no real role for you after that. I saw Garret FitzGerald do an extra term, I saw Albert Reynolds do an extra term and we don't have the tradition in Ireland really for people of that calibre to stay on in politics and, if you like, give their view without it being interpreted as "oh you're having a cut at the new fella". When what you have to say won't be accepted on face value there is not much point in hanging around. You'd like to have the freedom of making your contribution. I just felt, for myself … there is no future for me on the backbenches because I have seen other former taoisigh not being afforded that opportunity.'

Cowen decided to do what a former Fine Gael taoiseach had

done. 'So I said, "step out". I'm of what I call the Liam Cosgrave school of retirement. Step back.'

Most politicians, when reflecting on an end to their career, do so with bitterness. Cowen, who had the most tumultuous term in office of any taoiseach, is rancour-free. 'I had no complaints. I wasn't leaving upset with anybody. The people had spoken, no problem. My relationships with all my former colleagues were good: my relationship with the present leader [Micheál Martin] is good. I have no adverse comment to make. I only try to be helpful whenever I can be, locally here at constituency level. There is absolutely no animus.'

Cowen had a long and distinguished career in Cabinet before the dramatic denouement. 'I had a good career, I can't complain with the level of responsibility I was given by two other taoisigh and I'm just grateful for the opportunity to serve.'

He was at the helm when the economy came crashing down and he did not shirk responsibility for that throughout his discussions with us. But he also believes he left a legacy. 'Yes, my taoiseach term was a difficult time but I think over time people are maybe realising that we did get through that period, that what we did was part of the necessary recovery.'

He believes there was a basis for recovery left for the Fine Gael and Labour coalition that followed.

'And that government has done commendably well,' Cowen concludes.

Epilogue

Fianna Fáil, the party of power for the best part of eighty-four years, was decimated in the 2011 general election. The party's national vote had collapsed from 41.6% to 17.4% in four years. The party lost fifty-eight of its seventy-eight seats in the Dáil. Fianna Fáil had not a single female TD. It had just one deputy, Brian Lenihan, in Dublin. The Soldiers of Destiny were on the brink of extinction.

Brian Cowen emerged from the wreckage a private citizen, and he told us, 'As a committed democrat I accept the judgement of the people on the performance of the government I led, which was a pretty damning judgement really.'

He became something of a pariah figure. All the justifiable anger of citizens seemed to be focused on him. He believes that history will be kinder to him as the anger subsides. 'But over time maybe people will see the nature of the difficulties we were dealing with,' he says, 'and I think the most important duty of any person when they are in government is, you have to be prepared to make whatever decisions are necessary for the time you're there. And I always felt that we certainly couldn't be accused of taking the short-term view, we certainly couldn't be accused of trying to save the party at the expense of the country.' Cowen remained a member of the party, unlike his predecessor, Bertie Ahern, who resigned in 2012 in the wake of the publication of the Mahon Tribunal.

Micheál Martin became the eighth leader of Fianna Fáil. 'It was the worst defeat in the party's electoral history,' he said of the 2011 election, in 2015, after a revival of the party's fortunes, which had seen it secure 25% of the vote in the previous year's local elections.

He watched the former minister for finance struggle through the harsh February 2011 election. 'Brian Lenihan did his damnedest, you know. He would come in every morning and want to do press conferences. And we were worried at that stage, because he was certainly under physical pressure, but he loved the idea of coming in to head a press conference.'

Former tánaiste and Progressive Democrats TD Mary Harney left the Dáil for good. Asked whether she pined for politics, she said, 'No, I follow it intensely but I don't miss it that much.' She told us on the day after her Banking Inquiry appearance in July 2015, 'Yesterday was only my second time back in Leinster House. When I went in there first in 1977 a lot of former politicians were constantly in there having their lunch or in the bar and I used to say, "What a sad life, I'd never do that."'

The Green Party was annihilated in the 2011 election and had no TDs in the 31st Dáil. The party's time on the broad sunlit uplands of power had lasted less than four years. Eamon Ryan has 'regrets', not least about his complicity in the budgets of 2008 and 2009. 'I think we should have applied the brakes earlier and we should have seen it and we were putting through increases in social welfare that would subsequently not happen. That is one of the things that I look back at and say we should have acted faster, in hindsight.'

There is a mutual respect between the Green Party and Fianna Fáil. 'I think Brian Cowen deserves certain credit. You know, people can make their own judgement on that but internally in terms of managing a Cabinet in incredibly difficult times, when he could have just upped and said, "I'm out of here", he didn't and I would respect him for that,' says Ryan.

Slashing and burning in those final months, one Cabinet decision in particular stuck in Ryan's throat: 'One of the ones that I was particularly … pissed off about at the end was the minimum wage. That was a mistake. I hated it, it was the only thing Cowen insisted on and I do not know why.' One of the first measures the succeeding government enacted was to restore the €1 that had been cut from the minimum wage.

Fine Gael leader Enda Kenny became taoiseach in a coalition government with Labour, thanks to a total seat haul of 113. No government before it had entered power with such a resounding mandate. However, the political aftershocks continued long after the earthquakes of 2008 to 2011. Labour leader and tánaiste Eamon Gilmore was ousted in 2014 after appalling local and European election results. By mid-2015 the government had lost twelve TDs due to various disagreements.

Irish politics will not be the same for the foreseeable future, as the behemoth that was Fianna Fáil is badly wounded. The shift in the political landscape caused by the 2011 election was replicated somewhat in the 2016 election. Fine Gael and Labour lost fifty-seven seats between them, and while Fianna Fáil recovered ground, it still suffered its second worst election ever.

The party laments that there is no longer a member of the great Lenihan political dynasty in the Dáil. Brian Lenihan Senior had entered the Dáil in 1957. His sister Mary O'Rourke followed him into the Dáil but then lost her seat in 2011, along with her nephew Conor Lenihan. Both have left politics.

Brian Lenihan Junior, the former minister for finance, and beacon of hope during the crisis, was the only Fianna Fáil TD in Dublin to be returned in 2011. After the election Lenihan gave Micheál Martin an honest, and typically provocative, appraisal of the downfall: 'He came in to me afterwards and, you know, he was giving out about dynasties, because he felt that dynasties had left the party in weak states in some constituencies and that the organisation wasn't as strong.'

The Lenihan dynasty was soon to end its unbroken fifty-four year presence in the Oireachtas. Brian was dying. John Lee met him in Leinster House in April 2011 and, along with journalist Sam Smyth, they repaired to the Dáil self-service restaurant. He didn't seem too ill and he remained as intellectually sharp as ever, ribbing Sam about his northern Protestant heritage as he displayed his in-depth knowledge of Protestant theology. He noted that John Wesley, the founder of Methodism, liked to preach outdoors. Segueing in sparkling style, he then related a story about his father chairing a Fianna Fáil convention in Connemara in the 1960s. The local organisation had employed an old trick to stop the convention going ahead. They had ensured that the venue, the parish hall, had been double-booked and announced that, sadly, there could be no selection of headquarters' favoured candidate. Brian Lenihan Senior, a well-read man himself, declared, 'We shall take to the fields so, like John Wesley.' Laughing loudly he told us that his father procured a table and some chairs and held the convention in a field.

Billy Kelleher met Lenihan in Leinster House before he died. 'I had a cup of tea with him down in the coffee dock around eleven or twelve days before he passed away,' says Kelleher. 'We all had a cup of tea with him. It was very evident that there was very little time left for Brian. I distinctly remember hearing him talking about this government [Fine Gael and Labour], the bravado of this government in burning bondholders.'

Lenihan said to the TDs, 'Do you not think that we did not try all those things? Of course our first step was to protect the country, protect the taxpayer. It wasn't just about protecting the banks, we would have gladly burnt bondholders, but there was no way and there is no way that this crowd will.'

Kelleher says they continued their conversation away from the rest. 'He spoke at length and I explained to him that I didn't support him for the leadership and all those things but he was just very emotional about the fact that Fianna Fáil had just got destroyed in Dublin.'

John McGuinness and Lenihan had socialised and conspired against the leader throughout the preceding years. A breach had opened between them in the final weeks of the government when they fell out on national radio. But neither man was the kind to hold a grudge. McGuinness remembers: 'When he was dying he rang me and he said, "I've just read your book [*The House Always Wins*] for the second time and I want to thank you for the way you complimented and spoke about me."'

Lenihan tried to fumble an apology for some of the misunderstandings. 'That's okay, Brian, don't worry about that, we're still friends,' said McGuinness.

'That's what I rang you about, John, I hope that we can call ourselves friends.'

'Yes, Brian, we can,' said McGuinness.

'That bit on the radio, can we forget that ever happened?' said Lenihan about their final schism.

'Brian, don't ever worry about that, I don't ever carry baggage,' said McGuinness. He recalls, 'We had a very short conversation about general stuff and we finished the conversation. I remember saying to my wife, Margaret, "Brian Lenihan is saying his goodbyes." And I was right.'

Micheál Martin, Brian's friend and rival for leadership, also saw him in his final days: 'I remember I met him – my final meeting. I didn't realise it was the last time he was in Leinster House, I would have had a longer cup of tea or something. I just had a chat with him. And he never made it back, and I rang him a couple of times at home. Yes, that was it.'

As can be the way with people, they rarely accept the end is imminent, and Mary Harney, too, regrets not spending time available with Lenihan. 'I met him on the street somewhere around here [Government Buildings] and we said we must have lunch. And the next thing I heard he was dying.'

In August 2010 Lenihan had spoken in West Cork where Michael Collins had been gunned down in his prime. He enjoyed the Béal na Bláth commemorations immensely, as his grandfather P. J. Lenihan had fought on Collins' pro-Treaty side. 'I told Diarmuid Collins, who is grand-nephew of Michael Collins, that you gave him some of the happiest hours of his life, and he did,' says Mary O'Rourke.

'Brian said "I am so honoured", that was because his father's background was Fine Gael or Cumann na nGaedhael. I went and I was so happy I went. He was in great form. He only had eight or nine months left to live. He stayed for hours and people kept coming up and up and up. He kept talking and talking.'

She reflects on his last years in government. 'People were willing to live through it if he was around. I think the nastiness crept in when he left. There was a feeling he would steer the ship right, that there was someone who would actually see it right.'

O'Rourke remembers Brian's description of his final summer with his family – they stayed in London for a week. 'We had a great week,' he told her. 'I think he must have known it was his last holiday because they got up on the tour buses. They did all the touristy stuff and they had a wonderful time.'

Brian Lenihan died at home on 10 June 2011 and his funeral mass was held at the small St Mochta's church, Porterstown, near his County Dublin home. There were twenty-three priests, including three from Belvedere College, his *alma mater*, at the mass. Joining his wife and two children, among the 1,000 mourners, was his extended family, the Fianna Fáil party. It was not clear at that time whether it would be the last great gathering of the Soldiers of Destiny. But it was clear that Fianna Fáil would never be the same again.

INDEX

A

Ahern, Bertie 15–20, 22, 27, 29–31,
   33, 42–46, 50, 109, 132, 134, 135,
   137, 138, 147, 153, 210, 211, 215,
   229, 233, 303
Ahern, Dermot 20, 23, 26, 139, 218,
   219, 253, 254, 256, 257, 287, 290
Ahern, Michael 298
Ahern, Miriam 15
Ahern, Noel 132
Ahearne, Alan 118, 122, 123, 128,
   168, 183, 184, 261
Allied Irish Bank (AIB) 58, 60, 67,
   73, 75, 116
An Bord Snip Nua (see also Mc-
   Carty report) 139–141
Andrews, Barry 102, 290, 300
Andrews, Chris 162, 298
Anglo Irish Bank 16, 38, 39, 47, 48,
   52, 65–67, 69, 71–76, 85, 88–91,
   113–117, 119, 129, 206, 207, 238
Ardagh, Seán 298
Ardilaun Hotel 215, 216, 220, 226,
   235, 236, 245
Atkinson, Caroline 263
Aylward, Bobby 219, 232
Aylward, Liam 232

B

Bacon, Peter 124, 130
Bank of Ireland 51, 66, 67, 71, 73,
   75, 88, 116
Barroso, José Manuel 83, 89, 258
Beades, Jerry 279
Beausang, William 68
Behan, Joe 99, 152
Bloomberg, Michael 46
Bowler, Gillian 51
Boyle, Dan 138, 200, 201, 287

Brady, Áine 132, 217, 219
Brennan, Séamus 138, 152
Brown, Gordon 83, 89
Browne, John 217
Bruton, Richard 39, 87
Burgess, Niall 43
Burrows, Richard 66, 67, 73, 75
Burton, Joan 88, 247
Byrne, David 124
Byrne, Thomas 99, 121

C

Calleary, Dara 25, 56, 98, 110, 111,
   113, 131, 132, 158, 178, 183, 194,
   203, 205, 206, 210, 247, 248, 262,
   280, 281, 291
Calleary, Seán 56
Cardiff, Kevin 47, 50, 57, 60, 68, 69,
   74, 76, 77, 115, 123, 256, 263
Carey, Brian 277
Carey, Pat 26, 30, 31, 82, 83, 85, 86,
   94, 101, 104, 106, 107, 121, 123,
   128, 134, 137, 147, 157, 160, 164,
   175, 181, 186, 204, 205, 210, 218,
   221, 228, 255, 276, 280, 287, 293,
   295, 297
Carruth, Grainne 15–17
Casby, Conor 125, 127
Central Bank of Ireland 47, 48, 50,
   51, 54, 61, 63, 65, 68, 71, 73, 84,
   90, 114, 115, 123, 246, 252, 260,
   262
Clinch, Peter 29, 38
Cluskey, Frank 234
Collins, Michael 134
Conlon, Margaret 134
Connick, Seán 121, 205, 219
Constâncio, Vitor 254
Corrigan, John 123, 124, 256

Coughlan, Mary 18, 23, 24–27, 31, 42, 73, 98, 99, 121, 132–134, 139, 140, 144, 162, 165, 204, 205, 210, 212, 217, 232, 242, 279, 293–295, 297
Coveney, Simon 215, 222–224, 226
Cowen, Barry 300
Cowen, Ber 21, 233
Cowen, Brian 11–13, 16–34, 38, 39, 41–51, 53–55, 57, 60, 63, 65, 68–78, 80, 83–87, 89–91, 93, 97–101, 103–111, 114–122, 124–128, 131–135, 137, 139–141, 143–152, 156–162, 164–166, 168, 172–175, 180–182, 187–189, 194–196, 199, 201, 202, 204–213, 215–246, 249, 252, 253, 256–258, 261–263, 265–269, 271, 272, 274–305
Cowen, Mary 50, 127, 297
Cregan, John 218, 219, 232
Croke Park Agreement 37, 156, 165, 208–212, 222
Crown, John 178, 180
Cuffe, Ciarán 205
Cullen, Martin 26, 204
Curran, John 205, 217, 218, 232, 279, 287, 297

D

Darling, Alistair 83, 89
Deauville 249, 250
Dempsey, Noel 23, 26, 138, 160, 254–257, 287, 290, 295
Desmond, Dermot 48, 51
Devins, Jimmy 132, 152
Doherty, Pearse 252
Dooley, Timmy 298
Dorgan, Eoin 34, 81, 175, 181
Doyle, David 35, 37, 38, 68, 115, 123
Druids Glen 48, 65, 277
Drumm, David 47, 48, 65, 66, 113
Drury, Fintan 48
Duffy, Joe 57–60
Dunne, Eileen 126
Dwane, Mike 196–198

E

EcoFin 247, 248, 258
Elderfield, Matthew 263
English, Rachael 261
European Central Bank (ECB) 13, 61–63, 70, 71, 84, 245, 248–252, 254, 257, 259–264, 266

F

Farrell, Jim 68
Fianna Fáil 11–13, 15–18, 20, 21, 23, 25, 26, 28, 29, 32, 42, 46, 49, 54, 55, 62, 69, 91, 93, 96, 97, 99, 101–107, 117, 119–123, 127, 131, 133, 135–139, 144, 146, 147, 150–152, 155, 157, 160, 161, 163, 165, 166, 182, 187–189, 199–203, 205, 207, 208, 215–217, 219, 220, 222, 223, 226, 228, 230–233, 235–237, 240, 241, 243, 268, 271–281, 284–287, 291, 297–301, 303–307, 309
Financial Regulator 39, 48, 50, 54, 58, 63, 68, 70, 72, 89, 114, 263
Fine Gael 31, 39, 71, 87–89, 96, 127, 137, 138, 143, 144, 170, 187, 195, 198, 199, 206, 215, 216, 223, 224, 226, 230, 266, 297, 300–302, 305, 306, 308
Finneran, Michael 99
Fitzpatrick, Michael 298
FitzPatrick, Seán 38, 47, 48, 65–67, 113, 206, 277
Flanagan, Charlie 127
Flannery, Frank 137, 144
Flynn, Beverley 18, 55
Flynn, Pádraig 55
Foxe, Ken 125, 153

G

Gallagher, Pat 137, 152
Gallagher, Paul 68, 86
Ganley, Declan 31
Geithner, Timothy 248, 265
Gilmore, Eamon 69, 88, 140, 143, 144, 155, 207, 213, 234, 305

Gleeson, Dermot 67, 73, 75, 76
Gogarty, Paul 293
Goggin, Brian 51, 66, 73
Gormley, John 26, 79, 117, 160, 199, 201, 202, 267, 268, 277, 287, 288, 290, 293–296, 298
Gowran Park 62
Gray, Alan 48, 65, 66, 73, 74
Grealish, Noel 128
Green Party 11, 13, 18, 26, 79, 99, 103, 117, 124, 125, 137–139, 189, 199–203, 205, 228, 256, 267, 268, 276, 277, 287, 291, 293, 294, 296, 298, 300, 304
Gregory, Tony 138
Grimes, Tony 68

H

Halligan, Ursula 225, 227
Hanafin, Mary 25–28, 80, 139, 205, 289, 295, 298, 300
Harney, Mary 11, 17, 26, 30, 58, 71, 76, 79, 95, 98, 99, 101, 102, 104, 124, 148, 152, 160, 171, 173, 174, 188, 211, 226, 227, 249, 258, 262, 274, 288–290, 304, 308
Haughey, Charles 21, 46, 79, 87, 97, 106, 123, 146, 147, 156, 237, 243, 284, 299
Haughey, Seán 298
Hayes, Tom 88
Healy-Rae, Jackie 18, 128, 152
Herbert, Cathy 34, 123, 175, 182
Hoctor, Máire 98, 132
Honohan, Patrick 71, 72, 91, 123, 246, 252, 259–266
Horan, Niamh 50
Hurley, John 47, 51, 61, 68–70, 73, 76, 123

I

International Monetary Fund (IMF) 13, 245, 248, 250, 258, 261, 263, 265, 266
Irish Life & Permanent 51, 113

Irish Nationwide Building Society 71, 72, 75, 119, 206

K

Kelleher, Billy 78, 79, 81, 82, 131, 191, 192, 243, 272, 273, 275, 284, 285, 289–291, 298, 306, 307
Kennedy, Michael 99, 127, 241
Kenny, Enda 31, 46, 88, 91, 105, 109, 137, 138, 144, 195, 206, 207, 234, 286, 293, 305
Kenny, Pat 133, 168
Killeen, Tony 204, 205, 221, 287, 290
Kirk, Seamus 155
Kitt, Michael 132, 217
Kitt, Proinsias 217
Kitt, Tom 99, 217, 241

L

Labour Party 69, 87, 88, 120, 140, 143, 155, 187, 207, 216, 230, 234, 247, 286, 297, 300, 302, 305, 306
Lagarde, Christine 83, 247
Larkin, Celia 15
Lee, George 59, 81, 138, 143
Lehman Brothers 46, 54, 56, 57, 65, 70, 91
Lenihan, Brian 11–14, 18, 21–27, 33–36, 38–42, 49, 51–54, 56–63, 67, 68, 70–78, 80–83, 85–89, 91–93, 95–97, 99, 104, 109–111, 114–116, 118–124, 127–131, 134, 135, 139–141, 143–145, 148, 150, 153, 156–162, 164–189, 198, 206–213, 216, 217, 219, 221, 236–245, 247, 250, 252, 254–269, 271–274, 278–283, 285, 295, 296, 298, 299, 300, 303–308
Lenihan Snr, Brian 169, 170, 234, 305, 306
Lenihan, Conor 22, 27, 32–36, 41, 42, 51, 52, 61, 67, 72, 92, 94, 101, 103, 104, 106, 108–110, 121, 140, 141, 143, 162, 165, 168–170, 176, 177, 186–189, 193, 194, 210, 235,

239, 241, 244, 271, 272, 282, 292, 293, 296, 297, 300, 305
Lenihan, Patricia 171, 176, 178
Lennon, Joe 29, 68, 80, 81, 220
Lisbon Treaty referendum 31, 32, 47, 49, 151–153
Lowry, Michael 18, 128, 152

M

Mac Coille, Cathal 215, 218, 220, 221, 224
MacSharry, Ray 22, 33, 34, 186
Mahon Tribunal 15–18, 303
Mansergh, Martin 121
Mara, P. J. 147
Martin, Micheál 11, 13, 17–19, 23, 26, 28, 80, 85, 86, 124, 134, 141, 149, 151, 153, 167, 179, 180, 211, 212, 218, 225, 226, 243, 244, 266, 268, 269, 272–280, 282–289, 291, 293, 295–300, 302, 303, 305, 307
Martin, Shay 185
McAuley, Pearse 197
McCague, Eugene 68
McCann, Gary 48
McCarthy, Colm 88, 139, 140, 142
McCarthy, Dermot 68, 80, 81, 158
McCarthy report 140, 141, 143, 144
McCreevy, Charlie 34, 48, 109, 168
McDaid, Jim 99, 122, 152
McDonagh, Brendan 124
McDonagh, Joe 217, 223
McEntee, Gerry 169, 170, 172
McEntee, Seán 22
McEntee, Shane 170
McGrath, Finian 18, 100, 102, 152
McGrath, Mattie 99, 147, 162, 225
McGrath, Michael 99, 121, 298
McGuinness, John 20, 28, 62, 63, 97, 103, 108, 116, 121, 132–135, 188, 208, 209, 212, 213, 231, 232, 236, 237, 239, 240, 271, 272, 274, 279–282, 307
McPartland, Pat 219, 220
McWilliams, David 122

Meenan, Brian 34
Merkel, Angela 249
Moloney, John 97, 119, 120
Mooney, Derek 200
Moylan, Dermot 184, 259
Moynihan, Michael 99
Mulcahy, Michael 298
Murphy, Brian 29, 30
Murphy, David 81

N

National Asset Management Agency (NAMA) 129, 130, 138, 139, 151, 152, 172, 208, 246
National Recovery Plan 249
National Treasury Management Agency (NTMA) 57, 63, 114, 115, 123, 124, 130, 252
Neary, Patrick 68, 70, 72
Noonan, Michael 22, 222
Northern Rock 51, 57, 60, 84

O

O'Brien, Darragh 99, 218
O'Brien, Jim 123
Ó Cuív, Éamon 20, 22, 26, 59, 60, 63, 77, 140, 205, 287, 295, 298, 299
O'Dea, Willie 13, 19, 25, 26, 29, 31, 32, 41, 63, 71, 79, 85, 86, 117, 118, 150, 151, 168, 170, 181, 192, 193, 196–204, 208, 238, 239, 244, 255, 257, 283, 298
O'Donoghue, John 153–155, 298
Offaly 19, 21, 24, 27, 28, 32, 43, 101, 126, 195, 202, 233, 242, 290
O'Flynn, Noel 99, 134, 208, 216, 298
O'Keeffe, Batt 26, 139, 191, 204, 218, 232, 253, 288, 290, 291, 293
O'Keeffe, Ned 54, 55, 221, 298
Ó Neachtain, Eoghan 29, 68, 79, 80, 114, 126, 127, 220, 227, 254, 255
O'Rourke, Mary 14, 19, 49, 107, 108, 122, 129, 145, 146, 161–164, 167, 169, 170, 178, 183, 185, 186, 209,

210, 216, 220, 221, 235, 239, 241, 242, 256, 257, 259–261, 269, 283, 285, 305, 308

O'Rourke, Seán 110, 181, 183, 281, 282

Osborne, George 259

O'Sullivan, Christy 99

O'Sullivan, Maureen 138

P

Paulson, Hank 91, 92

Power, Peter 298

Power, Seán 132, 298

Progressive Democrats 18, 102, 152, 202, 211, 304

Q

Quinlivan, Maurice 196–198

Quinlivan, Nessan 197

Quinn, Seán 48

R

Reeves, Jim 21

Regan, Eugene 198

Rehn, Ollie 250, 251

Reynolds, Albert 21, 46, 301

Ring, Michael 96

Roche, Dick 200, 201

Ryan, Eamon 11, 18, 26, 32, 39, 40, 60, 94, 95, 97, 102, 103, 124, 125, 138, 139, 158–161, 164, 199, 228, 247, 256, 261, 268, 287, 289, 292, 295, 296, 304, 305

Ryan, Eoin 137

S

Sargent, Trevor 203, 204

Sarkozy, Nicolas 47, 87, 249

Scallon, Rosemary 31

Scanlon, Eamon 152

Schauble, Wolfgang 257, 258

Sinn Féin 31, 87, 137, 196, 197, 230, 252

Smith, Brendan 26, 165, 295

Somers, Michael 57, 124

Strauss-Kahn, Dominic 13, 248

T

Trethowan, John 224

Trichet, Jean-Claude 13, 61–63, 70, 86, 248, 250–252, 257, 263–265

Troika, the 12, 245, 246, 248, 258, 265, 281

Tullamore 12, 27, 28, 242, 297

U

Universal Social Charge (USC) 280, 281

V

Van Rompuy, Herman 257

W

Wallace, Mary 132, 221, 276

Whelan, John 120

White, Mary 138, 205

White, Victoria 124, 125

MERCIER PRESS

IRISH PUBLISHER - IRISH STORY

We hope you enjoyed this book.

Since 1944, Mercier Press has published books that have been critically important to Irish life and culture. Books that dealt with subjects that informed readers about Irish scholars, Irish writers, Irish history and Ireland's rich heritage.

We believe in the importance of providing accessible histories and cultural books for all readers and all who are interested in Irish cultural life.

Our website is the best place to find out more information about Mercier, our books, authors, news and the best deals on a wide variety of books. Mercier tracks the best prices for our books online and we seek to offer the best value to our customers, offering free delivery within Ireland.

Sign up on our website to receive updates and special offers.

www.mercierpress.ie
www.facebook.com/mercier.press
www.twitter.com/irishpublisher

Mercier Press, Unit 3b, Oak House, Bessboro Rd, Blackrock, Cork, Ireland